D1233388

Assumption-Based Planning

Unwelcome surprises in the life of any organization can often be traced to the failure of an assumption that the organization's leadership didn't anticipate or had "forgotten" it was making. Assumption-based planning (ABP) is a tool for identifying as many of the assumptions underlying the plans of an organization as possible and bringing those assumptions explicitly into the planning process.

This book presents a variety of techniques for rooting out those vulnerable, crucial assumptions that, through familiarity or other reasons, have gotten buried in one's thinking. The book also presents steps for monitoring all the vulnerable assumptions of a plan, for taking actions to control those vulnerable assumptions where possible, and for preparing the organization for the potential failure of those assumptions where control is not possible.

The book provides a variety of examples and practical advice for those interested in carrying out an application of ABP in the fields of business, management, strategic planning, and engineering and in military applications.

James A. Dewar is Director of the RAND Frederick S. Pardee Center for Longer Range Global Policy and the Future Human Condition and Frederick S. Pardee Professor of Long-Term Policy Analysis at the RAND Graduate School. He is also a senior mathematician and Director of Research Quality Assurance at RAND. For the past 15 years, Dr. Dewar's main research interest has been strategic planning. He led the development and application of the concept of assumption-based planning, and his planning experiences include projects for all four U.S. military services, higher education institutions, public corporations, and Fortune 100 companies.

Dr. Dewar's ongoing work in pure mathematics is also closely related to ABP, as the assumptions underlying a plan are similar to the axioms underlying a mathematical system.

Dr. Dewar has written and lectured on a variety of topics related to policy analysis, including a prize-winning paper for the Military Operations Research Society.

RAND Studies in Policy Analysis

Editor: Charles Wolf, Jr., Senior Economic Advisor and Corporate Fellow in International Economics, RAND

Policy analysis is the application of scientific methods to develop and test alternative ways of addressing social, economic, legal, international, national security, and other problems. The RAND Studies in Policy Analysis series aims to include several significant, timely, and innovative works each year in this broad field. Selection is guided by an editorial board consisting of Charles Wolf, Jr. (editor), and Paul K. Davis, Lynn Karoly, and Thomas McNaugher (associate editors).

Also in the series:

David C. Gompert and F. Stephen Larrabee (eds.), *America and Europe: A Partnership for a New Era*

John W. Peabody, M. Omar Rahman, Paul J. Gertler, Joyce Mann, Donna O. Farley, Jeff Luck, David Robalino, and Grace M. Carter, *Policy and Health: Implications for Development in Asia*

Samantha F. Ravich, *Marketization and Democracy: East Asian Experiences*

Gregory F. Treverton, *Reshaping National Intelligence for an Age of Information*

Robert J. MacCoun and Peter Reuter, *Drug War Heresies: Learning from Other Vices, Times, and Places*

Daniel Byman and Matthew Waxman, *The Dynamics of Coercion: American Foreign Policy and the Limits of Military Might*

Assumption-Based Planning

A Tool for Reducing
Avoidable Surprises

James A. Dewar
RAND

CAMBRIDGE
UNIVERSITY PRESS

PUBLISHED BY THE PRESS SYNDICATE OF THE UNIVERSITY OF CAMBRIDGE
The Pitt Building, Trumpington Street, Cambridge, United Kingdom

CAMBRIDGE UNIVERSITY PRESS
The Edinburgh Building, Cambridge CB2 2RU, UK
40 West 20th Street, New York, NY 10011-4211, USA
477 Williamstown Road, Port Melbourne, VIC 3207, Australia
Ruiz de Alarcón 13, 28014 Madrid, Spain
Dock House, The Waterfront, Cape Town 8001, South Africa

http://www.cambridge.org

First published 2002

Printed in the United Kingdom at the University Press, Cambridge

Typeface Sabon 10/13 pt.   *System* MS Word [AU]

A catalog record for this book is available from the British Library.

Library of Congress Cataloging in Publication data

Dewar, James A.
   Assumption-based planning : a tool for reducing avoidable surprises / James A. Dewar.
      p. cm. — (RAND studies in policy analysis)
   Includes bibliographical references and index.
   ISBN 0-521-80653-4 – ISBN 0-521-00126-9 (pbk.)
   1. Planning. 2. Hypothesis.   I. Title. II. Series
   HD87.5 .D49 2002
   658.4′012–dc21   2002073460

ISBN 0 521 80653 4 hardback
ISBN 0 521 00126 9 paperback

To Don, Barb, Kits, and Carl

Contents

Figures

Preface

Assumption-Based Planning (ABP) started out in 1987 as an approach Morlie Hammer Levin and I developed to solve a U.S. Army strategic planning problem. Thanks to the fall of the Berlin Wall two years later, that early ABP work initiated an ongoing conversation with the Army about how to do planning in the Army's newly and differently uncertain times. The use of ABP was first described in James A. Dewar and Morlie H. Levin, *Assumption-Based Planning for Army 21*, Santa Monica, Calif.: RAND, R-4172-A, 1992, and ABP itself was first documented in James A. Dewar, Carl H. Builder, William M. Hix, and Morlie H. Levin, *Assumption-Based Planning: A Planning Tool for Very Uncertain Times*, Santa Monica, Calif.: RAND, MR-114-A, 1993. As ABP evolved through various Army and other applications, it turned into a planning tool—a self-contained process with a specific planning purpose—that is applicable to *any* kind of plan or planning process. ABP continues to evolve, but its fundamentals have changed little in its last several applications. For that reason, it seemed appropriate to document formally what we have learned about it.

The careful reader will already have noticed that I use both the singular and plural first-person pronouns in talking about ABP. My coauthors on the original ABP documentation were intimately involved in both the intellectual development of ABP and in the learning process that accompanied its application to real planning problems. When I talk about what I know about ABP, then, it would make me very uncomfortable to use the singular pronoun. However, I have no such reservations when giving personal opinions. For that reason, I have tried to be careful about who is implicated in any statement I make

xiii

about ABP—hoping to err on the side of including the many contributors to my understanding of ABP and of planning.

My hope for this book is that it speak to two planning audiences. I intend this book, first, for students of planning and want them to use it as I intend to use it—as a reference on both the "how" and the "why" of Assumption-Based Planning. As simple as the concept of ABP is, my colleagues and I have found a great many subtleties in its application. These subtleties are easily forgotten from one application to the next. A separate chapter is devoted to each of the five steps of ABP, and each chapter contains a road map that both details our understanding about that step and places those details in a logical sequence. The primary intent of the road map is to allow easy access to specific aspects of each step—particularly on a second or subsequent reading.

The second intended audience is practicing planners, who, I realize, are more interested in just the "how" of planning. The book is set up to address three levels of potential interest on the part of practicing planners.

At the first level of interest, a planner might wonder whether ABP would be useful for a particular planning problem. Chapter 1 is intended to give enough of the philosophy, mechanics, and strengths and weaknesses of ABP to help that planner make an informed decision about whether to proceed.

At the second level of interest, a planner might wish to apply ABP but would need to know more about it. Chapters 2 through 7 develop the concepts and mechanics of Assumption-Based Planning. Chapter 2 defines assumptions and builds a taxonomy of assumption types. Chapters 3 through 7 detail each of the five steps of ABP—defining the terms used in ABP and characterizing some of the subtleties that we have discovered over the years in applying ABP to planning situations for a variety of organizations, from domestic and foreign militaries, to public companies, to private businesses. Where possible, I have included examples to illustrate the concepts. In addition, I have used the planning of a lemonade stand as a compact example with which to illustrate, in turn, each of the five steps of ABP.

At the third level of interest, a planner would be applying ABP and running into practical problems. As with any planning system, there is an art to how ABP is conducted. Not all of what we have learned can be passed along as easily as the concepts and mechanics of ABP. Chapters 2 through 7 discuss some of the art as it pertains to the concepts and mechanics. Chapter 8 is aimed more at the art of conducting an ABP application. It is intended to help planners work the major practical problems that we have encountered in our applications.

Assumption-Based Planning is a planning tool that is primarily useful for improving the robustness and adaptability of existing plans. However, it is also useful as a part of any planning methodology—a topic taken up in Chapter 9.

The Appendix carries on the "why" of ABP and strives to connect the terms and concepts of ABP with the same or similar terms and concepts in the literature. It is for readers who are familiar with the terms, concepts, and methods of planning and wonder how and where ABP fits in. It is not a thorough treatment but covers most of the popular planning concepts that relate strongly to ABP.

Acknowledgments

My first debt of gratitude is to the codevelopers of Assumption-Based Planning. From the beginning, then–RAND colleague Morlie Levin and I thought about, discussed, and argued over the Army's strategic planning problem and how to go about formulating an alternative approach. Soon thereafter, Mike Hix joined in the ongoing practical and philosophical problems of ABP. The late Carl Builder, in addition to his practical contributions, provided an intellectual "sanity check" on our thinking. Without Morlie, Mike, and Carl, ABP would simply not have come into being.

Since the development and first publication on ABP, many have contributed to both the intellectual foundations and practical application of ABP. Maren Leed continues to bring interest and insight to the evolution of ABP. Particularly instrumental in solving the practical problems of applying ABP have been then–Lt. Col. Tim Daniel of the U.S. Army and RAND colleague Jed Peters. Rich Kedzior contributed much to our understanding of the planning literature, as did Gary Moody before him. The sections that deal with decision analysis owe most of their intellectual content to Kristine Kuhn. Judy Larson has been my touchstone for turning my understanding into readable prose. In the process, Judy often helped me think about what I really meant. Laurie Rennie has helped in so many ways over the years that the details would quickly overwhelm this brief section. Finally, any number of people have contributed in small, but sometimes important, ways to the current status of ABP.

The intellectual content and readability of this book owe much to reviewers of earlier drafts. I particularly appreciate the informal, collegial reviews of the earliest drafts by B. J. Duke, Jim Gillogly, Mike Hix, Bob Klitgaard, Judy Larson, Maren Leed, and Jed Peters. Three people gave the penultimate draft excellent, thorough, formal reviews. Paul

Bracken's review positively affected the style of the final draft and added important examples and references. Paul Davis suggested several examples, some crucial references, and some interesting related concepts. He is most responsible for the chapter on the art of conducting ABP. Yehezkel Dror was exactingly thorough in his review. His deep insights into planning challenged my thinking in several areas and caused me to seriously rethink some crucial concepts.

I have had manuscripts edited before, but not like Marian Branch edited this one. Her intellectual involvement equaled her technical prowess, and the book has benefited significantly from both.

I want also to acknowledge people along the way who have encouraged and championed the 15-year journey of discovery that has been ABP. This list includes Donna Betancourt, David Chu, Lynn Davis, Dave Kassing, Tom McNaugher, and Jim Quinlivan.

Not one of those (incredibly few, I suspect) authors who gleefully write books, I also owe a special debt to my wife, Ruth. Not only did she gently encourage me to write the book when I was agonizing over the decision, but she did so knowing she was likely to be (and was) saddled for several months with some of my routine, day-to-day tasks in order to accommodate the absent-mindedness that such projects seem to induce. She also contributed significantly to the book, masterfully walking a fine line between being my toughest critic and my biggest fan.

As with any book, the final responsibility for its content and style rest with the author. I begrudgingly accept it.

1

The essence of Assumption-Based Planning

You envision a romantic dinner with a special someone. You are nervous; you want to make sure nothing goes wrong. You make a list of all those steps you need to take to make that special dinner a reality. You keep adding and revising the steps as new eventualities come to mind.

A group of U.S. military officers gathers in 1940 to look into the future to identify events that could plausibly lead to conflict. One of them suggests an air attack by Japan on a U.S. Navy base in Hawaii––a suggestion that is dismissed out of hand.

We cannot know the future perfectly, but we can imagine the future and make plans for it by making some assumptions––or judgments––about what that future could be like. Some of the assumptions we make are pretty likely to come true; others are more vulnerable to uncontrollable and unforeseen events; still others seem quite unlikely. Some of the assumptions are likely to be very important to the success of the plan; others will be more peripheral. Assumption-Based Planning (ABP) is a tool designed for improving the robustness and adaptability of plans––for reducing the number of avoidable surprises in any plan or planning. It is primarily a "post-planning" tool (recognizing that planning is an iterative process) that concentrates on the assumptions in an already-developed plan that are most important to the plan's success and that are most uncertain. Specifically, ABP works to decrease the risks that assumptions represent.

1

Yet, how effective a plan might be or how likely it is to succeed does not drive ABP. The driving force behind ABP is the view that it is important to confront, explicitly and honestly, the uncertainties facing an organization and its planners.

HOW DOES ASSUMPTION-BASED PLANNING WORK?

The five basic steps in ABP are shown in Figure 1.1.

All plans—from the plan for dinner at a restaurant, to the plans of a global corporation, to the plans of an international alliance—make assumptions about the future.

The five steps of Assumption-Based Planning can be seen even in the plan for dinner at a restaurant. Think of someone who is making a plan for dinner at a nice restaurant for the very first time. Here the planning and its assumptions are much more intentional and visible, much less automatic.

The first step in ABP is to identify the assumptions in the plan. The plan for a quiet dinner on Friday for two on the patio of a nice restaurant contains several assumptions, the foremost being the availability of the two participants on Friday and the availability of a table on the patio at the restaurant, then the weather on the patio, the traffic around the restaurant, personal finances, and so on. The plans for an interna-

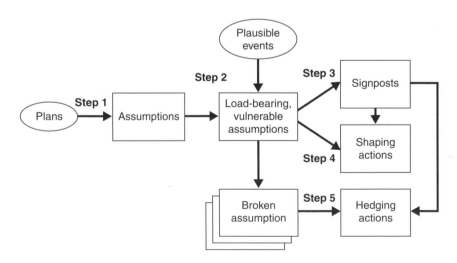

Figure 1.1. The Basic Steps and Flow of Assumption-Based Planning

tional alliance are likely to contain hundreds of assumptions at various levels of detail.

The next step in ABP is to identify the assumptions upon which the success of the plan most heavily rests—the "load-bearing" assumptions—and the assumptions that are most vulnerable to being overturned by future events. Assumptions that are both load-bearing and vulnerable are the most likely to produce nasty surprises as the plan unfolds.[1]

If the dinner plan contains a certain special someone, that someone's availability is a load-bearing assumption. If the plan is for a first date, that could be a very vulnerable assumption. If the dinner plan is for your spouse's birthday, an assumption about availability is probably pretty solid.

To deal with potential surprises, ABP produces three things: signposts, shaping actions, and hedging actions. *Signposts* are warning signs that can be used to monitor those assumptions that are most likely to produce surprises. Signposts are events or thresholds that, if detected, signify that a vulnerable assumption is broken or dangerously weak and that management or planning action is called for. In the dinner example with the special someone, a "no" response to your invitation is a clear sign that the plan is doomed and a new plan is called for. A corporation that has planned on the anticipation of a favorable future regulatory ruling faces the same kind of potentially heartbreaking signpost.

Another kind of signpost to monitor in the restaurant example would be the weather. The plan to dine on the patio undoubtedly contains an assumption about nice, warm weather—something that cannot be guaranteed beforehand or predicted with certainty. The vulnerability of that assumption can, however, be monitored through weather reports. A forecast for evening rain on the morning of the planned event would be a significant signpost. It would be a clear sign that the assumption of nice, warm weather is in trouble. If that signpost is detected, it may be time to postpone the quiet dinner to another day or to consider moving it indoors.

Shaping actions are intended to help shore up uncertain assumptions, to control the future as much as possible. Planners generally know how

1   In earlier documentation of ABP (Dewar and Levin 1992; Dewar et al. 1993), these were called the important, vulnerable assumptions. The reasoning behind the change is taken up in Chapter 2.

they would like an assumption to play out. Shaping actions are designed to help the assumption play out to the planners' liking. Not much can be done to control the weather, but an assumption about getting a nice table on the patio can be shored up by phoning ahead for a reservation. Similarly, an assumption about getting to the restaurant on time can be shored up by checking to be sure there is enough gas in the car.

Hedging actions better prepare for the possibility that an assumption will fail, despite efforts to shore it up. Hedging actions typically come from thinking through a plausible scenario in which an assumption collapses and asking what might be done now to prepare for that scenario. In the dining example, suppose the car has been acting up, but you are assuming it will get you to the restaurant. Now imagine the car breaking down. If it breaks down before you leave the house, maybe you could borrow a neighbor's car. A hedging action would be to talk with the neighbor today, explain the situation, and ask if it would be possible and permissible to borrow a car Friday night in the event yours were to break down. Now imagine the car breaking down on the way to the restaurant. One hedging action would be signing up for an auto club that could come rescue you in this situation. Insurance is a classic hedging action.

To further emphasize the difference between a shaping action and a hedging action, we view taking a balky car into the shop for repair to keep it from breaking down as a shaping action and taking steps to ensure you can get to the restaurant in the event the car *does* break down, as a hedging action. Shaping actions are usually easier to think about and generate than are hedging actions.

A planner using Assumption-Based Planning cannot hope to identify all the possible ways in which a plan could fail, nor hope to prepare a plan for any eventuality. There are any number of events that could intervene to disrupt any plan. In the dinner example, the eventual plan can still fall to a variety of events that range from common natural disasters such as mudslides, fires, or electricity outages, to man-made disasters such as a terrorist group taking over the restaurant, the kitchen crew going on strike, a family emergency, or an accident, to more fantastical disasters such as a meteorite strike or botulism scares. The primary aim of ABP is to ensure that a plan is cognizant of and responsive to the major uncertainties inherent in the assumptions that underlie it.

Many of the assumptions upon which the plan rests are voluntarily made by the planners. Those voluntarily made assumptions should be most explicitly recognized and dealt with. Surprises from the failure of those assumptions should be most avoidable.

WHAT IS THE VALUE-ADDED OF ABP?

Good planners confront uncertainties as a matter of course. The primary value-added of Assumption-Based Planning is in helping planners identify the important uncertainties that necessarily accompany the assumptions of any plan. What ABP adds is a double-check on the planners' awareness of uncertainties. ABP adds techniques for rooting out uncertainties that have been overlooked or forgotten, or that are buried. There are at least four ways ABP helps uncover these hidden—or implicit—assumptions.

Identifying implicit assumptions in the plan

Any significant plan contains dozens or hundreds of assumptions—most of them not explicitly stated and most of them either non–load-bearing or invulnerable. Assumptions such as "The sun will rise tomorrow" or "People will still buy electrical products" or "Life will go on pretty much as it has for the last few years" are all part of what most of us usually assume about the future. However, among all those "trivial" assumptions can lurk a hidden, implicit assumption that is both load-bearing and vulnerable and that can be dangerous.

In the dining example, the planner could well assume that the special someone would love the seafood menu at the restaurant. This is a load-bearing, vulnerable assumption that is likely to remain implicit and unconsidered. If it does, it carries with it the seeds for disaster if the other person is allergic to or hates seafood. If this assumption is recognized, planning for it becomes a rather trivial matter (make sure to check with the special someone during the invitation), and either enhances the probability for success of the plan or leads naturally to a different, more workable plan.

ABP offers specific techniques (see Chapter 3) for improving the chances of identifying the implicit, load-bearing, vulnerable assumptions of a plan.

Bringing other minds into the planning process

Identifying the assumptions underlying a plan provides a window into the thinking of planners, enabling other people to find implicit or hidden assumptions.

There is general agreement in the planning literature that it is important to the success of a plan to represent as many of an organization's diverse perspectives as possible in the planning process. From a practical standpoint, of course, it is not easy to get a diverse group together long enough to do planning or to figure out how to get them all talking the same language.

But planning occurs iteratively. ABP works as a "post-planning" tool that starts with the results of some planning effort.[2] By identifying the assumptions underlying the plan, ABP enables others to see not only what the planners came up with but the assumptions that underlie those results, making it easier for someone to come in after the fact and understand the planners' thinking. This insight into the planners' minds increases the chances for someone with a different perspective to identify implicit or hidden assumptions, particularly if a list of assumptions is presented with the caveat "These are all the load-bearing assumptions we could think of." This double-check encourages a fresh observer to add something that might seem obvious but that is not explicitly on the list. Some of the most critical implicit assumptions are found in exactly this way.

Uncovering assumptions caused by planning

The act of planning can itself introduce unrecognized or implicit assumptions to a plan, and ABP can help uncover them.

The typical planning process includes an analysis of the *external environment*—the part of the world that is largely beyond the control of

2   Post-planning is in quotes to acknowledge both that planning is never completed and the more recent view that even strategic planning needs to be viewed as a continuous process. However, even where the planning processes are supposed to be continuous, there is usually a point at which the planning is "frozen" long enough to have management give it the blessing it needs in order for the actions it recommends to be put into operation.

the organization—for threats and opportunities. Part of the planning process concentrates on producing a plan or strategy for handling those threats and opportunities. However, the process of creating the strategy or plan that addresses external threats and opportunities can introduce *new* threats or opportunities. This is a bit difficult to see in the simplicity of the dining example, so let me shift to a business example.

Suppose Company A is faced with a situation in which a major competitor has just revamped its manufacturing capabilities and is about to be able to produce what Company A manufactures, at equivalent quality and lower cost—clearly a threat to Company A. This threat becomes part of the strategy problem facing Company A, which has several ways to approach it.

Company A may decide as its strategy to revamp its own manufacturing capability in a somewhat novel way. That novelty itself may introduce new uncertainties about, say, equipment delivery that were not part of the original analysis of the external environment. Further, it may stretch the financial capabilities of Company A and introduce an implicit assumption that interest rates will stay stable for three years, a vulnerability that was not part of the original vulnerabilities and one that the company may overlook in its enthusiasm for dealing with the challenges of the novel strategy. In this way, the creation of a plan has itself introduced both explicit and implicit load-bearing, vulnerable assumptions that were not part of the original environmental analysis.

Revisiting old assumptions

ABP can help an organization identify assumptions that were once explicit but that have become implicit.

All too often, an organization will create and successfully execute a strategic plan, only to forget the original assumptions that made it work. Those original assumptions can get buried and forgotten in the standard operating procedures and the culture of the organization (the habits and attitudes that define how things are done in an organization). Worse, they can become unchallengeable because they are accepted by everyone in the organization. ABP provides an organization with a tool for systematically revisiting the assumptions of even a plan that is succeeding, to make sure those assumptions are still valid.

WHO HAS USED ABP AND HOW DID IT FARE?

ABP was developed in a military setting, and the ABP developers and others have used Assumption-Based Planning in a variety of planning settings. ABP has now been applied to U.S. Army, Navy, Air Force, and Marines planning and has been used by planners in at least two foreign militaries. ABP has been used to improve plans for public enterprises, ranging from a small nonprofit firm to a large water district. It has been applied to test plans in private businesses, ranging from a small specialty shop to a Fortune 100 company. It has been used to test plans in higher education, at individual institutions as well as at the state board level. Although those applications were often proprietary, many of the lessons learned and some of the examples in this book come directly from those experiences. Two applications of ABP can be found in Dewar and Levin (1992) and Peters, Larson, and Dewar (1998).

As to how ABP has fared, it is difficult to measure directly the number of surprises ABP has prevented. However, prevented surprises can be measured indirectly by talking about the two mechanisms of ABP that have proven especially effective.

- First, in using ABP techniques for identifying assumptions underlying an organization's plans, we *have* identified load-bearing, vulnerable, implicit assumptions—often to the amazement of the planners. In a recent application for a manufacturing company, the planning portfolio appeared to assume that the economy would continue along its ahistorical bullish way for the foreseeable future. When we suggested this as an assumption to the head of planning, he seemed a bit taken aback—which took *us* aback. On reflection, however, he agreed that thinking about a couple of downturn situations would be a prudent step. That was in late 2000. The market turned bearish before the organization had a chance to fully consider such situations. Although the organization was not entirely prepared for a downturn, it also was not entirely surprised.

  Another, military application of ABP offers a contrast of no surprise. We uncovered an implicit assumption in proposed doctrine that the United States would maintain its lead in sophisticated long-range weapons. At the time, 1987, that was a reasonable, but not forcordained, assumption. It has since become a more secure (if somewhat less relevant) assumption. But in 1987, identifying it as a load-bearing, vulnerable assumption led to changes in the doctrine that explicitly addressed the importance of the United States' maintaining its lead in long-range weapons. A typical application of ABP identifies at least one or two such implicit assumptions. At the least, planning surprises from those assumptions become less likely.

- The generation of scenarios, or alternative futures, is the other ABP mechanism of interest that demonstrates its worth. Royal Dutch/Shell (see, for example, Schwartz 1991) and others have shown that the generation of scenarios can be an effective means of avoiding planning surprise. ABP generates scenarios from broken load-bearing, vulnerable assumptions as a means of identifying hedging actions.

WHAT ARE ABP'S STRENGTHS AND WEAKNESSES?

Numerous applications of ABP in a variety of planning situations have given us an appreciation of both its strengths and weaknesses.[3] In addition to the value-added aspects described above, ABP has some arguable strengths.

Strengths

ABP works well in very uncertain times. In more stable times, an organization's world changes slowly and there are likely to be fewer vulnerable assumptions or uncertainties about the future. The fewer uncertainties there are about that future, the fewer are the assumptions that need to be made about that future. The fewer assumptions there are, the less likely it is that load-bearing, vulnerable assumptions will slip past planners. In a fairly stable world, ABP is not likely to uncover much of surprise or add much in robustness. The more chaotic the

3   In 1995, I participated in a U.S. Air Force–sponsored symposium on different strategic planning methodologies. Mine was the only presentation that included a discussion of the methodology's strengths and weaknesses. I thought it odd then, and still do, that developers of planning tools and methods do not do a better job of discussing the limitations of their approaches. I understand the desire to emphasize the strengths. My sympathies, however, are with beleaguered planners faced with a plethora of planning methodologies and tools. No one knows better than the developers of a planning method or tool what its limitations are. I consider it an abdication of responsibility (if not somewhat dangerous) to leave to others an evaluation of where a method or tool is most and least appropriate.

times and the greater the uncertainty about the future, the more assumptions planners are likely to have to make in order to develop a plan—and the more likely it is that some load-bearing, vulnerable assumptions will slip past their notice. It is here that ABP is most likely to add value.

ABP generates relevant scenarios systematically. Scenarios are a common means for thinking about the future during planning. However, the generation of those scenarios is generally done in an *ad hoc* manner. Often, outside consultants are asked to prepare scenarios for an organization to use in its planning. Generally wonderfully researched and detailed, these scenarios are often developed without seriously involving the requesting organization, and the resulting scenarios are often difficult to relate to the exact planning challenges of the organization. Further, the scenarios are not generally "complete": They do not cover all the organization's planning challenges. If, as with ABP, planners identify the major assumptions an organization is making about the future, scenarios generated from broken assumptions are *automatically* relevant to the organization. Generating scenarios in this way will not guarantee a complete set of scenarios, but starting with the heaviest load-bearing and vulnerable assumptions provides greater confidence that the most important scenarios have been considered.

ABP can help connect environmental scanning to planning. To try to understand business environments, businesses today do a good deal of environmental scanning to produce characteristics of the external world to which the organization wants to pay attention. But, as with the scenarios above, connecting those characteristics to the organization's plans can be difficult. By understanding explicitly what assumptions about the world *led* to the plans, it is easier to relate the assumptions themselves more directly to the results of an environmental scan or the characteristics of a business environment.

ABP ties actions to specific assumptions. Using ABP allows signposts and shaping/hedging actions to be associated with specific assumptions about the future. As the vulnerability of a given assumption changes, those changes can be quickly connected to the corresponding shaping and hedging actions for that assumption. This level of traceability of actions to assumptions is rare in planning methodologies.

ABP applies to any and all plans. Since all plans contain *some* assumptions about the future, Assumption-Based Planning can be used to test the robustness and adaptability of any plan to uncertainties in those assumptions.

Weaknesses[4]

ABP requires an initial plan or concept. The strength of ABP is as a tester of plans, which implies that there is an output from some planning process that is tied into ABP. The current operations or most recent plan of any ongoing organization can always serve as an input to an Assumption-Based Planning exercise. However, ABP is not particularly helpful at the "blank-sheet-of-paper" planning stage. A brand-new company, for example, will not be able to make good use of ABP until it produces some kind of planning output.

ABP produces plan fragments, not complete plans. ABP produces planning actions that address *individual* uncertainties about the future. The result can be a plan in which a particular shaping action seems to be working at odds with a particular hedging action. For example, a shaping action that advertised electric vehicles as the *only* sensible solution to energy and environmental concerns would seem to contradict hedging actions that continued research on fuel-cell and hybrid alternatives to electric vehicles. From a planning standpoint, both of these are defensible actions. Together, however, they ruin the coherence of the overall plan. *Coherence* is an important characteristic for an organizational leadership worried about rallying the troops and inspiring a target audience.

ABP handles threats better than opportunities. For risk-averse organizations, ABP's strength is that it does a good job of identifying the threats to or vulnerabilities of a plan. The fact that it does not do as well at identifying opportunities is a weakness for more-aggressive en-

---

4   There is no shortage of criticism of planning methods and tools, but little in the way of systematic evaluations. Mintzberg and Lampel (1999) is the only recent categorization of planning methods I know of in the open literature. Most comparisons of methods or tools that I have seen have been in company-private documents. Chapter Twelve in Mason and Mitroff (1981) gives a brief comparison of five different strategic planning methodologies. A more in-depth comparison of a number of methodologies and tools can be found in Davis and Khalilzad (1996), which explains how different methods apply to different phases of planning.

terprises. ABP *does* help identify opportunities by presenting situations to planners that require creativity. Further, it can also be argued that few methodologies or tools are particularly good at identifying opportunities. Generally, it is fair to say that ABP underaddresses opportunities. One of Drucker's five deadly business sins is "feeding problems and starving opportunities" (1999: 49). In this sense, ABP directly feeds problems and only indirectly feeds opportunities.

You cannot ensure that all load-bearing assumptions have been identified by ABP. The utility of Assumption-Based Planning is based on its ability to identify the assumptions underlying an organization's plans. Therefore, it is only as good as the assumptions it can identify. As should become clear in Chapters 2 and 3, great care has been taken in developing techniques for identifying the assumptions underlying a given plan. That said, there is no guarantee that *all* the load-bearing assumptions will be identified. ABP is a means for improving an organization's ability to avoid surprises, not a guaranteed means of eliminating them.

HOW DO YOU KNOW ROBUST PLANS ARE BETTER?

The clear goal of Assumption-Based Planning is to make plans more robust and sophisticated in the face of uncertainty. Teisberg (1993: 3) makes a good point when she worries about robustness as a goal in planning:

> The scenario analysis literature often recommends choosing a "robust" strategy, that is, a strategy that will enable the firm to do well in many different possible future scenarios. Undoubtedly, if a firm *can*, it should pursue a strategy in which it will be very successful no matter what future events occur. Unfortunately, such situations are unusual. . . . "Robust" strategies then often imply mediocre returns because firms reduce possible gains from some outcomes, while reducing possible losses from others . . . we see that pursuing a robust strategy could undermine a firm's chance for superior profits by forcing managers to avoid risky commitments with potentially high payoffs. [Emphasis in the original.]

The ultimate goal of ABP is to have an organization *understand and confront* all the load-bearing assumptions it is making in its plan. ABP makes no judgments about the risks inherent in the plan. Its application is designed to ensure that *whatever* risk is in the plan is recognized and that the shaping and hedging actions that are developed will do as much as possible to ensure that the plan is as robust as it can be to the uncertainties and risks the plan has already accepted.

* * * *

This chapter has presented the rudiments of Assumption-Based Planning. Chapter 2 defines assumptions more precisely and develops a taxonomy of assumptions. Chapters 3 through 7 detail each of the five steps of Assumption-Based Planning. Chapter 8 describes some of the practical art that has evolved from a variety of ABP applications. Chapter 9 describes extensions of Assumption-Based Planning into planning methodologies and Assumption-Based *Thinking*.

The Appendix connects the terms and concepts of ABP with the same or similar terms and concepts in the literature. It is for readers who are familiar with the terms, concepts, and methods of planning and wonder how and where ABP fits in.

2

A taxonomy of assumptions

A primary aim of Assumption-Based Planning is to identify certain types of assumptions underlying a plan: those that are load-bearing and vulnerable. This suggests that there are different kinds of assumptions. Indeed, we have found it useful to distinguish among several different types. In addition to making clear exactly what we mean in general by *assumption*, it is also important to make the distinctions among the different types of assumptions clear.

WHAT IS A PLANNING ASSUMPTION?

Webster's New World Dictionary defines *assumption* as "the supposition that something is true" or "a fact or statement taken for granted." (The 1998 version defines *assumption* as "an assuming that something is true.") The assumptions we are interested in fit these definitions, but they are more restricted. We are interested only in *planning* assumptions. For ease of discussion, we drop the *planning*, but it is implicit in what we have come to mean by "assumption" in Assumption-Based Planning:

A *[planning] assumption* is a judgment or evaluation about some characteristic of the future that underlies the plans of an organization.

All planning requires some judgments about, or evaluations of, the future. The more uncertain the future, the more likely it is that the planner will have to make judgments or "guesstimates" to help narrow the range and number of uncertainties about the future into a manageable few before progress can be made. As soon as you narrow the pos-

14

sibilities for the future by deciding, "I just don't think that's likely" or "I'm not going to consider that any further," you are making a judgment or assumption about the future.

To be useful to planning, the judgments in these assumptions *need to be about aspects of the future that concern the organization*. Despite strong concerns and opinions members of the organization might have about the future of, say, rock and roll, it is a planning assumption only if it is demonstrably related to the organization's plans and its future. This is a practical consideration for minimizing the number of assumptions that need to be considered.

The *plans* in the definition above include any type of actions directed toward the future, whether in draft form or implied by current operations. Preferably, these plans will be written out, at least sketchily. In general, but particularly if the plans are not written, it is important to have access to the planners. Without carefully documented plans or access to someone who knows what went into creating them, the plans will still contain assumptions—but little can be done about them.

The requirement that an assumption be about the future is subtle but noteworthy. As denoted in the dictionary, assumptions can be about the present or past as well as the future. Judgments or assumptions made about the present or past are useful for planning *only* if they translate into judgments about the future, too. For example, an organization may judge that its position relative to the market is eroding today and has been doing so for the past six months. This becomes an assumption only if there is a feeling or judgment that the erosion in market position, left unaddressed, will continue into the future or that it has already reached a critical point. Only if a judgment about the present or past is also a judgment about the future should it concern planners.

Judgments about the future can also overlap with planned actions in the sense of Alan Kay's famous pronouncement that "the best way to predict the future is to invent it" (1989). In the "can-do" world of modern capitalism, this overlap is very common. "Dot coms," for example, race to be "first to market" because they generally recognize that being first often confers a distinct advantage in the battle to capture a dominant market share. There is nothing wrong with trying to invent the future in this way. However, if an organization plans to capture a major market share by being first to market, it needs to recognize that there are assumptions buried in that plan, both about the organization's ability to *be* first to market and about whether being first actually translates into a dominant market share. Optimistic judgments about the future are fine as long as they are recognized and dealt with as assumptions, not inevitabilities.

We have deliberately defined *assumption* very broadly. What one person may not consider an assumption another may recognize as a crucial assumption. Where one observer may be so convinced of a trend in consumer preferences as to consider it a fact of life, another may see it as an assumption that is vulnerable within the planning horizon. In that case, it should be treated as an assumption.

By casting the net widely for assumptions, we intend, on the one hand, that as few assumptions as possible escape. On the other hand, the catch of assumptions can become quite large, leading to problems with handling them all. We deal with such problems in the next chapter.

THE TAXONOMIC TREE OF ASSUMPTIONS

The title for this chapter promises a taxonomy. That is, it suggests not only that there are different kinds of assumptions, but that they can be arranged in a tree-like structure. That (inverted) tree is shown in Figure 2.1.

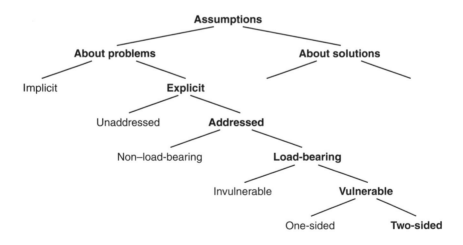

Figure 2.1. A Taxonomy of Assumptions, Emphasizing the Main Branches

The bold print in the figure further suggests that one particular branch of the tree is more important than any other. This is indeed the case. Not surprisingly, it is the branch that contains both load-bearing and vulnerable assumptions. Each level in the structure of Figure 2.1 represents a different distinction among assumptions. I address each in turn.

Assumptions about problems vs. assumptions about solutions

A *plan* is a tentative solution to the inexact problems posed by an uncertain future. Even if the future could be known with certainty, there are likely to be uncertainties about whether a given plan is the proper solution or approach for that future. Any plan, then, contains assumptions both about what the future holds (the problems) and about whether the plan will perform as hoped (the solutions).

A good deal of the planning literature is taken up with solutions to or means for approaching planning problems, including such solutions and/or means as Total Quality Management, benchmarking, time-based competition, outsourcing, partnering, reengineering, change management, and downsizing. Each of these solutions, or means, introduces assumptions about the outcome of the plan. It is as important to pay attention to the assumptions about outcomes as it is to pay attention to the assumptions about the future.

Suppose an assumption about the future is that a rival will introduce a lesser-quality, low-cost version of your best-selling product. The organization's plan to retain market share and profit margin might be to increase the number of features on its product and to emphasize the resulting product's quality in its ads. There is no doubt about the organization's ability to add features and to alter its ad campaign. One assumption being made is that the plan will work: that by adding features and changing the ads the organization will retain market share and profit margin.

Adding in assumptions about a plan's performance would seem to double the number of assumptions facing the Assumption-Based planner. Usually, it does. But usually, planners are very sensitive to the assumptions they make about *solutions*. In an ABP sense, planners already generally do the right things by these assumptions: They establish and monitor signposts related to these assumptions at least once a quarter; they take shaping actions by a variety of means to keep the assumptions sound, including advertising, providing incentives and penalties, and putting on motivational seminars; and they generally have a sense of hedging actions to be taken if the plan fails to meet some of its goals.

Assumptions about solutions in a plan, then, tend to get more and better ABP-like attention than do assumptions about the problem. On the one hand, this should not be surprising. The behavior of a plan is typically much more controllable for an organization than is the behavior of the world that the plan addresses. On the other hand, if the organization treated the assumptions it makes about the world more as it treats the assumptions it makes about its plan, it would already be doing Assumption-Based Planning.

We saw this curious dichotomy of treatment in a somewhat different way when we worked with the U.S. Army. On the tactical battlefield, the Army uses a methodology called Intelligence Preparation of the Battlefield (IPB) to help plan its operations (U.S. Army 1996). IPB contains many of the elements of ABP, albeit with different names. It identifies facts and assumptions about the battlefield environment. It makes assumptions about enemy Courses of Action and constantly updates those assumptions through monitoring Targeted Areas of Interest (signposts) that help distinguish among the enemy's possible courses. In its operational plans, the Army has both shaping actions to "encourage" the enemy to take a preferred Course of Action and hedging actions in the form of contingency plans, if the enemy does not behave as desired.

But if the Army's tactical planning with IPB is very much like Assumption-Based Planning, its strategic planning process has not been. Until the early 1990s, the Army did its strategic planning by developing a most-likely scenario of the global future (sometimes with variations) and then developing a strategic plan to handle that most-likely future.[1] The Army's tactical battlefield planning methodology did a much better job of confronting tactical uncertainties than its strategic planning methodology did of confronting strategic uncertainties.

1 In fairness, we have argued that the Army did not really have an uncertain *strategic* future until the Berlin Wall fell. Before then, it made sense to project the Soviet Union, with its known capabilities and its projected technologies, as the primary strategic problem. After 1989, it made more sense for the Army to adopt a more IPB-like approach to the strategic future as well. See Builder and Dewar (1994).

Implicit vs. explicit assumptions

The primary goal of Assumption-Based Planning is to make sure that as many as possible of the load-bearing assumptions underlying a plan have been made explicit and have been confronted.

If you talked to the developers of a given plan, they would be able to detail many of the assumptions that they factored into their thinking in plan development. Are these explicit assumptions because the planners can call them to mind when asked? Or might they be implicit assumptions if they have not been documented anywhere and could therefore be easily forgotten the next time the question is asked? The line between explicit and implicit assumptions is not crisp, but the general notion is that

> An *implicit assumption* is an assumption that planners are not (yet) consciously aware they are making.

It is important that planners recognize and deal with the assumptions they are making. However, this definition assumes (implicitly) that planners *document* the assumptions they are consciously aware of making. If they do not, the assumptions that planners are explicitly aware of might not be recognized by other observers or users of the plan.

Unfortunately, not all planners document the assumptions of which they are consciously aware. The above definition of an implicit assumption leads to a problem in trying to define what an explicit assumption is. Is it an assumption that planners are consciously aware they are making, or does the assumption also have to be documented in order that it might be explicit to everybody?

In the best of worlds, *explicit assumptions* are documented. In reality, there will be a confusion about *to whom* an assumption is not explicit. In a slight expansion of the definition, we allow an assumption to be implicit to anyone to whom it is not explicit—whether because it is implicit to the planners or because the planners have failed to make it explicit to everyone.

The other aspect of the definition that is important is the element of time. Since a major goal of ABP is to make implicit assumptions explicit, the shorter the time that an assumption remains implicit, the better.

In any case, implicit assumptions as they are defined above are the most potentially damaging to a plan. They are usually recognized only in retrospect, as they were in 1997, when excess capacity in the automobile industry led manufacturers to slash prices and offer large rebates to purchasers. As one planning manager at an automotive manufacturer said (in a quote from the *Wall Street Journal* article "Fears of Overcapacity Continue to Grow," March 2, 1998, in Corporate Strategy Board 1998: 45),

> There wasn't a clear understanding of the excess capacity situation, either by us or anyone else in the auto industry. Everyone *implicitly assumed* they could safely add capacity. [Though it was painful], the healthiest thing for the industry was for the top guys to understand as distinctly as possible what a mess the industry had gotten into.

There are any number of reasons why some of the assumptions underlying a plan are implicit. A common reason is that the assumption, which was once explicit, has through time become so ingrained that it has slipped below the level of conscious thinking and has been "forgotten." For example, market research could determine something important about customers in a given income bracket that is explicitly dealt with in the organization's plans. Over time, and without further market research, the organization may have come to depend on that original characterization even as the buying habits of those in the income bracket are changing significantly. The organization might no longer be aware that it is making that characterization in its customer projections.

A particularly dangerous type of implicit assumption is one that has become load-bearing without anyone realizing it until it breaks and the plan collapses with it. Assumptions such as "Sylvia will be here throughout the plan" may be explicit if Sylvia is a "star" and highly sought after elsewhere. If, however, Sylvia is intensely loyal to the organization, has never missed a day of work, and has become crucial to the workings of the organization, her availability (which cannot be guaranteed) may be both crucial and implicitly assumed. If Sylvia is suddenly not available at a crucial juncture in the plan's implementation, the plan could run into serious trouble without anyone having recognized that Sylvia was so crucial. The availability of crucial people, things, or capabilities can easily become load-bearing, vulnerable, *and* implicit assumptions underlying a plan.

There are several other reasons that an assumption may be implicit:

- It has been suppressed for organizational or external political reasons.

- It has been repressed by the planners.

- The planners have "cultural blinders."

- Recognition of the assumption is blocked by the planners' cognitive maps or previous attributions.[2]

For whatever reason, though, if a load-bearing assumption underlying a plan is *implicit*, it needs to be identified and confronted *explicitly*.

Note that a given assumption need not be made explicit to *everybody*. But it must be made explicit to the planners and decisionmakers. This is a subtle point. For reasons such as competitive advantage or pride, an organization may not want to expose some of its load-bearing assumptions widely. However, the planners and decisionmakers must be aware of, and deal with, even otherwise-unmentionable assumptions before they can develop and implement a plan that is as robust as possible.

Addressed vs. unaddressed assumptions

Whether an assumption has been addressed is an intermediate characteristic of assumptions about the future that needs to be discussed before going on to discussions of load-bearing and vulnerable characteristics. An assumption is *addressed* if there are specific actions in the plan that are directed at its validity—if you can form a statement of the form, "We are assuming [assumption], and, because of that, we will [take actions]."

The documentation of a typical plan generally contains, among other things, two major sections: one on what the future will be like and the other on what the organization is going to do about the future. It is not uncommon for the section on the future to contain assumptions that are not addressed in the section on actions. By being unaddressed, these assumptions cannot be load-bearing in an ABP sense, because their failure cannot cause replanning of any current planned actions. Nonetheless, they should be of concern to planners because such assumptions represent unfinished business—and they *should* be addressed. Only after

---

2   I am indebted to Yehezkel Dror of The Hebrew University for much of the discussion on additional sources of implicit assumptions.

they have been addressed can they can be judged for whether they are load-bearing, vulnerable, etc.

In our experience, unaddressed assumptions about the world— because they often represent issues that planners put into the "too-hard" box and leave until later—should be of particular concern to planners. In the late 1980s, a small professional organization explicitly assumed that the Internet *could* affect its publications in the future. However, because the World Wide Web had not yet exploded onto the scene, the plan made no mention of the Internet. Not until the planning cycle of the next year, when it was clear that the Internet and the World Wide Web were going to have a growing influence, did the planners come up with some actions to address the potential effect of the Internet. In another example, the U.S. Army explicitly assumed that operations in the future would more likely be carried out in urban terrain than in traditional theaters. How to carry out urban operations was unaddressed in the proposed plan and has subsequently been the topic of wide-ranging debate and development.

Load-bearing vs. non–load-bearing assumptions

In Chapter 1, the definition of *load-bearing* was left a bit vague. *Load-bearing* means something very specific in ABP, so it is here that we need to be explicit about what makes an assumption load-bearing:

> An assumption is *load-bearing* if its failure would require significant changes in the organization's plans.

This is not the usual sense of a critical or important assumption. Load-bearing in an ABP sense is akin to load-bearing for a physical structure. If you take away a load-bearing piece of a building, part of the building collapses. If you take a load-bearing assumption away from a plan, part of the plan collapses.

In physical structures, there are degrees of damage to load-bearing elements and there are degrees of collapse. The same is true of load-bearing assumptions and how much damage to the validity of the assumption is required before significant changes need to be made.

The definition of load-bearing takes an absolute position by talking about the *failure* of an assumption: that point at which the assumption will no longer be able to "support the weight of the plan" and replanning will be necessary.

The value of defining *load-bearing* as above became clear to us when we were working with U.S. Army planners. In one version of proposed doctrine, the Army explicitly assumed that it would not go to war in the future without the aid of forces from other nations. Therefore, it assumed that it would have to combine with the forces from other nations for future operations—a very important issue because of the vast requirements involved in being able to conduct operations with forces whose equipment, training, and language are different from the U.S. Army's. It is also an assumption in the sense that it is a judgment about how the Army would conduct its operations in the future. But, in the ABP sense, it was not a load-bearing assumption in the proposed doctrine.

How could that be? This assumption would have failed if the U.S. Army found itself conducting operations on its own. But the Army produces equipment and runs much of its training on its own. Because of this, the Army is already prepared for the potential failure of the assumption. The assumption's failure would not require the Army to change its plans. Therefore, the assumption is not load-bearing by definition. Suppose, however, that the Army were to embed the assumption about fighting with other nations' forces into its training practices and operational plans, and rarely or never train on its own. In that plan, the assumption's failure could be very disruptive and would qualify as load-bearing.

One of the load-bearing assumptions in that same proposed Army doctrine was the expectation that the United States would have superiority in long-range battlefield weapons. The plan hinged on the Army's ability to use those weapons to gain an advantage. If the Army did *not* have superiority in long-range battlefield weapons, advantage would be lost and plans would have to be adjusted significantly.

In a business context, if a company is risking everything on being "first to market," the assumption that it *will be* the first one to introduce a given product is clearly load-bearing. However, if the company also has a plan for capitalizing by being a "fast follower" (being able to catch up quickly if someone else is first to market), then its assumption that it will or can be first to market is not load-bearing in the ABP sense. The latter plan is a more robust one.[3]

---

3   One could argue that risking everything on a single assumption brings an important urgency to an organization's operations that a robust plan lacks. While a robust plan does lack that urgency, it also lacks the risk. In risk-

Whether or not an assumption is load-bearing, then, depends on whether other elements of the plan have been introduced to carry part of the load. Because the process of determining whether an assumption is load-bearing (as defined above) requires a broad understanding of the overall plan, that process should be done separately from the process of identifying assumptions.

Vulnerable vs. invulnerable assumptions

If a load-bearing assumption is one whose failure is of concern, then the potential for the failure of that assumption clearly plays a significant role. Indeed,

> An assumption is *vulnerable* if plausible events could cause it to fail within the expected lifetime of the plan.

Time is clearly an important aspect of vulnerability. Few judgments about the future are likely to fail from any cause in the next few minutes; most (time-unconstrained) judgments about the future of life on earth are vulnerable if you go far enough out in time.

All plans have at least implicit expected lifetimes, and many have explicit ones, usually measured in whole numbers of months or years. The strategic plans of businesses in the 1970s and 1980s commonly covered three to five years. More recently, those businesses that still admit to doing strategic planning tend to use shorter lifetimes. Whereas the setting of the lifetimes of some plans *can* be clear and precise—4 hours at most for the implemented game plan of a football team, for example—the setting of most plan lifetimes is usually rather arbitrary and inexact. This is not surprising. Given common business uncertainties about the future (such as customer behavior), planners could hardly be expected to know precisely how long a given plan is likely to be effective. That said, we believe a bit more rigor should be brought to the issue of understanding the expected lifetime of plans.

> averse organizations (such as the military), robust planning is more important than having a sense of urgency. In addition, any organization can add urgency back in, for example, with incentives for not having to go to a backup plan. Similarly, the organization may recognize the vulnerability of some load-bearing assumptions and be satisfied that its shaping and hedging actions are sufficient to allow it to go ahead and accept the remaining risks.

However the lifetime of a plan is measured or established, it sets the time frame for thinking about the vulnerabilities of assumptions. In a 3-year plan in the year 2001, an assumption that there will be a Republican administration in Washington, D.C., throughout the plan is not vulnerable. The same assumption in a 5-year plan in 2001 *is* vulnerable.

The question of just how plausible the events should be before deciding that an assumption is vulnerable is addressed in Chapter 3. One thing that should be clear at this point is that the longer the expected lifetime of the plan is, the more likely it is that assumptions *will be* vulnerable. That is, of course, why planning well into the future is so difficult.

There is one further taxonomic distinction that is important to make, and that involves how an assumption *might* fail.

One-sided vs. two-sided vulnerabilities

Vulnerability is typically defined in terms of being susceptible to wounds or damage, which suggests that a vulnerable assumption is one whose failure would lead to bad consequences and, generally, that an assumption would fail in a way that the organization does not like (for example, people *don't* flock to the new, improved product or service). In Assumption-Based Planning, vulnerabilities are intended also to point to the possibility that an assumption could fail in a way that the organization *does* like, yet still require the organization to change its plans.[4] To have to add production capability because of unexpectedly high consumer demand may be a happy change of plans, but it could be a significant change of plans nonetheless. We say that assumptions of this type have *two-sided vulnerabilities*, because they can fail in either good or bad directions.

By *one-sided vulnerabilities*, we mean assumptions that are vulnerable to failure *only* in one direction during the plan's lifetime: in the or-

4 Unfortunately, the connection between failures an organization likes or does not like and whether those failures lead to threats or opportunities, is not clear. However, it is fair to say that assumption "failures" that an organization likes are more likely to be thought of as leading to opportunities than to threats. In this way, ABP does have something to say about planning opportunities.

ganization's favor.[5] "Worst-case assumptions" is another term for assumptions of this type, because they have generally been deliberately chosen so that the future is very unlikely ever to be worse than that. Assumptions with one-sided vulnerabilities have shown up in all of the plans we have studied, but they are more likely to be found in the plans of what we think of as risk-averse organizations, such as public companies or the military. In planning for the large water district with which we worked, planners made several worst-case assumptions about the frequency and duration of droughts—exactly the kind of planning we want our water district to be doing to ensure adequate water supplies under even dreadful circumstances.

The U.S. Army assumption about the likelihood of having to conduct military operations in combination with the forces of other countries is an assumption with a one-sided vulnerability. If it breaks, it does so in the direction of the Army's having to conduct unilateral operations (which is what it actually prepares for and would prefer to conduct in the first place).

The difference between one-sided and two-sided vulnerabilities illustrates an important point about planning and robustness. A plan designed to handle a future built around nothing but worst-case assumptions (or assumptions with one-sided vulnerabilities) would be quite robust. The only "failures" its assumptions might suffer would be ones the organization would like. Such a plan would not really need improving (assuming the organization can figure out what it should do in the event of any happy assumption "failure").

Planning for the worst case only. If the goal is to develop a plan that is robust, why not just generate a worst-case future and develop a plan to handle that future? It is clear how to develop a worst-case future: Look at all the major uncertainties facing the organization, choose the worst case for each uncertainty, and generate a future based on those worst cases. Developing a plan to handle that worst-case scenario

---

5   Yes, we recognize that, logically, there is another type of one-sided vulnerability—one that fails only in a bad way. Assumptions with this kind of one-sided vulnerability might be called "Pollyanna assumptions" in light of their excessive optimism. Since we have never seen these kinds of assumptions/vulnerabilities in practice, we have commandeered the name for the particular type of one-sided vulnerability associated with worst-case assumptions.

might be challenging. If you could achieve one, you would have a good, robust plan.

Not only has such an approach been used in planning cases (particularly military ones), it is an approach worth thinking about in almost any circumstance. In fact, for very risk-averse organizations or for organizations facing a very likely worst-case future, it may be imperative to plan this way.

However, anyone who has seriously tried to plan to a worst-case future has run into practical problems. In the first place, I dare you to develop a worst-case future that I cannot make worse.[6] Imagination has its limits. The worst case you can possibly imagine is not guaranteed to be the worst case *possible*. For example, the French Army in World War II could not imagine that the German Army would slog through the dense Ardennes forest to go around their fabled Maginot Line. Some people had worried about a commercial airliner being used as a weapon, but no one imagined anything like the September 11, 2001, terrorist attack on the World Trade Center and the Pentagon. In practice, a worst-case scenario is settled upon by agreeing that a given worst case is bad enough. However, it is important to recognize that no worst-case scenario is truly without potential nasty surprises.

The more serious drawback to worst-case plans is that they are likely to be (much) more expensive than plans that permit some risk. For public safety or national security, cost may not be a significant constraint.[7] For most businesses, the cost of a plan must be weighed against its risks, and a plan that handles all possible risks is likely to be too expensive. This high cost decreases the likelihood that a worst-case plan will be implemented and increases the likelihood that the plan that is implemented will contain some risks and load-bearing, vulnerable assumptions.

6   In a private correspondence, colleague Paul Davis of RAND said he has seen a lot of supposedly "worst-case" plans that are "bizarre combinations of best-case and worst-case assumptions." As an example, he pointed to Defense Planning Guidance scenarios that assumed plenty of warning time and excellent allied support (best case) on the one-hand and "very big threats who fight heroically like the Japanese at Iwo Jima (worst case)" on the other.

7   There is another, more subtle danger in worst-case planning. Even if the costs can be borne, there is an implicit assumption in such planning that if the worst case can be handled, everything else can be handled, too. This assumption that everything else is a "lesser-included case" may not hold.

This brings up a more general planning point: There is always some freedom in choosing assumptions about the future, because choosing assumptions and developing plans to handle those assumptions is an iterative process. Starting out with a very risk-averse mind-set and choosing a lot of worst-case assumptions may cause the plan developed to handle those assumptions either not to be acceptable or not to fit the budget. Therefore, some risk is accepted, which involves changing some of the assumptions to accept more risk. And the planning process continues. Or the future may be viewed so optimistically that the planner gets nervous, so more risk-averse assumptions are made and replanning is done.

Dealing with two-sided vulnerabilities first. The last thing to be said about assumptions with one-sided and two-sided vulnerabilities is that it is better to deal with those assumptions that have two-sided vulnerabilities first. The vulnerabilities of one-sided assumptions are generally less destructive to the plan, so dealing with such assumptions can be deferred. This emphasis is reflected in Figure 2.1.

OTHER CHARACTERISTICS OF ASSUMPTIONS

Three other characteristics of assumptions do not really qualify as parts of the taxonomic tree in Figure 2.1 but are worth mentioning before we proceed.

Good vs. bad assumptions

A general discussion of assumptions is not complete without talking about "good" and "bad" assumptions. The entire thrust of planning is to make a few assumptions about the future and to develop a plan for that future that takes into account that some of those assumptions may not hold throughout the expected lifetime of the plan. Said in this way, there are no normative evaluations of the assumptions, only judgments about the future. Assumptions may turn out to be right or wrong, but they are not "good" or "bad."

Conversely, by listing all of the assumptions underlying a given plan and asking which of the assumptions is vulnerable within the expected lifetime of the plan, it is virtually impossible not to get judgmental about the assumptions: "I don't think this is a good assumption" (which usually indicates that someone thinks it is vulnerable or invalid), or "A better assumption would be . . ." (by which is typically meant a less vulnerable or more valid one), and so forth.

In an Assumption-Based Planning sense, an assumption is "bad" only if it is demonstrably broken already. "Interest rates will stay below 8 percent for the next three years" is not a good assumption if interest rates just went above 8 percent this afternoon. If that assumption is a load-bearing assumption, it may be time to start replanning right now. Otherwise, judgments about the goodness or badness of assumptions are not useful. Either an assumption is vulnerable or it is not.

Since assumptions are about the future, "We will assume that interest rates will be below 8 percent by the end of the fiscal year" may not be a "good" assumption, but it is not broken already no matter what interest rates are: It is a judgment about what is going to happen to interest rates in the coming months. That may well be a vulnerable assumption. If it is a load-bearing assumption, shaping and hedging actions should be developed. If shaping and hedging actions are infeasible (for whatever reason), it may make sense to replan, using new assumptions.

This avoidance of normative labels is a serious effort to bring focus to judgments about assumptions. Concentrating on the vulnerability of assumptions, whether or not they have already failed, and whether or not they can be shored up, is more useful and productive than judging assumptions to be "good" or "bad." In applications of Assumption-Based Planning that use someone familiar with ABP to assist in the process (what we call a *facilitator*), having a strong facilitator is the best insurance against the natural tendency to judge the goodness or badness of assumptions. The facilitator may need to step in from time to time if the discussion of assumptions starts to drift to the wild or frivolous. The subject of using a facilitator and maintaining a discussion on assumptions is taken up again in Chapter 8, "The art of conducting ABP."

Levels of assumptions

Unlike evaluations about "good" or "bad" assumptions, evaluations can reasonably be made about the "level" of an assumption within a hierarchy of assumptions. An assumption about geopolitical stability is at a different level from an assumption about a specific official in a particular country. Similarly, an assumption about the future of the electronics industry is at a different level from an assumption about the behavior of a particular electronics firm in a specific market segment. The first assumption in each case is likely to have wider-ranging consequences than the second and should be treated with greater attention in Assumption-Based Planning.

However, whereas it is generally useful to distinguish between levels of assumptions, the trouble comes in trying to set up those levels beforehand, in a systematic way. It is easy to imagine a hierarchical tree of assumptions of decreasing abstraction for a given situation. The tree could start with goals and values, move to how those goals and values will play out in various regional headquarters, move down to departments within headquarters, and so forth. Unfortunately, the hierarchical tree could as easily start with an organization's product lines or functional units or some other "top level." There are probably as many defensible abstraction trees as there are organizational forms.

In practice, we have found no particular advantage to setting up the levels before identifying the assumptions. Sometimes, doing so has been a distraction—possibly a constraint on the assumption-identification process. We have found that it is more efficient to identify assumptions without a preconceived notion of systematic levels. It is fairly easy—and useful—to take a preliminary list of assumptions and group them into levels and sublevels as a means of organizing what is usually an extensive list of assumptions.

Assigning levels, about which a fair amount has been written,[8] is an underexplored area in Assumption-Based Planning. One potentially fruitful area for further study is cognitive maps: the internal scheme that planners develop to navigate their way through the planning process. That map is likely to contain assumptions nested by their perceived importance to the problem.

Directed vs. elected assumptions

Up to this point, the discussion has proceeded as though the planners were completely free to elect which assumptions about the future they will develop into a plan. Unless top management is involved in the planning and the planning is being done at the highest level in the organization, this is rarely the case. More commonly, higher management will *direct* several of the parameters or assumptions to be used in plan-

8   I am indebted to Paul Davis for raising this issue.

ning at lower levels. These parameters often include budgetary constraints and can include specific assumptions to be made about some aspects of the world. These directed assumptions can be implicit or explicit. For example, when a higher headquarters asks for the plans of a division, it is often implicit that the division is to assume that the organization's divisional structure will remain as it is currently throughout the lifetime of the plan.

The most important and visible directed assumptions are the goals and values of the organization. They describe where the organization is trying to go and how it is trying to get there. They are the beacons and touchstones that will remain while everything around them is in turmoil. But they, too, are subject to change, and within the planning horizon. Goals can become unrealistic and cease to inspire or they can be overrun in advance and require resetting. Even *values*—those deeper parts of an organization's culture that define "how and why we do business"—can be overwhelmed by circumstances and become ignored. *Goals and values are load-bearing, vulnerable assumptions.*

Directed assumptions, then, should be treated like any other assumptions—that is, in theory they should. In practice, because of their sources, it is difficult to treat directed assumptions like any other assumptions. Perhaps in Assumption-Based Planning they should be treated as first among equals, shaped and hedged as vigorously as the planners can muster, but ABP planners should not treat them as immutable, which they are not. They are vulnerable, and they are load-bearing. If they fail, the organization could fail with them. Perhaps it is acceptable for the organization to fail; however, the planners owe the organization their best efforts to avoid failure. The best way for planners to do that is to confront the vulnerable aspects of directed assumptions at least as vigorously as they do the vulnerable aspects of elected assumptions.

That said, it is time to move on to the question of *how* to identify the assumptions underlying a plan.

3

Step 1: identifying assumptions

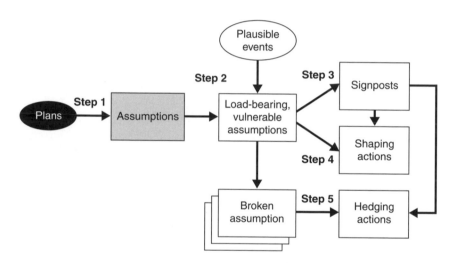

Figure 3.1. Highlighting Step 1 of ABP: Identifying the Assumptions
Underlying a Plan

Planners are generally aware of many of the key assumptions they are making in a given plan. How can they be sure they have identified all of their key assumptions? Some of the assumptions underlying a given plan are easy to identify, others are more difficult to determine, some may never be known, and history has shown on many occasions that some may be recognized only in retrospect, when they have failed with catastrophic consequences. Since it is this last category that we are most interested in avoiding, the goal of the first step in Assumption-Based Planning is to help planners identify as many of the assumptions underlying a given plan as possible. As depicted in Figure 3.1, this step involves taking what is known about the plans of the organization and identifying the assumptions underlying them, as though the plans had already been generated. Indeed, our experiences with ABP have largely been with after-the-fact plan improvement. The techniques that we developed are weighted toward identifying assumptions *after* rather than *during* planning. ABP helps improve plans rather than helping to generate them.

But planning itself is an iterative process. Organizations typically follow planning cycles. During a given planning cycle, planners come up with tentative ideas or plans, they evaluate those ideas or plans by a variety of means, and they make changes as necessary. ABP is also a means for testing the robustness of the ideas or plans *during* the iterations of the planning process. The one time and place that it can make a difference whether ABP is being applied during or after planning comes in where you look for assumptions, the first stop in the logical road map for identification of assumptions, shown in Figure 3.2.

WHERE TO LOOK FOR ASSUMPTIONS

After planning has been completed

When applying Assumption-Based Planning *after* planning has been completed, there are two primary places to look for assumptions: in the documentation and with the people involved in planning.

Looking in the documentation for the plans is often not that easy. Although most organizations document their planned actions—often in glossy brochures available for public dissemination—few organizations document their plans systematically, particularly the part that would reveal the assumptions being made about the future. To get at the details of the planned actions, along with the plans for monitoring those actions, we need to get at the underlying documentation for those glossy brochures. The documentation and details often exist, but usually only in fragments. Still, we have found that *any* documentation surrounding the plans is useful in the search for assumptions: Vu-graphs, handwritten notes, glossy brochures, computer files. Documentation in electronic format is particularly useful because of the powerful full-document search capabilities that are available on computers.

It is usually not difficult to find the second source of assumptions, the people who have the intimate knowledge of the planning process

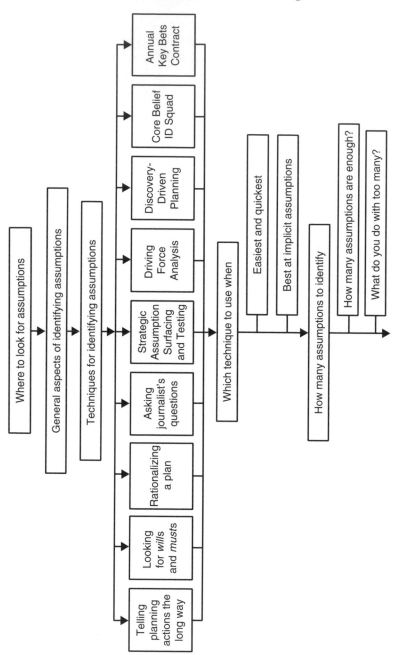

Figure 3.2. Logical Road Map of Chapter 3

and its outputs. These people may not be the planners themselves. In a large, private manufacturing company, we talked with the vice president in charge of planning. At one small college, we talked with long-time faculty who were involved in the planning, because they had the historical perspective on the college as well as a planning perspective. In a large public utility, we talked with planning department personnel—not the director of planning—because the department personnel had the important details, as well as a broader perspective. In some of the applications for the U.S. Army, we talked with both the leadership and personnel in the Directorate for Strategy, Plans and Policy. Although getting time with the right people can be difficult, a couple of 2- to 3-hour sessions is usually sufficient.

During planning

In applying ABP *during* the planning process, tentative plans can be tested in the same way that completed plans are. Written documentation is unlikely to be available, but the planners should be. Their thinking about the plan should be fresh in their minds.

As planning is just getting started

If no new or tentative plans exist—that is, if the planning is just getting started—ABP can still be applied, but it is more difficult. Here, the best place to start is by looking either at the previous plans (which are presumably guiding current operations) or at current operations themselves. In the case where planning is just getting started, it is even less likely than in a during-planning application of ABP that the plan and its assumptions are easily accessible in written form. Finding people who are still familiar with the planning effort that led to current operations may also be difficult. However, the probable reason for thinking about planning at any point is that one or more of the assumptions underlying current operations is either in jeopardy or has already broken. If little or nothing can be found of the planning process that led to current operations, it is still useful to try to identify the assumptions underlying those operations. Some of the techniques in this chapter are useful for doing so.

One reason for talking about where to look for assumptions is to reinforce the notion that documentation of plans and the assumptions underlying them is a *good thing*. It facilitates plan improvement and plan monitoring. Using ABP to improve one generation of an organization's plans can actually encourage the organization to make the kind of documentation effort that will facilitate using ABP (or other means) to improve plans in the future. I describe some documentation schemes later in this chapter.

GENERAL ASPECTS OF IDENTIFYING ASSUMPTIONS

To be done well, identifying a plan's assumptions—unearthing those judgments or evaluations being made about characteristics of the future that underlie the planned actions—requires a good deal of judgment and creativity. The first few assumptions are usually easy to identify. They tend to be invulnerable assumptions of great generality, and the planners are comfortable using them to set the basic parameters of their planning solution. For example, planners in a large manufacturing company identified several assumptions about the future, which included "globally diverse market," "brutal competition," "accelerating industry speed," and "unforgiving customers." These were all *current* realities that the planners presumed would continue throughout the planning time frame. Just about any business today could have these as planning assumptions. Notice that these are all "worst-case" assumptions (or assumptions with one-sided vulnerabilities) in that they are only likely to fail in favor of the organization.

In light of these assumed characteristics of the future, the planners at the manufacturing company decided the key organizational responses should be "innovation and market responsiveness." At this high level of assumptions and actions, it is hard to argue with either response. It is at lower levels of detail in a plan where finding assumptions is generally both more difficult and more fruitful. It is also at lower levels that real planning decisions, or "bets," are more likely to be made. When the planners make a "bet" on how the future is going to turn out and plan actions based on that bet, they are making an assumption that is likely to have two-sided vulnerabilities.

In this case, one of the lower-level actions was to concentrate international market responsiveness in several specific growth markets. That action makes assumptions not only about those markets but also about the markets that were not chosen. And failure in those assumptions can have good *and* bad consequences for the organization.

Write it down

As a general rule, an assumption should be presumed to be implicit until it has been explicitly stated and documented. However obvious an assumption may seem, it is always better to articulate the assumption and write it down than to presume that everyone else also realizes how obvious it is. This is particularly true when identifying assumptions in an ongoing planning effort, in which assumptions are likely to have been discussed but unlikely to have been written down. In a free-flowing discussion, assumptions can easily be forgotten. Assumptions that are not written down are as good as lost to a post-planning search and must be remembered, deduced, or reconstructed.

Know who is/was involved—and contact them

Another important aspect of identifying assumptions is knowing who is involved. The more planners who can be contacted or the better the available documentation, the easier will be the job of identifying assumptions. In the worst case, the assumptions will have to be largely deduced from what exists of the plan and the planners; therefore, it is helpful to have broad expertise and experience represented in the group that is doing the search for assumptions, as well. In the same way that planning benefits from a variety of expertise and experience inside an organization, so does searching for assumptions.

TECHNIQUES FOR IDENTIFYING ASSUMPTIONS

Over the years, we have developed or discovered a variety of techniques for identifying assumptions underlying a plan. The techniques we developed were expressly aimed at identifying assumptions. Those we discovered are more of a mixed bag: A couple are directly aimed at identifying assumptions; the remaining ones need some interpretation to be applicable. I begin by describing the four techniques we developed, then the five we discovered. I then compare them along several dimensions and discuss their strengths and weaknesses. This chapter concludes with a simple example of an Assumption-Based Planning exercise that is intended to illustrate some of the techniques.

The nine techniques for identifying assumptions are as follows:

- "Telling planned actions the long way"
- Looking for *will*s and *must*s
- Rationalizing a plan
- Asking the journalist's questions
- Strategic Assumption Surfacing and Testing (SAST)
- Driving Force Analysis
- Discovery-Driven Planning
- Core Belief Identification Squad
- Annual Key Bets Contract.

"Telling planned actions the long way"

"Telling planned actions the long way"—a lengthy narrative of the form "we are planning to take this action because we think it will help us achieve these goals in light of these characteristics we assume are plausible in the future"—is a good general tool for getting at the assumptions underlying a specific planned action. Every planned action is implicitly part of a longer narrative of this form. In general, such a telling is something that would be asked of a planner after the fact or that a planner would want to be able to answer during planning.

There is no single, correct way to tell the long story. However, it should generally answer the question, "Why are we planning to take this action?" The large manufacturing company mentioned above was planning to be more innovative and responsive to the market. Saying that the long way might take the form, "We are planning to be innovative and responsive to the market because we feel that is the best way to maintain and increase market share in light of our assumptions about a globally more diverse market, brutal competition, accelerating industry speed, and unforgiving customers."

At a more detailed planning level, a planned action to "increase presence in Country A" told out the long way might sound something like, "We are planning to increase our presence in Country A in order to increase our international market share (and thus our bottom line) because we feel that while Country B has a potentially larger market, we are assuming Country A will be an easier market to penetrate." The more detail you can put into telling a planned action the long way, the more likely you are to identify a potentially load-bearing and vulnerable assumption, such as, "We are assuming that Country B has a large potential market, but that it will be hard to penetrate."

There are, of course, many potential stories that could be told for a given planned action, and the same planned action could have a different story told the long way at two different times. The planned action "increase presence in Country A" could show up in the same organization's plans the next year with a completely different story: "We are planning to increase our presence in Country A in order to offset projected (assumed) losses in our domestic market and in light of the fact that we feel the foreign market will continue to show the strength it has during the recent product-recall problem."

This second story points up an important aspect not just of telling planned actions the long way but of the search for assumptions in general: brutal honesty. Planning, by its nature, is an optimistic undertaking. Hope springs eternal in humans, who then compound the situation by being generally overconfident in the accuracy of their hopeful forecasts (Hogarth and Makridakis 1981). Searching for assumptions is a time for realism and honesty. Putting a happy face on a plan can wait until it has been made robust by frankly assessing its strengths and weaknesses. The story of a planned action told the long way should be as blunt and forthright as possible.

It should also be recognized that a planned action can address more than one goal of the organization and more than one characteristic of the uncertain future. Telling this kind of action the long way may require a rather extensive story. But that's the point: If you are a planner, tell the story the long way. If you are talking to a planner, encourage him or her to tell the story the long way. The longer, the better: Telling the narrative forces thinking about how that planned action serves the plan's goals and addresses the uncertainties the plan faces. Also, when the story is told the long way, others get to hear it. Different people might be making different assumptions about why a given action is being taken, and those differences can be important.

Looking for wills *and* musts

Early on in our experiences with ABP, we happened upon this surprisingly effective way for pulling assumptions out of a plan's documentation. *Wills* help identify both assumptions about the future and about the organization's planned actions; *must*s also help identify actions. Here's how.

Across a wide variety of documented plans, we have seen an overwhelming tendency for planners to use the future-tense verb *will* in describing the world of the future. "For the foreseeable future, competition *will* be brutal." "Change *will* continue." "Development in information technology *will* revolutionize. . . ." "Population growth *will* strain the resources and social structures. . . ." "Organizations *will* be flatter. . . ." "Global incidence of obesity *will* increase." "Next-generation nickel-metal hydride batteries *will* extend range and battery life for electric vehicles." "Paper use in offices *will* not decline, but the nature of its use *will* change significantly." The sentences about the future with *will* in them are rarely factual. Most often, they state clearly an assumption that is being made about the future. Finding these sentences with *will* in them has proven to be a very good means of identifying assumptions being made about the future.

In one 45-page draft of an Army plan, TRADOC Pamphlet 525-5, *A Concept for the Evolution of Full-Dimensional Operations for the Strategic Army of the Early Twenty-First Century* (U.S. Army 1994), the word *will* appeared over 470 times.[1] To help us find all of them more easily in an electronic copy, we used editing capabilities to turn the *will*s bold and red. The document looked like it had the measles (the italicized *will*s in the paragraph above demonstrate the general effect). Early on, we concluded that it was in the nature of the military to be forceful about its projections and that this technique would be useful, but only in other military contexts.

Shortly after reaching that conclusion, I was reading the airline magazine on a flight home when I came upon an article on the future of the airline. There were no fewer than two *will*s per paragraph throughout the 3-page article. The wider hypothesis that planners in general share this somewhat surprising certainty (at least when writing about the future) has since been borne out in a variety of ABP applications. This tendency to use *will*s in talking about the future has been very helpful in identifying assumptions being made about the future.

If the *will*s help identify the assumptions about the future, what identifies the planned actions? Many also use *will*. "We *will* adopt a competitor-friendly posture." "The organization *will* consist of . . ."

---

1 In the pamphlet, *can* and *may* occurred about 45 times each and *must* appeared 93 times. *Could* occurred three times, and *might* occurred once.

"The Army *will* be at the emerging edge of . . ." The other popular verb for identifying planned actions is *must*. "We *must* look at reducing manpower . . ." "The logistics system *must* be capable of . . ." "The department *must* be able to regulate power . . ." "We *must* reduce the time to market of new products to no more than . . ." These are the planned actions.

This technique requires that there be documentation of the plan that includes both what the planners are assuming about the future and what they are recommending the organization do about that future. It works best for electronic documentation, because of the powerful tools available on computers for conducting searches. The technique will, however, work for any written record.

In practice, although "Looking for *will*s and *must*s" has been surprisingly effective in getting at a plan's assumptions, it has always been augmented by the search for other words that suggest future behavior or action. *Can, may, should, might, could,* even *cannot,* are all useful words to search for in a document because they are likely to occur in conjunction with a judgment about the future or a planned action by the organization.

Even after the sentences with all these verbs have been scanned for assumptions, it is useful to look at the remaining sentences in the plan for the occasional assumption introduced by some other syntactical construct.

It is still fair to say that looking for occurrences of *will* has been far and away the most useful means of identifying assumptions in the written plans we have looked at—so successful, in fact, that it leads to problems of its own (see shaded box on p. 42).

Rationalizing a plan

The primary goal of "Rationalizing a plan" is to identify implicit assumptions. Think of it as Step 1.5 in the Assumption-Based Planning process: It goes beyond just identifying assumptions, using the connections between assumptions about the future and planned actions to uncover implicit assumptions.

Rationalizing a plan can be done with any plan. However, it is easiest to describe for a plan that is well-documented. It starts with the typical documentation of a plan, which is largely written in two parts: The first describes what the world could be like; the second describes

Note to Plan Documenters: Using Too Many *Wills*

Even as we have made effective use of looking for *wills*, it is clear that they are overused. Using *will* to document assumptions about the future suggests certainty exactly where it is most important to admit uncertainty. All too many *wills*, deathlessly captured in the documentation of a plan, have helped us identify assumptions that we subsequently judged to be vulnerable to plausible events during the expected lifetime of the plan. It would be better to admit uncertainty where it exists, both because it is more realistic and because it would make the job of identifying vulnerable assumptions easier.

Here, planners might argue that, when presenting a plan, it is important to be optimistic and confident about the future and the organization's ability to bend it to advantage—which is understandable for eventual company-wide motivation or public dissemination. However, for purposes of developing a sound plan, uncertainties should be clearly spelled out and confronted. Here is where language is not only important but can be very helpful in making plans and planning more robust:

- Use *will* in documenting a plan, but sparingly.
- When there is any doubt about a statement with *will* in it, preface the statement with a qualifying phrase, such as, "We are assuming in this case that . . ."
- Use *will* when the assumption it documents is thought to be invulnerable.
- Use *might, could,* or *may* when the assumption being documented is more uncertain.
- Use *will* or *must* in documenting the planned *actions* of the organization. Doing so is acceptable, because the actions to be taken are generally more under the control of the organization: The organization can decide that it truly *must* or *will* do something.

Even if a plan were documented as we would prefer, searching for verbs that suggest future behavior or action would still be an appropriate means of looking for assumptions. In fact, if a plan were documented as we would prefer, this means of identifying assumptions would be even more helpful because the verbs would also be a record of whether the planners thought the particular assumption was vulnerable or not. *Will* would suggest invulnerability; *could, might,* and *may* would all suggest vulnerability. If all planners adopted this more logical approach to plan documentation, we would be forced to change the name of this particular technique for identifying assumptions—small price to pay for such progress.

what the organization plans to do about that world. This common documentation approach separates assumptions about the future from actions the organization plans to take. In the same way that telling planned assumptions out the long way does, rationalizing a plan makes explicit the connections between what could happen in the future and what the organization plans to do about it. It supplies the understood *therefore*s to a plan: "We assume that the world could be like this, *therefore* we are going to do that about it."

The first step in Rationalizing a plan is to disassemble the plan: to separate out the assumptions being made about the future and the actions the organization plans to take, as illustrated in Figure 3.3. To be clear, we have assumed in this technique that the organization's planned actions and the *explicit* assumptions about the future have been identified. If the explicit assumptions and planned actions are not spelled out explicitly, then some *other* technique for identifying them must be used.

Rationalizing the plan then consists of connecting assumptions about the world to those planned actions that address them, as represented in Figure 3.4. However, most plans are too large to physically make the connections as in Figure 3.4.

Typically, what we have done is indent under each documented world assumption the actions that are responsive to it. So, for example, a part of the rationalized plan might look like this:

Penetrating markets in other regions is likely to continue to take a long time, be costly, and present marketing difficulties.

- We will establish relationships with existing companies in the region and build strategic alliances.
- We will give priority to eight growth markets: China, India, . . .

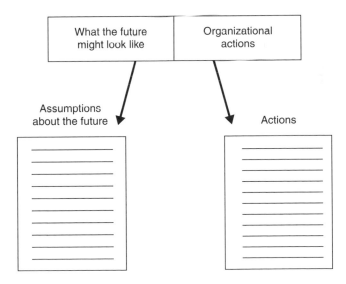

Figure 3.3. Disassembling a Plan into Assumptions About the Future and Actions

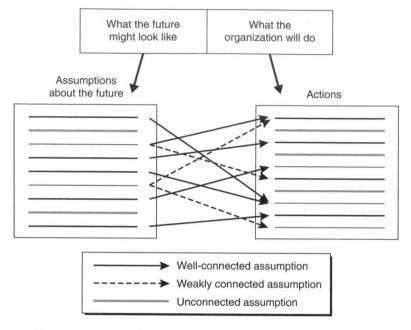

Figure 3.4. Rationalizing a Plan—Connecting Assumptions About the Future with Actions

- We will develop products aimed specifically at those regional markets.

- ...

Meanwhile, to keep track of which actions are connected with which assumptions, it is also important to mark those actions from the action list that are responsive to some assumption. For further ease in checking, each of the assumptions about the future and each of the actions could be numbered. The numbers of corresponding connections could then be appended to both world assumptions and actions. Those assumptions without appended numbers would be the unconnected assumptions and actions. However the connections are made, it should be clear that this matching requires an intensive effort.

This format also has two other interesting facets, both of which are illustrated in Figure 3.4. The first is the multiplicity of connections between assumptions about the future and actions. Some assumptions about the future are very broad generalities and have many actions associated with them. Some actions can be responsive to quite a few assumptions.

The second facet is that not all assumptions about the future or actions get connected. In fact, the connections that get made fall into four general classes:

- Well-connected assumptions about the future (represented by solid arrows in the figure). These are assumptions about the future for which the planned actions appear to be adequately responsive.

- Weakly connected assumptions about the future (dashed arrows). An organization's actions can be associated with these assumptions, but they appear to be only partially responsive to the assumption.

- Unconnected assumptions about the future (thick gray lines in the "Assumptions about the future" box in the figure), to which no actions appear responsive.

- Unconnected actions (thick gray lines in the "Actions" box in the figure). These are organization actions that do not appear to be responsive to any specific assumptions about the future.

The last class, unconnected actions, is what rationalizing a plan is aimed at. Unconnected actions are a good source of implicit assumptions. Planners do not usually plan useless actions. Figuring out why an unconnected action is being planned usually reveals an assumption about the future that has yet to be explicitly stated. It may be an invulnerable assumption, and it may be obvious and trivial, but it may also be a load-bearing, vulnerable assumption that would otherwise have slipped through the cracks to resurface somewhere down the road.[2]

In one application of rationalizing a plan, the company—using the fact that people trust the company brand—was taking several actions related to "branding." Behind those actions was the implicit assumption that branding would continue to be important in that industry. That assumption may be sound, but nowhere in the plan was that assumption spelled out. Until such an assumption is explicitly recognized and stated, the discussion of how important branding might be in the future cannot take place.

---

2   Another, more sinister possibility is that an unconnected action is unconnected because it is just something the organization wants to do and there is no good external rationale for doing it. While admitting this possibility, we need to emphasize that actions that appear to be "playing the game" like this often do have useful, but implicit, external rationales that can be brought out in an exercise such as Rationalizing a plan.

Note to Planners: Finding Weaknesses in a Plan

Two connections that result from rationalizing a plan—weakly connected assumptions and unconnected assumptions about the future—are very useful to planners and the planning process. *Weakly connected assumptions about the future* suggest areas where the planners may want to do additional shoring up of the plan. *Unconnected assumptions about the future* indicate either that the planners have some serious additional planning work to do or that that aspect of the future is not very important to the organization.

The ideal rationalized plan would seem to consist of nothing but well-connected assumptions about the future and planned actions. None of the plans we have rationalized achieved the ideal. Most had both unconnected actions that revealed vulnerable, load-bearing assumptions and "holes," either from weakly connected assumptions or unconnected assumptions about the future.

Note to Plan Documenters: Improving Plan Documentation

Documenting a plan well is very difficult. Computer languages, such as Hypertext Markup Language (HTML), which enable World Wide Web pages to embed links to one another, could facilitate this task.

We have identified four characteristics[a] of a good plan:

- Completeness/consistency. Both the assumptions about the future and the organization's action plan should be as comprehensive as possible: The assumptions about the future should contain as many as possible of the aspects and uncertainties of the future that are important to the organization, and the action plan should cover the important steps the organization can take to achieve its planning goals.

- Responsiveness. The actions should appropriately address the assumptions about and the uncertainties in the future. Each assumption should be adequately dealt with in the action plan.

- Traceability. Each action should be identifiable as the response to one or more of the assumptions about the future.

- Parsimony. There should be no extraneous assumptions about the future or actions.

It is very difficult to document a plan in such a way that it is easy to establish all four characteristics at once. There are two choices for documenting what the plan assumes about the future and what actions the plan recommends for handling the future and its uncertainties—the two major elements of a plan.[b]

(continued)

---

[a] By these characteristics, weakly connected assumptions about the future fail the responsiveness characteristic; unconnected assumptions about the future fail either the responsiveness characteristic or the parsimony characteristic; and unconnected actions fail either the traceability or parsimony characteristic.

[b] This description of a documented plan represents typical plan documentation, not ideal plan documentation. For the latter, I agree with Yehezkel Dror's notion that the ideal would include "a discussion and elaboration of the main values and goals at which it [the plan] is directed; a mapping of likely and possible relevant futures, including explication of the main uncertainties and domains of inconceivability; a set of intended actions; and an outlook on expected ranges of results and their vulnerabilities" (private communication).

Note to Plan Documenters: Improving Plan Documentation (continued)

The first, and most popular, is to document the assumptions about the future and the organization's plans separately (as depicted, for example, in Figures 3.3 and 3.4, where the assumptions about the future and the assumptions about actions are collected separately). This approach permits relatively easy checking of the completeness and logical consistency of each of the two separate parts. However, it separates the assumptions about the future from their *therefores*—the actions—which seriously complicates checking for responsiveness, traceability, and parsimony.

The second option for documentation would maintain all the connections between the assumptions about the future and the planned actions—a difficult process simply because of the multiple connections occurring between assumptions about the future and planned actions. The difficulties in documenting a plan in this way become evident quickly in rationalizing a plan, although this option eases checking for responsiveness, traceability, and parsimony while complicating the task of checking for completeness and consistency.

There is now a means of doing both styles of documentation simultaneously, thanks to computer languages like HTML. HTML makes Web documents two-dimensional in the sense that a document can either be read straight through, as one would a newspaper article, or paused to continually dip into the second dimension of links. Hypertext links would enable a plan to have links from each assumption about the future to its associated actions and vice versa. This two-dimensionality would enable a straight-through read of either the world assumptions or the actions while retaining easily navigated links that keep the connections between them.

Asking the journalist's questions

The six questions journalists are taught to ask are Who? What? When? Where? How? and Why? We have incorporated these six questions into five two-part questions, with the "Why" as the second part of each of the other five. This technique is useful for identifying assumptions, particularly when little information is available on the plans, either in documentation or narrative from planners.

Asking the journalist's questions consists of asking for detailed answers to the following five two-part questions:

- What is it that you do (and why)?
- Who does it (and why them)?
- When do you do it (and why then)?
- Where do you do it (and why there)?
- How do you do it (and why that way)?

We have used these questions as a semi-structured interview technique both with planners and with managers of operations.

A significant part of the power of this technique lies in having people listen to themselves as they explain their business. We once interviewed the vice president of a Fortune 100 company (who had already been briefed on Assumption-Based Planning) for three hours, asking him to explain and defend his product portfolio. Several times during that interview, he paused, then added as an afterthought to something he had just said, "Of course, I suppose that's an assumption." We took the results of that interview and laid out the assumptions we heard in his recitation and identified those assumptions we thought were vulnerable. We then had another interview with him and reviewed the assumptions we had identified. By the end of the second session, we had a list of assumptions and the vice president had a much better understanding of his product portfolio.

That was a particularly short application of Asking the journalist's questions. At the other end of the spectrum in applying this technique, we ran a week-long conference with a few dozen U.S. Army Non-commissioned Officers (NCOs), looking at their system for leader development. We divided the participants into groups aligned with the five questions above and did a thorough investigation of what/who/when/where/how they did their current business and why they did it that way, making sure that NCOs from every branch of the Army were represented in each of the groups.

An unusual thing happened: There was more energy in the room on the last day of the week than there had been on the first. By our having played the part of journalists who were naive about the NCO leader-development process (not a bad approximation to the truth), we started an energetic conversation among the various parts of the NCO leader-development system that was constructively questioning the foundations of the current system. In addition, we and they identified a set of assumptions about the current system that were vulnerable to changes looming on the horizon.

The weeklong exercise was a prelude to a serious planning exercise the NCOs' leader-development community was about to undertake. As such, it provided a clear understanding of their business at the start of the planning exercise.

Institutions as old as the Army tend to have more traditions than other organizations. Traditions are good places to look for assumptions. Often starting as the solution to a particular, urgent problem, they then become routinized to the point that their original justification has been lost. That original justification can be overtaken by events without anyone noticing—threatening the tradition itself.

An interesting example of a justification getting lost came out at the Army NCO conference. The Army has long had a tradition that all of its soldiers must be able-bodied: capable of running, jumping, climbing, carrying and shooting a gun, etc. This tradition made good sense in the days when all soldiers routinely operated close to the front lines and thus needed to rely on their bodies to escape potential dangers. Today, some soldiers get no closer than hundreds of miles from the front lines; the Army is becoming increasingly inclusive (to the point, for example, that it now accepts women, who are not allowed in combat); some Army jobs (e.g., staring at a computer screen all day) might actually be handled just as well by a physically challenged person; and the rights of physically challenged people are increasingly being broadened and protected in society. The tradition that all soldiers and warfighters will be able-bodied is more clearly seen as an assumption, and as an assumption that is increasingly vulnerable.

* * * *

In addition to the above four techniques for identifying assumptions, we have, over the years, come across the following five additional techniques that can help identify assumptions. Only two were intended specifically for identifying assumptions; the other three can be modified for that purpose.

Strategic Assumption Surfacing and Testing

Strategic Assumption Surfacing and Testing (SAST) was developed by Mason and Mitroff (1981) as a means of identifying not only assumptions, but load-bearing and vulnerable assumptions underlying a strategy option. After the five steps in the SAST process are completed, all of the identified assumptions can be arrayed in a two-dimensional graph and weights assigned according to how load-bearing and uncertain each is. In Assumption-Based Planning terms, the load-bearing and vulnerable assumptions are in one quadrant of the graph. For our purposes here, I describe only the step involved in assumption surfacing and defer later steps to their appropriate place in the ABP process.

In SAST, a group with broad expertise and experience is assigned to identify—"surface"—the assumptions underlying a strategy. The group uses what Mason and Mitroff call the "stakeholder method" to do the surfacing. In the stakeholder method, the group first identifies the stakeholders of a given strategy, then asks what must be assumed about each set of stakeholders to make the strategy optimal (Mason and Mitroff call this the "inverse optimal question"). The stakeholders of a strategy thus include groups such as stockholders, creditors, customers, labor unions, capital markets, federal government agencies, and competitors.

The group has only the presented strategy from which to work. Members of the group must have familiarity with the various stakeholders and be able to determine how each set of stakeholders would react to the strategy. The group then determines what reaction each stakeholder must have for the strategy to be most successful. The reactions are the assumptions of the strategy. As an example, for one strategy to work well, the strategy may have to assume that the Environmental Protection Agency (as part of the "federal government agencies" stakeholders) would not enact any regulations that would divert investment from a planned technology-expansion program. The assumptions underlying that strategy are the stakeholder reactions that are required for optimal performance of the strategy.

Driving Force Analysis

Clayton M. Christensen (1997) developed Driving Force Analysis to get at the root causes of the issues a company needs to address in planning. Driving forces are akin to implicit assumptions. Before making that connection, I describe Christensen's technique.

Christensen defines *driving forces* as the "the economic, demographic, technological, or competitive factors in the company's environment that either constitute threats or create opportunities." Identifying driving forces requires two steps. The first step is to generate driving-force candidates through brainstorming, which is done by a team consisting of the company's senior executives and managers representing each of the organization's functional groups. The team then clusters the resulting driving-force candidates around topics or themes. Christensen says 50 to 60 candidates usually yield 10 to 15 clusters. The team is then divided into subteams of three or four people and tasked to distill each cluster they are given into a single statement as summarizing the ideas in the cluster. The single statements are almost always manifestations of deeper causal forces: for example, Christensen gives as a hypothesized driving force, "several competitors can profitably undercut [the company's] most aggressive prices."

The second step tests the driving force clusters through a process Christensen calls "mapping." Mapping is an iterative, visual tool, again used by small teams. Team members search for two or three factors that could bring about the idea expressed in the cluster statement. They then plot those factors on the axes of a diagram or matrix, working with the diagram or matrix until they are comfortable that it explains the root causes of the candidate driving force. The hypothesized driving force of "several competitors can profitably undercut [the company's] most aggressive prices" driving force was mapped to "[the company's] costs are high relative to competitors' because of new technologies that enable cost-effective manufacturing at low volumes, and because of the complexity of managing our broad product line with our present configuration of plant and equipment" (Christensen 1997: 145).

There is more to Driving Force Analysis, but it is the driving forces themselves that are of interest to Assumption-Based Planning. Driving forces are related, somewhat tangentially but importantly, to the search for implicit assumptions in ABP. The search for driving forces is a search for implicit assumptions that have been overtaken or are being overtaken by events. In the example above, the company had been implicitly assuming that, through economies of scale and scope, it would maintain its dominant position in the market. What it did not realize was that, through new technologies, competitors were undermining its economies of scale and that, through its own ineconomies of scale created by a broad product line, it was further undermining its own assumption. When it is obvious that something is wrong with the current strategy, Driving Force Analysis is a technique for uncovering those implicit assumptions underlying the strategy that have caused or are causing it to fail.

Discovery-Driven Planning

Discovery-Driven Planning offers "a systematic way to uncover the dangerous implicit assumption that would otherwise slip unnoticed and thus unchallenged into the plan" for a new venture (McGrath and MacMillan 1999: 115). Discovery-Driven Planning is aimed at new business ventures for which there is usually a "high ratio of assumption to knowledge" (1999). The developers draw a clear distinction between planning for a conventional business (which they describe as extrapolating future results from well-understood past experience) and planning for a new venture (which they characterize as trying to envision what is unknown, uncertain, and not yet obvious to the competition). Planning for a new venture must rely not only on more assumptions than planning for a conventional business, but on more assumptions that Assumption-Based Planning would characterize as vulnerable and load-bearing.

The Discovery-Driven Planning process is captured in four separate documents, but the first two, reverse income statement and pro forma operations specifications, capture the process for identifying assumptions. Instead of starting with the projected revenues of a new venture and working to derive profits, the reverse income statement process starts with required profits and works backward, to determine the revenues and allowable costs of the new venture that are necessary to reach those required profits.

Given the necessary revenues and allowable costs, the required pro forma operations specifications on sales, manufacturing, shipping, equipment, and depreciation can be determined. McGrath and MacMillan recommend using industry standards where possible to determine these specifications and adapting standards from similar industries where industry standards do not exist. These pro forma specifications then become the assumptions underlying the potential profitability of the proposed venture. If the profitability goals cannot be met, either the venture should be scrapped or the first two steps of the process should be repeated with revised information until a set of reasonable operations specifications is produced that leads to the required bottom line.

In an Assumption-Based Planning sense, the Discovery-Driven Planning technique concentrates primarily on assumptions about the effectiveness of planned actions. Although some assumptions about the future might be embedded in some of the specifications, this method is primarily aimed at whether or not performing the planned actions will be effective.

In a new business venture, assumptions about the effectiveness of planned actions are likely to be much more vulnerable than in a well-understood venture. In Chapter 2, we suggested that assumptions about the problems facing an organization are generally more crucial than assumptions about the solutions to those problems, because the assumptions about solutions are typically better handled by the organization's experiences. For a venture into a new business area, the load-bearing, vulnerable assumptions about planned actions (or solutions) are just as crucial as the load-bearing, vulnerable assumptions made about the surrounding environment (or problems). This technique is well-suited to bringing out those load-bearing, vulnerable assumptions about solutions.[3]

The last two techniques come from *Proceeding in Daylight: Frontier Practices for Challenging Strategic Assumptions* (Corporate Strategy Board 1999). The Corporate Strategy Board is part of the Corporate Executive Board, a membership organization headquartered in Washington, D.C., that "provides best practices research and executive education to a membership of the world's leading corporations and not-for-profit institutions."[4] Based on Assumption-Based Planning,[5] *Proceeding in Daylight* followed from work the Corporate Strategy Board had done on "growth stalls"—serious flattenings or downturns in corporate growth—in large corporate enterprises (Corporate Strategy Board 1998). The Board blamed many of these stalls on "outdated, untested

3   In a vein similar to that of Discovery-Driven Planning, Paul Davis does something in the military context he calls "mission system analysis," which he describes as taking a systems approach to the capabilities required to accomplish a given mission. From a system perspective, there are many ways a mission can fail. Said more positively, there are many components—weapons systems, communications, command and control, etc.—that must succeed. Through fault trees, Davis can construct the minimum capabilities required for completing the mission (private communication, June 4, 2001).

4   For more, see the Corporate Strategy Board's Web site at http://www. executiveboard.com/ (visited June 2001).

5   "The focus on assumptions in strategy has its roots in U.S. national security planning. A methodology called assumption-based planning was formally developed in the 1980s at RAND . . ." (Corporate Strategy Board 1999: 12).

strategic assumptions" that failed. For *Proceeding in Daylight*, the Board researched how best-practice companies made their strategic assumptions explicit and dealt with them to avoid growth stalls. The Board identified four approaches for "surfacing deeply held corporate beliefs" (1999: 50). One, called an "Assumption Surfacing Competition," is a variation of the Strategic Assumption Surfacing and Testing technique that was described to them by one of the developers of SAST (Mitroff). A second approach was Christensen's Driving Force Analysis. The last two are the "Core Belief Identification Squad" and the "Annual Key Bets Contract."

Core Belief Identification Squad

The Core Belief Identification Squad is composed of 25 to 30 employees from across the company who get together for short, frequent brainstorming sessions aimed at identifying the company's implicit core beliefs. Members of the squad are drawn from across the company and vary by "age, gender, job function, tenure with the company, geographic location, and diversity of perspectives" (Corporate Strategy Board 1999: 52). Membership in the squad is purposely biased toward younger, newer employees who are less wedded to current orthodoxies and more willing to challenge convention. By asking provocative questions about both internal and industry orthodoxies, the squad aggressively seeks out those canonical beliefs that are worth reexamining and readdressing. Representative questions include the following:

- What do industry leaders believe about . . .
  - who the customer is?
  - how to reach them?
- Who has succeeded by breaking the established "rules" of the industry?
- What major innovations has our company missed?
- What do we believe about . . .
  - what industry we are in?
  - what our customers want?
  - how we make money?
  - what values and behaviors we promote?

Answers to these questions get directly at the assumptions the company is making about itself, its industry, and the way it plays in that industry. The question about what innovations the company has missed is an interesting one in that it drives toward implicit assumptions that were vulnerable and taken advantage of (by someone else) in the past.

Annual Key Bets Contract

The Annual Key Bets Contract technique not only identifies the assumptions underlying the plan but further codifies the load-bearing and vulnerable assumptions in the same process. The key bets (or load-bearing, vulnerable assumptions) are monitored throughout the year and reevaluated if the bets are proving unfavorable. The inputs to the Annual Key Bets Contract method come from a network of internal and external industry experts who are interviewed yearly about the primary challenges facing the company. Business managers and senior executives convert the inputs into a list of measurable "key bets" the company will make. These bets are the critical but uncertain assumptions that the company is willing to make (and to put into contracts for the business units) as part of the business strategy. ABP would call these the load-bearing, vulnerable assumptions underlying the strategy.

The actual process for identifying the assumptions (and for determining load-bearing and vulnerability) is interviews with the network of experts, followed by discussions and negotiations among business managers and senior executives—seemingly not rigorous enough for identifying the (load-bearing, vulnerable) assumptions. The primary factor this technique brings to the table is the significant stakes attached to getting right the assumptions about the uncertainties the company faces. The company is going to literally bet on the resultant assumptions, so there is great incentive to making sure that the discussions aimed at identifying those assumptions are rigorous, unvarnished, and thorough.

Other techniques?

The nine techniques described above are by no means the last word on identifying assumptions. The search for practical and effective techniques continues. We encourage anyone interested in assumptions or ABP to explore other means for eliciting assumptions. For example, more-formal techniques for bringing structure to a plan could be applied. One technique might involve collaborating with a planner to draw a map of the entire plan. This map would be a more complete rationalization of the plan than described above under Rationalizing a plan. It would include all the interconnections among assumptions and actions and might reveal subtle assumptions that the cruder "assumption, therefore action" approach of Rationalizing a plan would miss.

There is a rich literature on how people think and reason that could be applied in clever ways to get at the assumptions and reasoning behind a plan or a planner's concept. Any technique aimed at understanding a person's reasoning would also be a candidate technique for identifying assumptions. I would not be surprised if there were several more techniques that could be created to assist in finding assumptions in a plan.

WHICH TECHNIQUE TO USE WHEN

In describing the nine techniques for identifying assumptions, I have suggested that some are particularly useful in specific situations. What can be said about which techniques are most effective in which situations?

Several characteristics are of interest when choosing a technique for identifying assumptions:

- Whether or not documentation of the plan is required.
- Whether the technique is more appropriate for use during planning or after the planning has been done. Some are only useful after the plan and its documentation are complete.
- How long the technique is likely to take.
- How many people need to be involved.
- How easy it is to learn and use the technique.
- How broadly the technique can be applied. Most of the techniques are broadly applicable; a couple are intended for more-specific situations.

Table 3.1, which shows a rough rating in each of these six characteristics of applicability for each of the nine assumption-identifying techniques, provides an overview of the regions of applicability of the nine techniques. Clearly, these techniques can be used in combination; how-

Table 3.1. *A comparison of techniques for identifying assumptions*

Technique	Documentation Needed?	Best During or After?	Time Required to Complete	Number of People Required	Ease in Applying	Breadth of Applicability
Telling actions the long way	No	During	Could drag on	A few	Fairly easy	Broad
Looking for *wills/musts*	Yes	After	Fairly short	A few	Quite easy	Broad
Rationalizing a plan	Yes	After	Takes quite a while	A few	Complex	Broad
Asking journalist's questions	No	Either	Can range from short to long	A few to many	Quite easy	Broad
SAST	No	After	Medium	Three groups	A bit tricky	Broad
Driving Force Analysis	No	During	Medium to long	Several	Mapping is tricky	Best on for-profit
Discovery-Driven Planning	No	During	Medium	A few	Needs some expertise	Best for new ventures
Core Beliefs	No	Either	Fairly short	Several	Easy	Broad
Key Bets	No	During	Medium	Several	Requires network	Fairly broad

ever, doing so can adversely affect other characteristics in the table, such as length of time, number of people involved, or ease of application.

What Table 3.1 does not address is the question of which technique is "best." All of the techniques in the table work. They have been used either for identifying assumptions directly or for identifying things such as key issues that can be turned into assumptions. The valuations given in the table portray important qualities of each technique. Nonetheless, after the usual caveats about "best" being a multidimensional concept and therefore an inappropriate question, I would nominate two kinds of "bests"—easiest and quickest, and best at identifying implicit assumptions.

Easiest and quickest

For plans with good documentation that is available in electronic form, the easiest and quickest is the Looking for *will*s and *must*s technique. The power of computers can be brought to bear in looking for telltale phrases that indicate an assumption is being made. The planners still have careful work to do interpreting the assumption candidates and sifting out assumptions about the future from planned actions, but using the computer in this way quickly narrows the list of promising candidates. With a well-documented plan, it is surprising how well this computer-aided technique works. The primary problem with employing this technique is that there are not too many cases (yet) of well-documented plans.

If the documentation of a plan is not good and assumptions must be elicited from people associated with the planning process, the winner for easiest and quickest is the Asking the journalist's questions technique. It is easy to ask the journalist's questions and to keep asking them (in the classic fashion of a three-year-old) of the people who are involved or have been involved in planning. The hard part is taking the answers to the questions and turning them into assumptions. The primary problem in applying this technique for the first time is that you realize as you are sifting through the answers that a question should have been phrased differently or a different question asked. After a couple of sessions of asking the journalist's questions and interpreting the answers, it becomes easier to see how to focus the questioning on driving out the load-bearing assumptions. This technique can yield reasonable results quickly, despite the difficulty of delving very deeply into a plan's assumptions in a short period of time.

Using the Asking the journalist's questions technique in discussing the product portfolio of the large manufacturing company described above, we elicited enough information in a single 3-hour session with the vice president for planning to enable us to identify a wide variety of candidate assumptions underlying the portfolio. However, we had to go away and carefully study the results of the session, then return for another session with the vice president after we were comfortable that we had identified the major assumptions. In the course of the later discussion, we identified a few additional assumptions and came to a consensus on the product portfolio's major assumptions.

If plan documentation is not good, second place in the easiest and quickest category is something like the Core Belief Identification Squad technique—just a fancy name for what was presented earlier as a general aspect of identifying assumptions. The process of identifying assumptions should involve a group of people chosen for their diversity of experience and training in the organization. Some of the more subtle aspects of getting such a group to function effectively and efficiently are discussed in Chapter 8.

Best at identifying implicit assumptions

Any technique aimed at identifying the assumptions of a plan, if conscientiously applied, can identify implicit assumptions. However, a couple of the techniques are focused more aggressively on identifying assumptions that might have been overlooked or forgotten.

The most aggressive of these implicit-assumption identifiers is the Rationalizing a plan technique. When enough documentation exists to apply this method, its identification of unconnected actions is a potent source for thinking about implicit assumptions being made that cause those actions to be appropriate. The major drawbacks to this technique are the time required and the need for reasonably good documentation of the thinking in the plan.

Second place in identifying implicit assumptions goes to Discovery-Driven Planning. Its narrowly focused field of applicability—new ventures—is particularly susceptible to burying assumptions in a wave of optimism. The rigor of having to derive all of the precursors to profitability in a balance-sheet format and translating those precursors to operational requirements is a powerful means for exposing implicit assumptions.

Honorable mention in the identifying-assumptions category goes to the Core Belief Identification Squad. Again, having a somewhat contrarian group convene periodically to think about the core beliefs of an organization is a good antidote to the tendency to forget that core beliefs are likely to be assumptions that can be overtaken by events.

HOW MANY ASSUMPTIONS TO IDENTIFY

The simple answer to how many assumptions should be identified is, "You never know if you have all, or even enough, of the assumptions underlying a plan." You can, however, have too many.

How many assumptions are enough?

The ultimate goal is not to identify a certain number of assumptions but to identify as many load-bearing, vulnerable assumptions as possible. The more creative and careful the process of identifying assumptions, the more assumptions it is likely to identify. Further, once an assumption is identified and listed, it remains an assumption (unless overtaken by events) for any subsequent assumption search or planning cycle. The list of assumptions will thus tend to get longer with each succeeding planning cycle. Revisiting the assumptions periodically, then, is a good means for improving the list of assumptions and increasing confidence that as many as possible of the load-bearing assumptions have been included.

A good example of improving a list of assumptions by revisiting them occurred in a small professional society that used ABP to develop a 3-year plan. The planning problem was modest, and the planners did a good job of documenting the load-bearing and vulnerable assumptions of the plan, the signposts for monitoring assumption vulnerabilities, and the shaping and hedging actions they identified in the ABP process. They were pleased with the plan and its performance. After a year, the planners revisited their planning assumptions and the organization's performance. In doing so, they realized that they had been making a load-bearing—and still implicit—assumption about electronic publishing that was clearly becoming problematic. They had been implicitly assuming that electronic publishing would not affect them or their publications. When the planners realized that electronic publishing *could* threaten their publication plans, they added an explicit assumption in that regard, and replanned to accommodate it.

Iteration is not a panacea, however. If the same set of people look for assumptions several times, there is no guarantee that the list will improve. Decision research has shown that even experts are often insensitive to missing information (see, for example, Fischhoff, Slovic, and Lichtenstein 1977: 330–34 and van Schie and van der Pligt 1990). Just as it is useful to have those involved in the search for assumptions represent a broad spectrum of expertise, it is useful to have those involved in a review of the assumptions include at least some people who represent perspectives different from those of the people on the original team. People relatively new to the organization, who may not yet have been captured by culturally ingrained implicit assumptions, can be particularly helpful here.

What if you have too many assumptions?

We have said that, as a general rule, the search for assumptions should err on the side of inclusion. If there is any doubt whether something is an assumption or a fact, it should be included in the list of assumptions. The point here is to encourage the identification of those judgments about the future that have been ossified into "facts" in an organization's thinking, for it is surely these that promise the greatest mischief in the organization's future.

This inclusiveness dictum makes it possible to get too many assumptions at this stage. As a general rule, anything over a few dozen assumptions is probably too many, even at the point before load-bearing and vulnerability have been determined. What should you do if the number of assumptions is creeping toward triple digits? Start getting rid of the clearly non–load-bearing ones. If an assumption's negation would not require any replanning, whether or not it is vulnerable is immaterial. It can be deleted. If this gets you down to a few dozen assumptions, stop.

If you still have too many assumptions, get rid of the clearly invulnerable assumptions: those of "The sun will rise in the east" variety. However, this rule can be tricky and should be applied with care. Seemingly invulnerable assumptions can harbor surprising vulnerabilities. My favorite extreme example is "gravity will be 32 ft/sec^2"— clearly an invulnerable assumption for any Earthbound plan and just as clearly inappropriate for any plan that contemplates space or lunar operations. Seemingly invulnerable assumptions ("East and West Germany will remain separated for the foreseeable future") can come crashing down in a surprising hurry.

Good candidates for pruning are the worst-case assumptions: those with one-sided vulnerabilities. If you truly have too many assumptions, it is important to concentrate on those that represent decisions with two-sided vulnerabilities that open the organization up to downside risks.

If you *still* have more than a few dozen assumptions, take advantage of the division of labor between planning and management. It is up to the organization's management to determine which additional assumptions can be tolerated without further action. It is a planning function to ensure that no assumption is left behind. It is a management function to decide that the risk of leaving a given assumption behind is acceptable. In any case, keep a list of any assumptions that have been pruned and any reasons for which they were pruned.

That completes Step 1 of the ABP process—identifying assumptions. Before going on to the next step, it may be helpful for some readers to get more immersed in a simple example. To provide that example, I will use the planning of a lemonade stand—the one type of enterprise about which I consider myself an expert—to illustrate some of the considerations and actions that take place in an ABP exercise. After the description of each step of the ABP process, I return to the lemonade stand to illustrate that step in terms of lemonade-stand planning.

Lemonade Stand—1

The following paragraphs illustrate considerations relating to identifying assumptions in the plan for the lemonade stand.

The plan

The important thing to know about the plan for our purposes is that it is the plan for a lemonade stand *six months in the future*. Let us say, then, that it is January and the plans are for the last weekend in June. The stand is to be run by a young entrepreneur named Margot. Her plan is to set up the stand in the front yard using materials readily found in the garage, lemons from the tree in the backyard, paper cups that will probably have to be purchased, sugar from the kitchen, and help from her friend, Chloe. There are plans for an advertising campaign (signs posted on telephone poles) and worries about competition. There are a few other details in the plan (including a rough budget), but these will be discussed later.

Identifying assumptions

Several of the assumptions Margot has made are explicit. First and foremost is about the weather. She assumes that the weather will be nice. If it rains that weekend, the lemonade stand is in trouble. She begins to worry about the weather, but then reminds herself that at this point she should just identify all the assumptions she can think of that underlie her plan. She begins to list her assumptions:

- The weather will be nice.[a]
- There won't be any competition (from other lemonade stands).
- The tree in the backyard will have plenty of lemons.
- Chloe will be available (i.e., not on vacation).
- She (Margot) will be available.

(continued)

---

[a] Note the number of *will*s in these assumptions. Margot is, in fact, expecting that these assumptions *will* be true. In later steps, she confronts the vulnerabilities in these assumptions and what can be done about them.

Lemonade Stand—1 (continued)

- There won't be road construction or something keeping people from walking or driving by.
- She (Margot) will be allowed to run the stand (i.e., she won't be "grounded").
- The yard will be available (i.e., they will still live there).
- The stand will draw at least 24 customers at $.25/cup.

At this point, Margot starts spinning out wilder and wilder schemes. She realizes that she is assuming that there will not be a sugar shortage, that there will not have been an earthquake within the last few days before the big weekend, that nothing will keep her from being able to make the advertising signs, that people will still like lemonade. She decides to write these assumptions on a separate sheet. Although they would cause problems if they occurred, they just don't pass some likelihood threshold. At the same time, she promises to keep thinking about her plan and its assumptions, and she promises to add anything to the assumption list that passes some likelihood threshold.

Margot could also think about breaking the assumptions into different levels, so that her availability is at one level and, for example, the assumption that she won't be grounded would then be a subassumption under the assumption about her availability. Because the lemonade-stand example is so limited, I will forgo any further discussion of levels of assumptions. However, it should be clear that those levels could be useful in a larger example.

The exercise has already been useful. Margot had not realized she was assuming Chloe would be available. That realization led her to the realization that she was assuming that *she* (Margot) would be available. She also had not been paying attention to the assumption that she would not be grounded or otherwise prevented from running the lemonade stand. Technically, this can be viewed as a vulnerability in the assumption about her availability. For now, she writes it on the list, because it is an important assumption in her mind.

She also realizes that thinking in terms of assumptions is different from thinking in terms of failure mechanisms. Thinking in terms of how she was *picturing, in detail, the plan working* is different from thinking about *how the plan could fail.* This is a subtle, but useful, distinction. She is ready at this point to think about which assumptions are load-bearing and vulnerable.

4

Step 2: identifying load-bearing, vulnerable assumptions

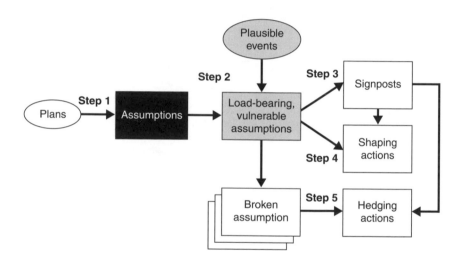

Figure 4.1. Highlighting Step 2 of ABP: Identifying the Load-Bearing, Vulnerable Assumptions

At this point in the application of Assumption-Based Planning, we have a collection of assumptions that underlie the plans of the organization. Whether they were implicit or explicit earlier, the assumptions are all explicit from here on in. We have made sure that there are not too many assumptions in the collection—maybe a few dozen. As depicted in Figure 4.1, the essence of Step 2 is to examine the assumptions and identify those that are both load-bearing in the plans and vulnerable to failure within the expected lifetime of the plans.

While identifying the assumptions underlying plans, it is impossible not to have opinions about the weight they carry and/or about their vulnerability. However, voicing or otherwise indicating such evaluations is expressly discouraged in the assumption-identification process, because it could cause the assumption to be discarded prematurely based on hasty judgments. Deciding whether an assumption is load-bearing or vulnerable requires judgments in each case. The pitfalls common in each type of judgment are worth thinking about carefully and, therefore, separately from the process of identifying assumptions.

Figure 4.2 shows a logical road map for this chapter as it describes the assessment of load-bearing, vulnerable assumptions.

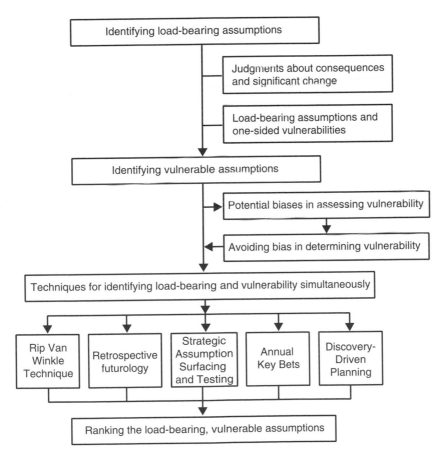

Figure 4.2. Logical Road Map of Chapter 4

It is not necessary or important to determine load-bearing and vulnerability separately *from each other*. But that is getting a bit ahead of the story. This chapter focuses first on means for, and common pitfalls in, judging how load-bearing and vulnerable an assumption is. Following that, it discusses means for identifying load-bearing and vulnerability simultaneously, then answers two frequently asked questions: "How do load-bearing, vulnerable assumptions relate to risk?" and "How many load-bearing, vulnerable assumptions will there be?"

IDENTIFYING LOAD-BEARING ASSUMPTIONS

As was discussed in Chapter 2, load-bearing has a specific meaning in ABP:

> An assumption is *load-bearing* if its failure would require significant changes in the organization's plans.

Notice that this definition of *load-bearing* subsumes the notion of vulnerability. This raises the question, "Can an invulnerable assumption be load-bearing?" If an invulnerable assumption cannot fail, it cannot require significant changes in an organization's plans and therefore cannot be load-bearing.

If an assumption underlying a plan is invulnerable, it does not matter whether or not it is load-bearing. From a logical standpoint, this suggests that, if load-bearing and vulnerability are to be determined independently, vulnerability should be determined first. Identifying load-bearing assumptions could then be done on the smaller set of vulnerable assumptions. From a more pragmatic standpoint, it is better to identify load-bearing first, because doing so leads to a better understanding of the *potential* for load-bearing assumptions to fail. Being clear about the consequences of a failed assumption can make it easier to be clear about the possibility that the assumption could fail, or at least to be more worried about its potential for failure.

To apply the definition of load-bearing, it is not necessary to know (yet) whether an assumption is vulnerable to failure. It is enough to consider what would happen if the assumption *did* fail. Identifying load-bearing assumptions is more about being a Chicken Little than a Pollyanna. If it is too difficult *not* to think about likelihoods, assume the worst and think about the consequences. If those consequences require a significant change in plans, the assumption is load-bearing. Further contemplation of likelihoods of failure will come in the assessment of vulnerabilities.

If load-bearing and vulnerability are determined separately, Step 2 of ABP has two separate substeps, shown schematically in Figure 4.3. In any case, the result of Step 2 is a subset of the original list of assumptions whose members are both load-bearing and vulnerable.

There are no special instructions, guidelines, or techniques for determining whether an assumption is load-bearing. In practice, it is not difficult for someone familiar with a plan to go through a list of assumptions and pick out those that are load-bearing. If there is no one available who is familiar with the plan, the process is more painstaking. Basically, it requires applying the definition. If the plan depends on whether the assumption holds or comes true, the assumption is load-bearing. That said, using the definition of *load-bearing* requires judgments about both the consequences of an assumption's failure and whether those consequences require significant changes to the plan.

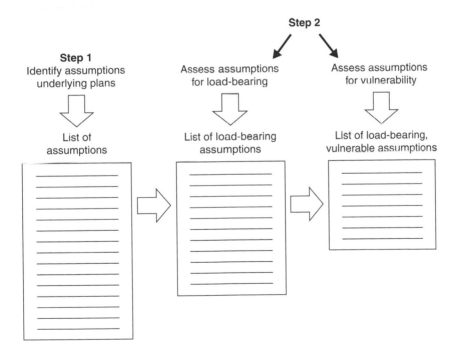

Figure 4.3. Winnowing the List of Assumptions to Those That Are Load-Bearing and Vulnerable

Judgments about consequences

Judging the consequences of a failed assumption requires imagining both the failed assumption and the implications of that failure for the plan.

In practice, thinking about a failed assumption is hard to separate from thinking about how it might have failed, which can lead to problems in clearly thinking through the possible consequences. A typical investor in early 1929 might have found the possibility of a stock market crash so remote that the consequences were either dismissed or seriously downplayed. But this is exactly where the discipline of thinking strictly about the consequences of an assumption failure and not about its *likelihood* of failure, can pay dividends.

Those dividends can be seen in the now-famous planning example of Royal Dutch/Shell in 1984. While the remainder of the oil industry assumed oil would not fall significantly below its then-current price of $28 per barrel, Royal Dutch/Shell planners contemplated a scenario in which oil was $15 a barrel (the details of the following scenario come from de Geus (1999: 52)). The planners wanted management to think about what it would do in that scenario. Interestingly, management refused to play until it was told "when the price is going to fall, how far it will fall, and how long the fall will last." Planners wanted management to think about $15 a barrel oil without having to convince them it could happen. The planners broke the ensuing impasse by describing a case in which the price of oil plummeted and prefaced it by saying, "though none of us knows whether the price is going to fall, we can agree that it would be pretty serious if it did. So we have written a case showing one of many possible ways by which the price of oil could fall" (de Geus 1999: 59). They then asked management to think about what the government would do, what competitors might do, and what, if anything, they—management—would do.

In this case, Royal Dutch/Shell planners can be said to have identified as load-bearing the assumption that "oil prices will not fall significantly below $28 a barrel during the planning period." It is likely that there was a difference of opinion between the planners and management about the vulnerability of that assumption, but neither doubted that the consequences of that assumption's failing were dramatic for the company and would require a serious change of plans. Both sides could then agree that, in an ABP sense, that assumption was load-bearing.

Getting management to think through those consequences (a later step in ABP) paid a handsome dividend to the planners and to the company. Royal Dutch/Shell was in a much better position when, in April 1986, the price of oil fell to $10 a barrel, and it weathered the collapse better than did other oil companies.

Getting management to agree on the load-bearing assumptions of a plan is easier than getting management to agree on the vulnerability of those assumptions, and such agreement will *facilitate* discussions of their vulnerabilities. Planners should work to get prior agreement with management on the set of load-bearing assumptions.

Judgments about significant change

The meat of the definition of *load-bearing* is whether the failure of an assumption requires significant changes to a plan. There are two major difficulties in deciding whether a significant change will be required as a result of an assumption failure. The first difficulty is that an assumption could fail without requiring significant changes to the plan, because what appears to require a significant change may be covered by hedges and contingencies. The idea behind making a plan robust, or "uncertainty-sophisticated," is to prepare for the uncertainties of the future as much as possible. This can mean making plans—hedges—that position the organization for a variety of futures; it can mean preparing alternative plans—contingencies—for specific futures; and so forth.

The plan itself, then, can contain actions that buttress a load-bearing assumption. In fact, to use the building metaphor, it is possible to buttress a load-bearing section so well that its failure would not require significant changes. An assumption that appears to be load-bearing, then, may be buttressed by actions taken elsewhere in the plan. Determining whether an assumption is truly load-bearing can require a thorough knowledge of the entire plan. It is possible to decide that an assumption is load-bearing without realizing that there is a hedge or contingency in the plan specifically designed to handle the assumption's failure. Clearly, it is better to identify those assumptions that *might* be load-bearing by definition and worry later whether adequate hedges or contingencies have been developed.

The second major difficulty in determining load-bearing assumptions is that assumptions may fail gradually, making it difficult to decide when a significant change is called for. Suppose a plan depends for its resources on the company's stock's achieving somewhat optimistic performance targets over each of the next four quarters. In what way does the plan's success depend on the assumption about stock performance? At one extreme, if the plan collapses catastrophically when the stock market fails to hit its targets, significant changes to the plan are in order and the assumption is clearly load-bearing. At the other extreme, if the plan's chances for success move relatively smoothly with the stock price, is it load-bearing? Said another way, "Is there a point at which the plan will need to be seriously rethought?" If so, the assumption is load-bearing.

Load-bearing assumptions in Discovery-Driven Planning

Sometimes, in the way a plan is developed, assessing which assumptions are load-bearing can be almost trivial. This is the case with the Discovery-Driven Planning process, which is aimed at making the plans for a new venture as robust as possible. Discovery-Driven Planning starts with the requirement that the bottom line of the new venture be positive/profitable and works backward to determine necessary revenues, allowable costs, and minimum operations specifications in order to meet the bottom-line requirements. Because each of these revenue, cost, and operations requirements is set as the minimum possible to achieve profitability, if any one of the requirements were to fail, the profitability goals could not be met and the new venture would fail.

In this sense, each of the derived requirements is a load-bearing assumption. On the one hand, this judgment is obviously a bit overblown in that none of the derived requirements can be determined so precisely that it acts as an absolute arbiter of the success or failure of the proposed venture. On the other hand, the Discovery-Driven Planning methodology was developed to derive assumptions about revenues, costs, and operations specifications that, if not reasonably achievable, would require either replanning or abandonment of the venture. If the venture goes forward, then each of these derived requirements becomes an assumption whose failure could require serious rethinking of the venture. That makes them load-bearing assumptions in an ABP sense.

Load-bearing assumptions and one-sided vulnerabilities

It is important to recognize that an assumption can be load-bearing even if it has one-sided vulnerabilities and potential failure appears only to be in favor of the organization. To ask if an assumption with a one-sided vulnerability is load-bearing is to ask if its failure would require significant changes in the organization's plans. The organization is likely to be unconcerned about formally replanning if the future is going to turn out less dreadful than it had feared. A better-than-feared future is the kind of situation an organization would appear to be happy to face without having a specific hedging or contingency plans in place.

Nonetheless, two cautions about assumptions with one-sided vulnerabilities need to be considered.

The first caution is that the assumption *could* fail on the negative side. Presumably, the plan has been designed to deal with the "worst case" that the assumption represents. However, no worst-case assumption is so bad that it could not be made worse yet. The assumption may not be *likely* to fail on the negative side, but it is worth thinking seriously about whether the worst-case assumption could actually fail worse than feared. If the future *did* turn out worse than assumed, it is likely that the plan would require significant changes.

The second caution about assumptions with one-sided vulnerabilities is that not having hedging actions or a contingency plan for an assumption that breaks in favor of the organization can cause serious problems. Imagine a plan that assumes that all the demand for a given product can be handled by one manufacturing site. Then suppose actual demand is almost double that. If the organization has not hedged for that possibility, it is easy to imagine severe shortages of the product; consumer anger and frustration; and, for something like medicines, maybe even a government investigation—all leading to a significant black eye for the company.

These two cautions suggest that, at the very least, assumptions with one-sided vulnerabilities be considered very carefully before being rejected as load-bearing.

IDENTIFYING VULNERABLE ASSUMPTIONS

An assumption is *vulnerable* if plausible events could cause it to fail within the expected lifetime of the plan. Determining vulnerability basically becomes the search—by whatever means available for thinking about the future—for a plausible event or events that could occur within the expected lifetime of the plan and would cause the assumption to fail. If one or more plausible paths to failure can be found, those failure paths should be captured (for later steps in the ABP process) and the assumption declared vulnerable. If no plausible means of failure can be found or if all potential means strain credibility within the expected lifetime of the plan, the assumption can be declared *invulnerable*. If all the plausible means of an assumption failure cause the assumption to fail only in favor of the organization, it is still a good idea to declare the assumption vulnerable and carry it forward to the next step.

The plan's time horizon is an important determining factor in assessing the vulnerability. It sets an important bound on the plausibility of events that would cause an assumption to fail. In the case of Royal Dutch/Shell and the price of oil, management might well have been more receptive to (but undoubtedly less interested in) the possibility of oil prices' falling to $15 a barrel during the succeeding 20-year period, but the likelihood of prices falling that far in a short period of time was, at least initially, implausible to them.

How can plausibility and the future, however near, be reconciled? Techniques for thinking about the future fall into roughly four major categories:

- Trend extrapolation and pattern recognition. Finding trends in historical data and extrapolating them into the future is a common means for thinking about the future, particularly the near-term future. Recognizing a trend in historical data is a specific example of the broader category of recognizing patterns in history that can be used to suggest similar patterns in the future.

- Expert opinion and experience-based intuition. An expert's greater knowledge and experience are generally thought to provide better insights into what is plausible and what is implausible in the future. Specific techniques for collecting expert opinion—such as gaming, interviewing, and focus groups—belong in this category. Also in this category are the experience-based intuitions and "gut feelings" of experts and non-experts about plausible future events.

- Theory and modeling. Theories about "how the world works" can be used to model a variety of plausible worlds. The different worlds arise from choosing a different set of values for the underlying factors. This category includes computerized models.

- Imagination. This category covers the more creative and visionary approaches to peering into the future. Included here are both true visionaries and false prophets, because only time reliably separates one from the other.

Some of these techniques, such as trend extrapolations and modeling, are typically used for forecasting or predicting the future. It is important to keep in mind that we are *not* trying to *predict* whether or not an assumption will fail. We are only trying to assess whether an assumption is vulnerable to failure or could plausibly fail during the lifetime of the plan.

All of these techniques, then, are useful only in the sense of establishing the *plausibility* of an event's occurring within a given time period and whose occurrence would cause an assumption to fail.

The more convincing the potential failure of an assumption can be made, the better. And at some point it will be important to have an assumption's vulnerability be convincing to a potentially hostile audience. Therefore, employing two or more of the above four techniques in tandem is a means of increasing the plausibility of a seemingly implausible assumption failure. For example, expert opinion backed up by models is likely to be more convincing than either alone.

The techniques above for thinking about the future are generally well-known in the business community. For example, they are employed regularly to do environmental scanning. However, I must re-emphasize that the purpose here is not to *forecast* the future, but to identify plausible events that could undermine assumptions.

Deciding on the vulnerability of an assumption rests on judging the plausibility of the event or events that could undermine it—one of the great difficulties in assessing vulnerability. What is plausible or likely to one viewer may be completely implausible to another. A good deal of this mismatch between views of vulnerabilities can come from biases that can creep into the assessments. Unfortunately, a large number of biases can affect judgments about plausibility.

Potential biases in assessing vulnerability

Nothing will eliminate all possible mismatches in vulnerability judgments. In fact, except for probability judgments of 0 percent or 100 percent, the *accuracy* of a vulnerability judgment for a nonrepeatable event generally cannot be established. For example, even if everyone agreed that a certain assumption had, say, a 15-percent chance of failure within the planning horizon, there is no way of determining—even after the fact—whether that was an accurate assessment.[1]

Research and practice suggest that there are several sources of potential bias in making likelihood judgments and that those potential biases act in predictable ways. Moreover, research suggests that experts are susceptible to these biases and that simply warning people about potential biases may not reduce those biases (Freudenburg 1992; Fischhoff et al. 1977).

Seven specific bias sources are worth discussing:

- Confirmation processing
- The availability heuristic
- Difficulty in generating plausible causes
- Incomplete search for plausible causes
- Failure to foresee cumulative causes
- Organizational culture and politics
- Conjunction fallacy.

Interestingly, the first five tend to introduce biases toward underestimating vulnerability; the sixth can introduce biases in either direction; and the seventh tends to introduce a bias toward overestimation of vulnerability.

People typically pay more attention to evidence that supports—confirms—their views than to evidence that conflicts with them, a bias known as *confirmation processing*. It is also easier for people to generate reasons that support their beliefs than those that contradict them. So, people tend to be overconfident in the accuracy of their forecasts, tending to deny uncertainty and vulnerability.

---

1 There *are* means of assessing the reliability/accuracy of forecasts and forecasters of repeatable events, such as weather forecasts. If, for example, it actually rains 15 percent of the time that a given forecaster predicts a 15-percent chance of rain (and so on with the forecaster's other numerical predictions), then the forecaster and his/her forecasts are accurate. For more on this, see Murphy and Winkler (1974).

In general, the likelihood of an assumption's failure will be determined by the possible causes of failure that a person can imagine. This tendency to base likelihood judgments of an event on the ease with which instances or occurrences of that or similar events can be brought to mind is referred to as the *availability heuristic* (Kahneman and Tversky 1982). This is a reasonable heuristic, considering that those events we can easily imagine or recall are often those that are most frequent. But availability can also lead to systematic bias. For example, judgments of the risk of various hazards or events will tend to be correlated with how often they are mentioned in the news media.

In thinking of such future events as assumption failures whose likelihoods cannot be based on past historical rates, people often construct their own simple causal scenarios of how the event could occur, using the difficulty of producing reasons for an event's occurrence as an *indicator* of the event's likelihood. If no plausible cause or scenario comes to mind, an assumption failure may be deemed impossible or highly unlikely. The more radical or counterintuitive the change, the more difficult it may be to imagine how that change could occur or how the assumption could fail to hold true. Thus, the probability that an assumption could fail may well be underestimated.

When people consider the possibility of significant change, they are likely to display a preference for simple, dramatic events as causal agents, rather than causes that are chronic and cumulative. On the one hand, it might be fairly easy to imagine the invention of a new technology or a sudden catastrophe creating dramatic change. The change would be given a relatively high probability or likelihood. On the other hand, an equivalent degree of change resulting from, for example, a slow shift in social attitudes might be more difficult to imagine. Thus, probabilities for events that could be produced by slow, incremental change often may be underestimated. Kahneman and Tversky (1982) have suggested also that the availability heuristic will result in events for which one plausible scenario will be viewed as more probable than events that seemingly can only be caused through a multitude of unlikely ways. Research in explanation-based tasks supports this hypothesis; the probability of propositions that can be true for multiple reasons may be underestimated as a matter of course (Sloman 1994).

Research in explanation-based tasks has found that information searches are often truncated once one possible cause or explanation for an event has been identified (Shaklee and Fischhoff 1982). Therefore, another source of underestimation bias in assessing the likelihood of an assumption's failure is *incomplete search for possible causes*. Again, if the possible cause or explanation is short of compelling, stopping the search for other causes at that point can mean that other, more compelling or more corroborating causes go undiscovered.

Whereas the sources of potential bias above generally work to cause the vulnerability of an assumption to be underestimated, the culture and politics of an organization can bias the assessment of vulnerability, but not necessarily in predictable ways. But the *culture* of an organization is generally more likely to lead to an underestimation of vulnerability because of the organization's understandable desire to have a plan succeed. However, subelements within a culture may tend to over- or underestimate vulnerabilities. For example, the marketing people may underestimate the vulnerabilities of a plan's assumptions while the finance people overestimate them.

Organizational politics—the internal dynamics leading to policy decisions—can be even less predictable in the estimation of vulnerability. Political factions that favor alternate plans may seek to overstate the vulnerabilities of assumptions underlying an adopted plan that they do not like and understate the vulnerabilities of the alternatives. As a result, the "winning" vulnerabilities may be underestimated.

The final source of potential bias, the conjunction fallacy, works toward *over*estimating vulnerability, and this overestimation can be (and is) used to help people contemplate vulnerabilities that they are otherwise unwilling to entertain. That is, it can be used to help *counteract* biases toward underestimation of vulnerability. Assumption failures for which possible causes can be convincingly pictured may receive high likelihood ratings.

Psychological researchers have demonstrated the existence of the *conjunction fallacy*, wherein an outcome paired with one likely cause is often judged (even by professional forecasters) to be more probable than the occurrence of the outcome alone (Kahneman and Tversky 1982). For example, suppose Tom Clancy were to write an embellished version of an unlikely event. His version of the event will tend to be seen as more likely to occur than would an unembellished version of the event, primarily because the embellishments themselves make the events seem more realistic. Although this is a violation of the laws of probability—the probability of the intersection of event A [the outcome] and event B [the specific cause] cannot be higher than the probability of event A—it makes intuitive sense when we consider that reasoning about the future is based primarily on causal thinking. In the Royal Dutch/Shell case about the price of oil, management asked for, and planners used, the conjunction fallacy—the embellished version—to help management engage with the scenario. Also noteworthy in this case was that the planners warned against the conjunction fallacy in their preface to the scenario.

Avoiding bias in determining vulnerable assumptions

Since most of the biases lead to underestimation of the vulnerability of assumptions, underestimation is important to guard against. The following rules of thumb can help minimize the underestimation of assumption vulnerabilities.

Above all, think "Chicken Little," not "Pollyanna." Thinking the worst is the single best rule of thumb for avoiding inappropriate certainty about the future. There is plenty of time later in the ABP process for more balanced assessments of vulnerabilities. Right here is the place to be thinking of everything that could possibly go wrong with an assumption. Worrying that the sky is going to fall is the best counterbalance to the tendency of people to deny uncertainty.

Get as many people with as many different backgrounds as possible involved in the search. Involving people with a variety of backgrounds will combat the tendency to be overconfident about the reliability of a judgment about the invulnerability of an assumption; increase the likelihood of identifying possible failure modes (weakening the availability heuristic); combat optimism in the assumptions (confirmation processing); and facilitate the search for multiple failure causes.

Concentrate on plausibility, not likelihood. Assess whether an assumption *could* fail in a given way, not whether it is likely to. This is the place to be thinking about failure *mechanisms*, not failure likelihoods, and to be suppressing statements such as, "Well, that *could* happen, but . . ." and "Yeah, but I don't think . . ." Anything that *could* happen within the expected lifetime of the plan should be accorded serious attention as a vulnerability.

Search for multiple causes of plausible failure. One of the sources of underestimation in assessing vulnerability comes from truncating the search for failure means after one failure mechanism is found. Pushing past that will not only minimize this bias, but will also help identify a vulnerability that is due to a collection of factors as opposed to the vulnerability that is due to a single catastrophic event.

Encourage creativity; discourage censorship. It never hurts to have a planning environment in which people feel comfortable "thinking the unthinkable." Only in such an environment will you get people to question cherished assumptions ("Our customers will always be loyal to us," "People will always need product A," "No one will ever make a better car than Detroit," "The Soviet Union will remain our implacable foe forever," etc.). Discouraging censorship could produce some potentially flaky vulnerabilities; however, at this point in the planning process, such "flakiness" can be tolerated.

* * * *

In identifying vulnerabilities in a plan's assumptions as realistically as possible, planners can do a great service to the organization. However, as with the prophetic visionary Cassandra, there is a danger that naysaying in this way will cause planners to be disregarded. Yet, unlike the mythical Cassandra, planners can move beyond the naysaying to identify actions that will strengthen the plan and make it more robust to the uncertainties of the future.

Techniques for identifying load-bearing and vulnerability simultaneously

To avoid prematurely dismissing potentially important assumptions, assessment of load-bearing and vulnerability must be performed separately from identification of the assumptions. How crucial is it to determine load-bearing and vulnerability separately from each other? Not very. In fact, decision literature suggests that it is difficult to make the assessment of load-bearing separately from that of vulnerability. Even our definition of *load-bearing* carries an element of the vulnerability of the assumption.

We have argued that *if* load-bearing and vulnerability are assessed separately, load-bearing should be assessed first. However, there are at least five techniques that combine the assessments of load-bearing and vulnerability simultaneously:

- Rip Van Winkle
- Retrospective futurology
- Strategic Assumption Surfacing and Testing
- Annual Key Bets
- Discovery-Driven Planning.

Rip Van Winkle technique

We developed the Rip Van Winkle technique over the course of several applications of Assumption-Based Planning. The technique is useful both in the planning itself and in assessing how load-bearing and vulnerable the assumptions that underlie a plan are. The Rip Van Winkle technique begins with the following setup:

> You have been asleep for the last 20 years. You know nothing about the world in which you awaken. Somewhat unfairly, you have been asked to guess what your company's operations are currently. To be somewhat more fair, before answering you are allowed to ask 10 questions about the world today. You are told that those questions must have yes or no answers and should not be contingent on the answers to other questions.[2]
> What are your 10 yes/no questions?

By being put in Rip Van Winkle's situation, you are thrust into the uncertainty of the future. Asking about your company's operations restricts your thinking to the company's future—and builds on your current knowledge of the company. Your questions automatically reveal aspects of the future about which you are uncertain. Restricting the number of questions forces you to think about the most important uncertainties that underlie what will drive the future business of the company. Requiring that the questions have yes or no answers and that they not be contingent on the answers to other questions requires that you think about the specifics of the future—and avoids unrevealing questions such as, "What is the world like?"

2   We have also had success posing this setup as a current-day exercise with a time traveler. The time traveler can only nod yes or no, but knows everything there is to know about the future. Participants must then create a list of questions to be asked of the time traveler.

Your 10 questions, then, lead to a set of issues that you consider most important and uncertain about the company's future. By looking at the current plan and what it assumes about these issues, you can derive the load-bearing, vulnerable assumptions of the plan.[3]

While the Rip Van Winkle technique could literally be aimed at an individual, it has primarily been used to collect the questions of a group of people interested in the future of an organization. The composition of this group is important: The more institutional diversity that is gathered in the group, the better. Getting at the combined sense of a diverse group requires a means of combining the questions from each of the participants and has led to two different formats: using the Delphi methodology and conducting a seminar.

Delphi format. The Delphi methodology is a means of running a group discussion anonymously and from a distance, as an alternative to the traditional method of obtaining group opinions: face-to-face discussions. Delphi was developed at RAND from studies on decisionmaking that began in 1948 (see the seminal work of Gordon and Helmer 1963; see also Dalkey 1968). The age-old adage "two heads are better than one" provides the primary rationale for the technique, particularly when an issue is debatable. Experimental studies had demonstrated several serious difficulties with face-to-face discussions, including dominant individuals exerting undue influence on the discussion, conversation unrelated to the discussion at hand creating "noise," and group pressure for conformity being applied. The Delphi technique sought specifically to avoid these difficulties. In its original form, it was used to gather expert opinion in hopes that its particular format would increase the quality of the group opinion. It has not proved as effective as hoped in that regard (see Sackman 1975 for a critique), but it is still in widespread use.

As used in Assumption-Based Planning, Delphi is primarily a means of polling a group of very busy people without having to compare calendars in search of a meeting time, with two basic features: (1) *anonymous response*, whereby opinions of the members of the group are solicited separately so that no one knows who else is participating and (2) *iteration and controlled feedback*, whereby interaction among partici-

---

3   This examination also provides a check on the completeness of the plan. If the important, uncertain issues are not addressed or are underaddressed in the plan, there is planning work still to be done.

pants takes place in several iterations, or rounds, with carefully controlled feedback between rounds.[4]

Procedurally, the Delphi technique begins with the group of participants receiving the Rip Van Winkle setup. Each member of the group then sends in a set of ten questions as a first-round response, usually via email or Internet. The responses from the first round are tabulated and fed back to the entire group without attribution, to protect the anonymity of the respondent. The members of the group are asked to rethink their list of responses/questions in the context of the knowledge of what everyone else has asked, and they are asked to resubmit a list of ten questions. Their resubmitted questions constitute a second round of the Delphi. The results of that round are tabulated and fed back to the group as in the first round, and the process continues, typically for three or four rounds. In the final round, the respondents are usually restricted to fewer (usually six) questions to further gauge the importance of each question to the respondent.

On the one hand, it is possible to do statistical summaries of the responses, but such summaries are rarely fruitful with a small number of participants and a wide variety of responses. On the other hand, two trends are generally visible in such an exercise: first, the questions in succeeding rounds worry less about current concerns and more about the future. An early-round question about the future of computers might ask if a specific microchip wafer technology had been successful. In later rounds, questions might focus more on fundamental barriers in computer technology, such as whether optical computers had become a reality. This change provides some reassurance that the Rip Van Winkle setup is working to focus people more on the future. Second, general convergence occurs on some issues. It is those convergent issues that are most crucial to check against the assumptions and actions of the current plan.

The major advantage of the Delphi technique is that it permits participants from widely scattered locations to participate in a group polling process, which often contributes significantly to the diversity that can be brought to the group. The major disadvantage is that the entire process can take up to three months, with each round taking a week or two.

---

4   In its original version, Delphi has a third step, *statistical group response*, in which the group opinion is defined as an appropriate statistical aggregate of individual opinions in the final round.

Seminar format. The seminar format of the Rip Van Winkle technique brings all the participants together in the same room. Participants are given the Rip Van Winkle setup and are either allowed time to frame their responses quietly or are asked to begin calling out the questions they would like to ask. Both approaches have been used successfully.

The questions are collected on paper or boards that all participants can see and read. The process of adding questions continues until the room is "played out." Creativity is encouraged; censorship is discouraged. Slight variations in questions are treated at this point as separate questions.

After the complete list of questions is generated (and after a well-deserved break), the group is then told that it must reduce that set of questions to the 10 questions allowable by the Rip Van Winkle setup. This begins a process of combining some questions and discarding others. We have found it quite useful to have someone in the room to note the major arguments of the ensuing discussion.

The group typically resists reducing the list of questions. The smaller the list gets, the greater the resistance becomes. Nonetheless, the discussions at this late point tend to be the most interesting because the participants are talking about what is *truly* important about the future and why. It is generally not worth the struggle to get to exactly 10 questions, so the process is typically cut off when the list gets to about 12 questions.

The resulting list of 12 or so Rip Van Winkle questions reveals the most important uncertainties about the organization's future. These important uncertainties must then be compared with the organization's plans to see what assumptions have been made about them. The load-bearing, vulnerable assumptions are derived in that comparison.

The major strength of this seminar variation of the Rip Van Winkle technique is that the discussions are often as valuable as the results in assessing what is important and vulnerable about the organization's future. Another strength is that the entire process can be done in a single, long day. The primary weakness is that the people you want to participate are generally very busy. It is therefore very difficult to schedule an entire day of their time simultaneously. This format also demands a strong moderator to keep the strongest personality or the highest-ranking participant from dominating the discussions.

Retrospective futurology[5]

Retrospective futurology begins with the failure of the company or division, to force the planner into thinking about the important vulnerabilities in the way his/her organization is currently operating. It is similar to the Rip Van Winkle technique and is particularly effective in identifying load-bearing, vulnerable assumptions in current operations. A sample setup is as follows:

> In two years your company/division will go broke. Describe how this happened.

Knowing that the outcome of the scenario is the failure of the company/division forces you to confront, in detail, how the current plans could be overwhelmed by plausible events in the time horizon called out by the retrospective futurology setup.

This technique works best as a written exercise, although writing a single scenario provides only a single failure mechanism for the company/division. To identify other failure mechanisms, this exercise can be presented to a wide variety of participants from across the company/division.

Strategic Assumption Surfacing and Testing

The Strategic Assumption Surfacing and Testing (SAST) method has a two-step process for determining load-bearing, vulnerable assumptions. SAST starts with three groups of people carefully chosen for intragroup compatibility and intergroup diversity, and with three different strategies, or planning approaches. In the first step of identifying assumptions, each of the groups is set the task of identifying the assumptions underlying the group's particular strategy.

The assumptions are numbered and arrayed on a two-dimensional graph, or matrix, like that shown in Figure 4.4. The numbered assumptions are placed in the matrix according to their relative importance (how load-bearing they are in the ABP sense) to the given strategy and the relative certainty to which they can be known. Each group then settles on the *pivotal*—most important and uncertain—assumptions underlying its plan. In Figure 4.4, the most important and uncertain as-

5   I am indebted to Paul Bracken for this technique. He says that he has used it "to great effect" in executive programs.

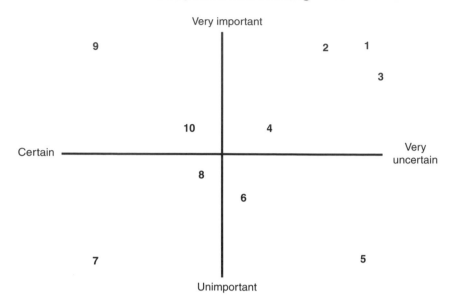

Figure 4.4. Assumptions Arrayed by Importance, Uncertainty

sumptions would certainly include assumptions 1 through 3 and may include assumption 4.

At the conclusion of this step, SAST brings the three groups together and has them engage in a dialectic debate. According to Mason and Mitroff (1981: 50), "*dialectic debate* occurs when a situation is examined systematically and logically from two or more points of view." Without going further into the technique, what is interesting from the SAST case studies is that the groups typically identify many of the same assumptions (even though they are dealing with different strategies), but they rate them quite differently on importance and certainty. Part of the dialectic debate, then, is to bring the larger group closer to consensus on the importance and certainty of overlapping assumptions. During a debate, the assumptions in Figure 4.4, for example, may well move around until a greater consensus is reached.

This SAST technique, then, is a method of getting different groups to assess importance and vulnerability of assumptions independently, then argue (constructively) about those assessments. When ABP has produced quite a few load-bearing, vulnerable assumptions, this technique might be an excellent means of differentiating among those assumptions.

Annual Key Bets

The Annual Key Bets methodology introduced in Chapter Three includes a matrix with the "key uncertainties" identified as being both high in importance to the company's strategy and high in uncertainty of understanding. However, the exact process by which these "most important, admittedly unknown" assumptions are identified is described only as taking place in annual interviews with the network of experts. Those interviews develop an updated understanding of the key uncertainties facing the company. In ABP terms, Annual Key Bets uses expert opinion to assess simultaneously those aspects of the future that are load-bearing and vulnerable (uncertain). Subsequently "placing bets" on how those uncertainties will play out turns the key uncertainties into load-bearing, vulnerable assumptions.

Discovery-Driven Planning

Discovery-Driven Planning, introduced in Chapter Three, derives a set of minimal requirements leveled on a new venture according to a presumed level of profitability. Each of these minimal requirements then represents a load-bearing assumption underlying the profitability of the venture. At the same time, Discovery-Driven Planning requires an assessment of the feasibility of achieving those minimal requirements. This is the same as assessing the vulnerability of those assumptions. If the vulnerabilities of those assumptions are too great, replanning is immediately necessary. Otherwise, the plan proceeds and the assumptions are carefully monitored. If an assumption is invulnerable, it is a candidate for accepting greater vulnerability as a means of reducing the vulnerability of another requirement elsewhere. In this way, the vulnerability of these assumptions is assessed at the same time that the assumptions themselves are developed.

RANKING THE LOAD-BEARING, VULNERABLE ASSUMPTIONS

At this point in the ABP process, we have a list of the load-bearing and vulnerable assumptions that underlie a company's plans. The dog that has not barked yet in these discussions is ranking: Any good planner or manager is going to want to know what the relative risks are of each load-bearing, vulnerable assumption.

The most straightforward means of ranking the load-bearing, vulnerable assumptions is by risk. Without delving too deeply into the fields of risk analysis and risk management, we define the *risk* associated with a load-bearing, vulnerable assumption roughly as the product of how load-bearing an assumption is and how likely it is to fail within the time horizon of the plan. On the one hand, such a mathematical formulation is better suited to a methodology that has assigned numerical values to load-bearing and likelihood, which we have studiously avoided. On the other hand, it captures the notion that the riskiest load-bearing, vulnerable assumptions are those that carry the most weight in the plan and/or organization and are most vulnerable to failure during the plan's lifetime. The problem with sorting by this definition of risk comes in comparing an assumption that is very vulnerable, but a bit less load-bearing, with one that is very load-bearing, but a bit less vulnerable.

There are two approaches for ranking assumptions by risk. The first approach deals with rank-ordering by arraying the assumptions or issues on a two-dimensional graph (or matrix) like the one in Figure 4.4. In Strategic Assumption Surfacing and Testing, a matrix like that in Figure 4.4 is used to identify the importance and uncertainty in the assumptions by placing the assumptions by judgments of how certain and how important the assumptions are. The farther to the right in Figure 4.4, the more uncertain; the higher up the vertical axis, the more important. Those that are farthest to the right and highest are the riskiest. These are clearly judgments. But once they are made, deciding which assumptions are riskiest becomes a matter of measuring to see which are farthest from the origin of the graph in Figure 4.4 and in the upper-right-hand quadrant. In Figure 4.4, the highest-ranking load-bearing, vulnerable assumption would be assumption 1. From the figure, assumption 2 is more important than assumption 3, but less uncertain or vulnerable. However, they are both about the same distance from the origin, so they would be tied for next riskiest.

The Annual Key Bets methodology uses a similar approach to arraying the importance and certainty of the challenges facing the company. The company then "makes bets" on the important and uncertain challenges.

The second approach to ranking assumptions is used by the Global Business Network (GBN) in assessing the most important and uncertain drivers of the future.[6] After brainstorming a list of key drivers of the future of an organization, each member of an assembled group is then given a small number of votes (say, 5). Each member of the group then votes for the most important and most uncertain drivers of the future. The rules for voting are interesting in that all the votes can be spent on one driver or can be spread as thinly as one per driver. A similar method could clearly be used to rank load-bearing, vulnerable assumptions.

To rank assumptions by some sense of risk is to compound judgments, producing judgments of judgments. However, it is a natural instinct to rank assumptions by some sense of their risk. The greater the number of load-bearing, vulnerable assumptions, the more sense it makes to use a more systematic method for identifying the riskiest ones. Ordering of load-bearing, vulnerable assumptions will come up again when we get to Step 5, developing hedging actions.

In practice, ranking the load-bearing, vulnerable assumptions has not been all that important, for two reasons: First, there have not been that many load-bearing, vulnerable assumptions. Second, it is reasonably easy to rank such assumptions after the long process of identifying which assumptions are load-bearing, which are vulnerable, and what their vulnerabilities are.

HOW MANY LOAD-BEARING, VULNERABLE ASSUMPTIONS WILL THERE BE?

It is theoretically possible to have a plan with no load-bearing, vulnerable assumptions. An affordable plan based entirely on worst-case assumptions or a plan that was brilliantly well shaped and hedged could have no remaining load-bearing, vulnerable assumptions. The theoretical minimum number of such assumptions, then, is zero.

I mention this theoretical limit to reinforce the idea that the number of load-bearing, vulnerable assumptions in a given plan is related to the care that has been taken to make it robust. In practice, a more decisive factor in guessing how many load-bearing, vulnerable assumptions there will be is the level at which the plan is aimed. The higher the level, the fewer the number of load-bearing, vulnerable assumptions there are likely to be. That is, if a plan is aimed at the strategic level, the assump-

6   This information comes from a GBN planning exercise in which I participated in 1999, after I received instruction in the GBN methodology.

tions tend to be very general and tend to be worst-case assumptions. If the plan is down at the budgetary level (such as in the Discovery-Driven Planning method, which concentrates on profitability), there are likely to be more load-bearing, vulnerable assumptions.

Clearly, the more load-bearing, vulnerable assumptions that have been identified, the longer the remaining ABP steps will take. There can easily be too many to comfortably carry out the remaining steps. If there are more than a dozen or so load-bearing, vulnerable assumptions at this point, it becomes all the more important to rank them by risk. Ranking them by risk is an important means of preparing them for pruning; further pruning mechanisms are presented in the coming two chapters.

Lemonade Stand—2

When we left our young lemonade-stand entrepreneur, she had a list of assumptions dealing with the weather, lemonade supplies, the availability of key personnel, competition, and customers. Since yesterday, however, she has thought about a couple of assumptions that she has added to the list, because it became clear to her that she was assuming they would happen:

- She and Chloe will be healthy.
- Somebody with a car will be available in case they need to be driven to the store for more supplies.
- There won't be a fire or something that diverts car and foot traffic from in front of the house (she added this assumption after she remembered the house down the block that had a fire in the garage that resulted in all car and foot traffic being diverted around their block for two days).

At this point, she is ready to identify those assumptions that are load-bearing and vulnerable.

Identifying load-bearing, vulnerable assumptions

Clearly, the assumption she is most worried about is the weather. If it rains, the whole concept of a lemonade stand is unlikely to be successful. This is definitely a load-bearing assumption. Further, it *could* rain that weekend (it *has* rained on the last weekend in June in the past), so this is also a vulnerable assumption. There is little that Margot can do at this point to resolve this uncertainty. It is a load-bearing, vulnerable assumption.

What about the other assumptions? Some were neither load-bearing nor vulnerable:

- *There won't be road construction or something keeping people from walking or driving by.* One year, she had moved her stand down to the corner because not enough people were wandering by. She and Chloe could do that again if they had to. Besides, the city repaved the street just last year, so it is unlikely there will be any road construction this coming summer.

(continued)

Lemonade Stand—2 (continued)

- *The yard will be available* (i.e., they'll still live there). Her parents had been talking about moving, so she was plenty worried about having to leave her school and friends. But at this point, it is just preliminary talk. It would be unlikely to happen before June. She could probably set up the lemonade stand in the new front yard if the family did move. *If* the family moved (and at this point it is a big "if"), the move would seriously disrupt her life, but not necessarily her lemonade-stand plans.

Some assumptions were load-bearing, but judged not vulnerable:

- *The tree in the backyard will have plenty of lemons.* If this assumption were to fail, it would not be devastating, but it would ruin her "organic lemonade" advertising campaign. In that sense, it is load-bearing in this particular plan. The tree has *always* had plenty of lemons. It is *possible* that something will happen, but unlikely. Margot *did* check the tree and everything seemed normal, so she has concluded that this is not really a vulnerable assumption. Just in case, though, she will keep it on the list of assumptions.

Some assumptions were vulnerable, but not load-bearing:

- *There won't be a fire or something that diverts car and foot traffic from in front of the house.* Margot could not rule out the possibility that a fire or explosion could happen in the neighborhood. And again, she and Chloe could move the stand if they had to.

- *Chloe will be available* (i.e., not on vacation). Chloe is often on vacation during the summer. If Chloe is gone that weekend, Margot can ask Brianna if she could do it. Even if Brianna could not do it, Margot is ready to run the stand by herself.

- *Somebody with a car will be available in case they need to be driven to the store for more supplies.* As soon as she realized she was assuming this, Margot started thinking about alternatives. She realized that if there was no one around to drive her to the store, she could get on her bike (with a backpack) and ride to the store. The assumption about the availability of a ride to the store could have become load-bearing, but in the (now) modified plan (in which technically she added a hedging action or contingency plan) it is no longer load-bearing. She has now added an assumption that her bike will not have a flat tire, but that, too, she can shape and hedge against. This assumption is easy to make non–load-bearing.

Besides the weather, Margot identified five other load-bearing, vulnerable assumptions:

- *Margot and Chloe will be healthy.* She was protected against Chloe being unhealthy (by having planned for a replacement because of the possibility that Chloe might be healthy but gone on vacation). However, Margot was not prepared for being sick or injured herself, nor could she absolutely guarantee that she would not be in six months. If she was not available, no one else would set up the lemonade stand and the plans would fail—definitely a load-bearing, vulnerable assumption.

- *There won't be any competition* (from other lemonade stands). Margot has made her assumption about the competition. But competition carries uncertainties. She can't be sure what the other entrepreneurs her age are going to do. She knows there is competition out there (people have several thirst-quenching choices), but she is presuming that she has the organic-lemonade-from-adorable-young-entrepreneurs niche to herself. If she does not, her plan could be in trouble. She cannot guarantee that there will not be competition—a load-bearing, vulnerable assumption.

(continued)

Lemonade Stand—2 (continued)

- *Margot, herself, will be available.* This is load-bearing. If she is not there, the lemonade stand will not happen. It is unlikely that her family will be on vacation (they usually go in August). Margot can also control the things she might schedule (like going to the movies). Other scheduling possibilities can be checked (will there be a softball game?). Many aspects of her availability, then, are under her control. But some aspects of her availability are not subject to her control and do not have to do with either regulatory matters ("being grounded") or injury. Suppose she were invited to a birthday party or a day at the beach. These would be hard to reschedule and equally hard to pass up. This has to be considered a vulnerable, as well as a load-bearing, assumption.

- *She will be allowed to run the lemonade stand* (e.g., she won't be "grounded"). This is clearly load-bearing. Further, this is different from being sick or injured in that it should be controllable. That is, this assumption should not even be vulnerable. Unfortunately for Margot, it is. She's been doing better lately, but . . .

- *The stand will draw at least 24 customers at $.25/cup.* Margot's rough budget and her previous experience has led her to conclude that she can charge $.25/cup and that she will have at least 24 paying customers. Further, she is confident (based on past experience) that this will make her lemonade stand financially successful. Nonetheless, she cannot guarantee at least 24 customers—load-bearing and vulnerable.

Counting the weather, Margot has identified six load-bearing, vulnerable assumptions in her plans for a lemonade stand. She is now ready to improve her plan's ability to handle these six important uncertainties.

5

Step 3: identifying signposts

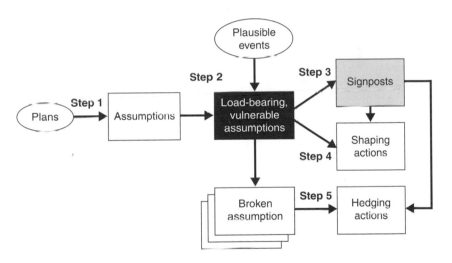

Figure 5.1. Highlighting Step 3 of ABP: Identifying Signposts

At this point in the Assumption-Based Planning process, we have the load-bearing, vulnerable assumptions (ordered by risk, if there are quite a few assumptions) underlying the plans of an organization. The first two steps of ABP identify the vulnerabilities of a plan. The final three steps work to improve the plan's handling of those vulnerabilities.

Because the last three steps all work with the load-bearing, vulnerable assumptions, each step must wait until those assumptions have been identified. However, once they *have* been identified, the final three steps are independent enough of one another that the order in which they are done is not critical. Ordinarily, we have done the steps as

91

shown in Figure 5.1, first developing signposts, then identifying shaping actions (Step 4), and finally determining hedging actions (Step 5). I keep them in that order in this chapter and the next two chapters.

The signposts we want to identify in Step 3 of ABP are intended to mark points in the unfolding future where turns from the current path may be necessary or advisable. More specifically, signposts are indicators, or warning signals, that the validity or vulnerability of an assumption is changing. As depicted in Figure 5.1, signposts can be developed once the load-bearing, vulnerable assumptions have been defined—in fact, planners can start developing signposts as the vulnerabilities of the load-bearing assumptions are being identified.

Although identified during the planning process, signposts find their primary utility in the more prosaic process of implementing and managing the plan. For example, signposts are commonly a part of a strategic control system, a formal system that monitors and manages a plan after its implementation has begun (see below and the Appendix). In fact, a more compact version of ABP might have just Steps 1, 2, 4, and 5 in Figure 5.1, with a postscript saying "and add a standard-issue strategic control system to monitor and control the plan itself."

But signposts have a more exalted intent in ABP. Signposts are formally part of the Assumption-Based Planning process for what they bring to the understanding of a plan and its assumptions. By being clear on specifically how and when a load-bearing, vulnerable assumption underlying a plan might fail, planners develop not only a better appreciation of the strengths and weaknesses of a given plan, but a better feel for whether the assumptions being made are the best ones for solving the essential planning problem. Thinking about signposts forces planners to confront whether there is sufficient indication and warning of an impending assumption failure to be able to take appropriate action. Signposts are a way to reinforce the notion that there is value in *thinking* in an assumption-based way while planning.

Figure 5.2 shows a logical roadmap for this chapter as it describes the identification of signposts.

DEFINITION OF *SIGNPOST*

Specifically, for Assumption-Based Planning,

A *signpost* is an event or threshold that indicates an important change in the validity or vulnerability of an assumption.

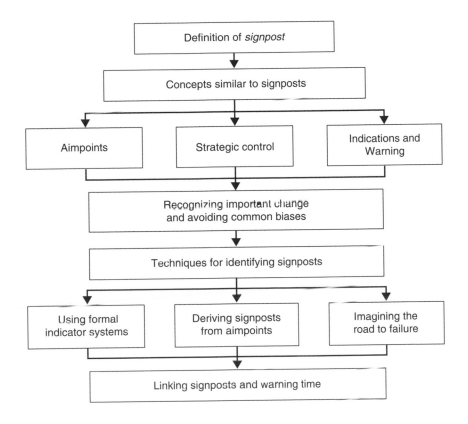

Figure 5.2. Logical Road Map of Chapter 5

This definition encompasses two important concerns: validity and vulnerability. We are interested in monitoring changes in the *validity*, or correctness, of load-bearing assumptions because, if a load-bearing assumption loses validity (if it fails), by definition, the plan that rests on it will also fail. Signposts should warn us when a load-bearing assumption has lost or is losing validity.

We are also interested in monitoring changes in the *vulnerability* of load-bearing assumptions because that vulnerability is what indicates that an assumption *could* fail (is subject to loss of validity). We are particularly interested in knowing whether there is an important *drop* in the vulnerability of an assumption. For example, suppose a company's plans rely heavily on the assumption of a favorable regulatory or judicial ruling at some point in the future. There are two possible outcomes: the ruling is not favorable—in which case the assumption fails—or the ruling is favorable—in which case the assumption remains valid *and the vulnerability surrounding that assumption disappears* (pending appeals). The signpost in this case can be the date on which the ruling will be made.

An increase in the vulnerability of an assumption might presage the failure of that assumption. For a judicial ruling, a preliminary ruling that damages the case for a favorable ruling increases the vulnerability of an assumption of a favorable ruling and is, itself, a signpost that the assumption may be failing.

CONCEPTS SIMILAR TO SIGNPOSTS

At least three concepts in planning—aimpoints, strategic control systems, and Indications and Warning—are similar to signposts. All three concepts overlap with signposts in ways that are important to understand.

Aimpoints

Aimpoints—goals, targets, and/or objectives—are important outputs of any plan. These aimpoints are structured so that, if met, they will make the plan a success. Said another way, the plan *assumes* that the aimpoints will be met—or, in the case of "stretch goals" (goals purposely chosen to be challenging), at least nearly so.

Aimpoints *can also be* signposts, although, usually, they are not. Usually, failure to reach an aimpoint would not cause a plan to fail—although it would certainly be cause for concern. Assumptions that the aimpoints will be met are usually vulnerable assumptions. *If, and only if, assumptions about meeting aimpoints are load-bearing, will the aimpoints also be signposts.* Failure to reach the aimpoints will be failure of a load-bearing assumption. We saw this in Discovery-Driven Planning, in which the assumptions about performance were minimal acceptable performance parameters and therefore load-bearing.

Load-bearing, vulnerable assumptions about meeting aimpoints may not make the best signposts, in any case. As signposts, they provide no warning time: Failure to meet a load-bearing aimpoint will already mean that the plan has failed. If possible, it would be better to select as a signpost something short of an aimpoint that would provide an indication that the plan was in trouble, providing more time to take corrective action. In Discovery-Driven Planning, load-bearing, vulnerable assumptions about meeting aimpoints are used more appropriately to decide whether or not to proceed with a plan. Signposts derived from such aimpoints are discussed further below in the Techniques for Identifying Signposts section.

Strategic control

Strategic control is the part of strategic management—which also includes strategy formulation and strategy implementation—that compares strategic goals with progress toward those goals and identifies shortfalls (for more details on the relation between strategic control and ABP, see the Appendix).

Strategic control, then, occurs during plan implementation and focuses on whether the plan is succeeding. However, a part of strategic control—premise control—is closely related to the objectives of signposts. *Premise control* is the process of checking whether the assumptions underlying the strategy are still valid. The primary difference between signposts and premise control is that signposts are identified during the planning process and are monitored thereafter. In premise control, planners scan the environment during the implementation phase of a plan and ask whether the assumptions of the plan are still valid. The significance of this difference is more evident in the third concept related to signposts—Indications and Warning.

Indications and Warning

Indications and Warning (I&W) is the name given to a military methodology used to determine a potential threat through analysis of indicators—military, political, or social changes—of a possible increase in imminent danger to U.S. forces or national security interests, and to issue appropriate levels of warning. Signposts are indicators of a possible increase of imminent danger to a load-bearing, vulnerable assumption.

I&W is generally part of a larger system called Intelligence Preparation of the Battlefield (or Battlespace) (IPB). In U.S. Army IPB, Areas of Interest (AOIs) are even more closely related to signposts. These physical locations, which are monitored for activity, help confirm or confound assumptions about enemy plans. Signposts are intended to indicate changes in either the validity of load-bearing, vulnerable assumptions or changes in the vulnerability of those assumptions.

The important similarities among indicators, AOIs, and signposts are that they are all identified *during* the planning process. It is the need to think about these indications during planning that encourages serious thought about and better understanding of the vulnerabilities of their associated assumptions. That is the true value of signposts.

HOW IMPORTANT IS *IMPORTANT*?

The most difficult criterion to establish in the definition is that a signpost represents an *important* change: significant enough either to require replanning or to raise seriously the issue of replanning.

But when is a change important or significant enough? Recognizing important change involves understanding both what data should be collected—*sensing*—and how those data should be interpreted—*making sense*. By establishing a signpost, we are suggesting what data should be collected and how the collected data should be interpreted: the classic intelligence-gathering process and history are littered with "intelligence failures."

Quite a bit is known about the general area of signposts and recognizing important change. The interpretation of signs is a field in its own right—semiotics. There is also a rich literature on the causes of intelligence failure and what might be done to avoid them. It is worth spending time, then, discussing some of the more common biases that can creep into defining important change. After that discussion, I describe three techniques that can work to counteract those biases.

Potential biases in recognizing important changes

Most of the problems in defining *important change* come not in deciding what data to collect but in deciding how to interpret the data. Bias in interpreting data comes from four basic sources:

- Defensive avoidance
- Cultural or organizational blinders

- Bad or missing information
- Failure to think through the consequences.

On the cognitive level, failing to recognize important signals can be at least partially explained by the concept of *defensive avoidance*: When unfavorable events begin to unfold that run counter to expectations, misperception of the events provides a shield from stress (Janis and Mann 1977). There is no known cure for defensive avoidance, but identification of and agreement on signposts during the planning process (and subsequent monitoring) will certainly help guard against this tendency.

This same kind of avoidance can be seen at cultural and organizational levels, as well as the personal level. Both *cultural and organizational avoidance*, or "blinders," were probably at work when U.S. auto manufacturers and Xerox misinterpreted the strength of Japanese competition.

A particularly pernicious source of misinterpretation of important changes is *bad or missing information*. Therefore, although the interpretation of the data might have been reasonable, the bad or missing data can lead to a misinterpretation of the underlying change. Bad data can come from a variety of sources, a common source in a competitive situation being deliberately bad data—misinformation. This is a serious concern for the military, because of the potential for loss of life, but it is also a concern for businesses because of the financial damage that can result.

Bad data can also come from sloppy collection techniques or from collecting the wrong data. A good example of collecting the wrong data comes from the plywood industry. For many years, plywood was the dominant source of structural panels in buildings and its growth trend in sales was smooth. In the late 1960s and early 1970s, analysts observed oscillations in plywood demand and attributed them to increased sales in waferboard. Had there been a signpost built around the increasing use of waferboard, analysts might have concluded that the signpost was upon them. With the industry in a panic about competition from waferboard, further research showed that fluctuations in fixed residential investment explained almost all of the oscillation in plywood sales (Corporate Strategy Board 1999; Pistorius and Utterback 1995). Thinking it had been collecting all the data it thought necessary to accurately monitor the sales of plywood, the industry discovered, fortunately, that it was missing some data necessary to give an accurate picture before something went wrong.

The last major source of misinterpretation of important changes is a *failure to think through the consequences of a change.* Paul Bracken (personal communication) provided a nice example of an assumption that had been true for so long that people ignored even obvious signposts because they failed to think through the consequences of a change. From 1998 through 2001, Japan introduced a zero-interest-rate policy in order to save the banking industry. It worked. The banking industry was saved. Unfortunately, the insurance industry was seriously damaged. Insurance companies depended on market returns to pay their claims. These returns vanished after the zero-interest rate was introduced, and the many insurance companies went bankrupt. Zero-interest rates were a signpost of insurance industry trouble that people failed to recognize.

Avoiding bias in recognizing important changes. If failing to think through the consequences of change is a major source of misinterpreting important changes, the very act of thinking about signposts counteracts this source of trouble. Taking the time, prospectively, to think through how failure might occur and how it might be spotted is a good antidote to many of the potential biases in recognizing important change. Thinking through both what data ought to be collected and how they ought to be interpreted helps clarify how to recognize the failure or impending failure of an assumption.

In addition to the act of developing signposts, there are two means of fighting bias in developing signposts:

- Getting agreement on signposts

- Thinking about who should monitor signposts.

Getting agreement on signposts. Not all signposts need to be, or should be, agreed on. However, when a very diverse group is developing the signposts, agreement on a signpost means agreement on the importance of that signpost as an indicator of change. Getting agreement on signposts gets more difficult the greater the diversity of the group that is developing the signposts. Paradoxically, it seems that the greater the difficulty in agreeing on signposts is, the greater is the chance the signposts will be useful.

Taking this process one step further, it is useful to take those consensual signposts (and their hard-fought justification) up the corporate ladder for further rounds of agreement. Doing so runs the usual risk that the signposts will get watered down, in the sense that an early indicator of trouble will be changed to an indicator that will not be triggered until trouble is well advanced. However, the more people who buy into a signpost, the more people there are who will have been sensitized to the vulnerability of its associated assumption.

Thinking about who should monitor signposts. Having the right signpost is only part of the problem. If a signpost cannot be recognized, it is useless. The same bias that makes a signpost difficult to identify can make it difficult to recognize. Business literature documents numerous examples of information that was ignored or misinterpreted and that, in hindsight, was a clear indication of important change. Both U.S. auto manufacturers and Xerox woefully misinterpreted the strength of Japanese competition, although the data were available. IBM ignored first minicomputers, then personal computers. Digital surprised IBM with its minicomputers and was surprised, in turn, by personal computers. The list goes on. Military literature, especially, details a long history of "intelligence failures," in which important information was ignored, misinterpreted, suppressed, or otherwise mishandled (see, for example, Lanning 1995 and Wirtz 1994). As long as there have been people looking for important change, there have been people *over*looking important change.

Thinking about who should monitor a given signpost can help decrease the bias in recognizing the signpost. Picking the right person or organization to monitor the signpost can make all the difference. Some signposts may require monitoring outside the planners' organization. A small business that does not have the resources to maintain its own macro-economic forecasting capability may be able to monitor market and industry trends by purchasing relevant reports or updates from government or private agencies. Other signposts may be better monitored outside the organization. An industry-wide indicator system, for example, is less likely to be subject to biases that are peculiar to a given organization. Although an industry-wide indicator system is likely to avoid a particular regional bias or a cultural bias within a single organization, it is likely to share biases that are common to the industry as a whole.

Planners may also ask other divisions (such as the financial division) in the organization to monitor specific signposts. This is common in the military, in which signposts dealing with, say, foreign technology may affect the doctrine community but may be better monitored by the intelligence community or the technology community.

TECHNIQUES FOR IDENTIFYING SIGNPOSTS

Signposts are as common in the management world as they are in the physical world: Every "corner"—event or trend—seems to have one or more. Monitoring and interpreting events and trends is common not just in the business world. Analysis of current events is hardly complete without the pundit being asked for and positing a sign to watch for as an indication of which way events will develop. But how are these signposts developed?

For all the talk about signposts, there is little talk about means for developing them systematically. We have come across only three essentially distinct means of identifying signposts:

- Using formal indicator systems
- Deriving signposts from aimpoints
- Imagining the road to failure.

Since each has its own heuristics for generating signposts and its own limitations, I describe each in more detail.

Using formal indicator systems

Most communities of practice have some kind of indicator system for predicting the future of a particular community. A good example of an indicator system is the Index of Leading Economic Indicators (LEI), perhaps the most celebrated of the formal systems. Used by economists, businesses, and policymakers to anticipate economic development, the LEI is itself a composite of ten leading indicators, including average workweek, building permits, and interest-rate spread.

The best formal indicator systems include a careful analysis of past events; statistical means, such as factor analysis, to determine which are the best predictors of the future; and an active community of researchers dedicated to keeping the indicator up to date and accurate. These indicators are generally made available to all interested parties.

How can formal indicators be used for signposting? A mechanism for indicating significant changes is generally built into these indicators.

With the LEI, for example, three consecutive monthly changes in the same direction suggest a turning point in the economy, consecutive negative readings indicating a possible recession. This, then, would be a signpost for an assumption about the economy and whether it is likely to go into a recession.

The difficulty with using indicator systems is having little control over whether the indicators apply to your signposting situation. Using indicator systems, then, requires ensuring that the indicator is appropriate for a given assumption. The LEI was definitely applicable to the large manufacturing company that was making the implicit assumption that the economy would not go into recession during the lifetime of its plan. The part of the LEI relating to building permits might also have been useful as a signpost for the plywood makers, who failed to monitor residential investment.

For the purposes of signposting, a major problem with indicator systems is that they generally require a long history of performance data from which to pick the most significant predictive indicators. Indicator systems are good at picking up recurring trends or shifts in the state of a community of practice, but they are not particularly good at picking up the spasmodic event that upsets an assumption. For that, you need another approach to identifying signposts.

Deriving signposts from aimpoints

Aimpoints—goals, targets or objectives—are a good place to look for signposts. Aimpoints are measures of a plan's success or failure. I want to reemphasize that signposts are intended to measure the success or failure of the assumptions underlying a plan, *not* of the plan itself. Aimpoints and signposts, then, may or may not be connected.

As above, they *are* directly connected in the special case in which an assumption about meeting an aimpoint is a load-bearing assumption. For example, suppose a company has a goal of raising $50 million by year's end to finance a fabrication plant for a new product. If the company is counting on that new plant and product, the assumption that it can raise the $50 million is load-bearing. That $50-million goal, then, could also be a signpost. The failure to meet that aimpoint will signal the failure of the plan.

This is a good example for two reasons. First, the $50 million is a "soft" number in that it need not be met exactly. If the company raises all but $3,000 of the goal, say, it would be likely to proceed with the plant and the plan. Second—and more important—the company would not wait until the end of the year to decide whether the goal had been met and whether the plan should change. That is, the $50-million goal by year's end is not a good signpost, but there is *some* number and *some* date that *would* be a good signpost. If the company has not raised *at least* $30 million by the end of April, they may decide that the final goal is unlikely to be reached and that the plan should change. The signpost of $30 million by the end of April has been *derived* from the aimpoint.

Derived signposts need not be numerical. The planners could decide that if the company cannot get the European subsidiary to help with the financing of the new plant, that they will not be able to put the financing together and the plan must change. The European subsidiary's decision, then, becomes the signpost.

It should also be clear that derived signposts need not come only from load-bearing assumptions about aimpoints. Aimpoints are used to measure the progress of a plan. Their ability to measure the plan may also be useful in measuring the vulnerability of a plan's associated assumptions. Tracking the number of hits on a World Wide Web page may help decide if banner ads are meeting their planned targets for effectiveness. Tracking the number of hits may also be used as part of a signpost to check the vulnerability of a load-bearing assumption that the World Wide Web is going to be increasingly important to the organization's outreach.

Imagining the road to failure

In our search for means of identifying signposts, no one seems to have come up with a better approach than the common-sense way of proceeding: Start with the vulnerability of an assumption and imagine a path along which the assumption could fail. Look around on that path for unique, unmistakable identifiers of that path. These are the signposts.

The more quantitative the assumptions are, the easier it is to identify signposts that are quantitative. These assumptions can either be about the world or about actions. "Oil prices will not fall below $15 a barrel during the plan's lifetime" is an example of a quantitative assumption about the world that leads directly to a quantitative signpost. "Sales must increase by at least 10 percent during the first year" is an example of an assumption about actions that leads directly to quantitative signposts. If sales for the first quarter are significantly below a seasonally adjusted 10-percent rate, the assumption is in serious jeopardy of failing.

Even so, these quantitative signposts reemphasize the highly judgmental nature of signposts. What if oil prices drop to $15.05 a barrel? Has the signpost arrived? Is it better to set the signpost at $16 a barrel? Should there be a "worry" signpost at $18 a barrel and a "take-action" signpost at $15? There are no easy one-size-fits-all answers to such questions. In some cases, sharp signposts can be set: "The minute we stop being profitable, the front office will shut us down." In most cases, the setting of signposts is somewhat arbitrary, and the less quantitative the signposts are, the more arbitrary they are likely to appear. "A competitor comes out with a striking new product" is a significant indicator of change—one that may require quick and decisive action. But, Which competitor? How striking? How difficult to react to? and Who's buying it? are among the questions it would be nice to have answers to before deciding if this is a signpost that should trigger change.

More so than with judgments in earlier steps, it is particularly useful to have a variety of perspectives and opinions involved in the identification of signposts. On the one hand, a variety of perspectives is likely to make it more difficult to get agreement on clear signposts. On the other hand, the dialog itself among the various perspectives is a good means of developing an understanding of the issues involved in developing a signpost. As a senior vice president at a Fortune 100 company told us, "We don't lack signposts, but there may be too much democracy." It is helpful to get those signposters and their signposts in a room and have them work together to hammer out a few select, consensual signposts. This group discussion also increases buy-in and helps minimize politics if and when information arises that may lead to undesirable consequences from one constituency's perspective.

* * * *

Just as assumptions may be vulnerable to anything from a simple, dramatic event to a combination of slow, subtle trends whose accumulation finally becomes destructive, signposts should be developed so that they reflect the spectrum of failure mechanisms. As difficult as it is to identify single events or thresholds that portend a significant change in the validity or vulnerability of an assumption, combinations of events, trends, or thresholds will be that much more difficult to both identify and defend. The Index of Leading Economic Indicators is a good example of a system made up of multiple trends that is used to monitor whether or not the economy is in a recession.

More than one signpost may be associated with a given assumption, and a given signpost can be associated with more than one assumption. In fact, multiple signposts may be appropriate for a single assumption, either to increase the likelihood of detecting an emerging threat or to monitor several ways in which an assumption might be threatened.

One crucial aspect of signposting is the amount of warning time a signpost affords.

LINKING SIGNPOSTS AND WARNING TIMES

Signposts are only useful if they can be recognized in time to take appropriate action. A street sign that is obscured by foliage until you are well into the intersection is of little help. Similarly, warning signs of a major accident are likely to come too late to prevent the accident. Dangers of this type require prevention: making sure they cannot or do not happen.

Dangers that permit adequate warning time allow for evasive action. This simple logic of signposts and warning times is shown in Figure 5.3. Considering what kind of warning time a given signpost affords a given vulnerable assumption is particularly important in developing signposts.

The adequacy of warning time helps draw a dividing line between signposts and the general field of risk management. *Risk management* primarily seeks to identify the possibility of and prevent catastrophic accidents that do not afford adequate warning time for evasive action. If warning time adequate for evasive action is not available, signposts are not particularly helpful. If an assumption could fail without adequate warning time, action must be taken either to prevent the assumption's failing (shaping actions) or to be prepared to clean up afterward (hedging and contingency actions).

In his book *Hypercompetition*, D'Aveni (1994) suggests that today's business climate is increasingly one in which sufficient warning time is *not* available. The faster the pace in a given market, the less time there is to see what is coming and the less time there is to take action—even if

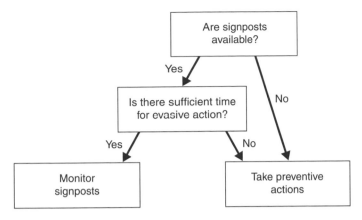

Figure 5.3. The Relationship Between Signposts and Warning Time

you can see what is coming. The process of trying to develop signposts is crucial in a fast-paced situation. Even when a signpost cannot be developed because of insufficient warning time, recognizing that situation can, itself, lead to improved preventive actions or important replanning. When warning time is too short to be helpful, developing shaping and hedging actions is likely to take precedence over identifying signposts.

Lemonade Stand—3

Margot, the young lemonade-stand planner, has identified six load-bearing, vulnerable assumptions in her plan for the coming summer:

- The weather will be nice.
- There won't be any competition from other lemonade stands.
- Margot will be available.
- Margot will be healthy.
- Margot will be allowed to run the stand.
- The stand will draw at least 24 customers at $.25/cup.

Margot is ready to identify signposts. She is looking for indications that load-bearing, vulnerable assumptions might be failing or that the vulnerability of those assumptions might be changing. She is also interested in whether or not those indications will give her sufficient warning time to take corrective or evasive action.

Identifying signposts

- *The weather will be nice.* The signpost for the weather will come from a formal indicator system: weather forecasts from the newspaper. For the sake of argument,

(continued)

Lemonade Stand—3 (continued)

let us say that, historically, there is a 30-percent chance of rain on a typical day at the end of June in Margot's town. If it rains either day, the stand is unlikely to make money. That means there is a 49-percent chance that the weather will be nice and the stand will make money. However, Margot knows that the weather forecasts two days ahead are pretty reliable. If the forecasts say there is only a 10-percent chance of rain, the prospects for a successful stand rise to 81 percent. The chance of rain as forecast the Friday before the big weekend, then, is a signpost. By checking the weather forecast the Friday before the weekend of the lemonade stand, Margot can reduce the unpredictability of the weather because the forecasts two days ahead are quite reliable. Unfortunately, she will not know what the actual weather prediction is going to be *until* that Friday. Still, the weather forecast is an important signpost, allowing her a chance to change her plans.

- *There won't be any competition from other lemonade stands.* Competition is more difficult than weather for identifying signposts. What indications might there be that there would be competition? Signposts will probably require paying attention to talk in school and the neighborhood about what other people are going to be doing during the summer. One signpost would be any talk of setting up a lemonade stand. Margot would then want to gather more information about when and where that stand will be. Other than talk around school or the neighborhood, any indication that there is going to be competition is likely to happen so close to the event that taking evasive action will be difficult. Margot will definitely want to think about shaping and hedging actions for this assumption.

- *Margot will be available.* Here, Margot has several possible signposts. She sets a signpost to check the softball calendar when it comes out to see if there is a conflict during the big weekend. This is a specific event that will help resolve some of the uncertainty surrounding her availability. Another signpost would be a "must-go" invitation (say, to the birthday party of a good friend). If that were to happen, it would seriously threaten Margot's availability. Either of these signposts might be cause for replanning the date of the lemonade stand. There are also catastrophic events (such as a death in the family) that could cancel her availability and that can't be resolved completely until the event is over. In the case of catastrophic events, there won't be enough warning time to do much. Margot will think about shaping and hedging actions, but hedging actions appear more likely than shaping actions.

- *Margot will be healthy.* Her signposts will include whether or not she is feeling bad in the days immediately before the scheduled weekend. This type of signpost may or may not give her enough time to take remedial action. Accidents could cause her health to "fail," but, again, for accidents, signposts are not likely to be as useful as shaping and hedging actions.

- *Margot will be allowed to run the stand.* Any serious grounding near the actual event would be a signpost. Margot cannot imagine any other road to failure for this assumption that would give more than a few days' warning time.

- *The stand will draw at least 24 customers at $.25/cup.* Here, Margot is on more familiar ground. This is budgetary stuff. Her past experience has led her not only to appreciate what she can charge and how many customers it will take to become profitable, but to have a reasonably good idea of what acceptable customer "rates"

(continued)

Lemonade Stand—3 (continued)

should be. She knows that if she does not have five customers by 1:00 p.m. the first day and ten customers by the end of the first day, she is likely to be in trouble.

These six items, then, become signposts for monitoring her assumption about the effectiveness of her plan. If Margot cannot identify signposts for any of the load-bearing, vulnerable assumptions of her plan, or there will not be sufficient time for evasive action from the signposts she *can* identify, she will be faced with taking preventive actions instead. That will lead her first to shaping actions and then, perhaps, to hedging actions.

6

Step 4: developing shaping actions

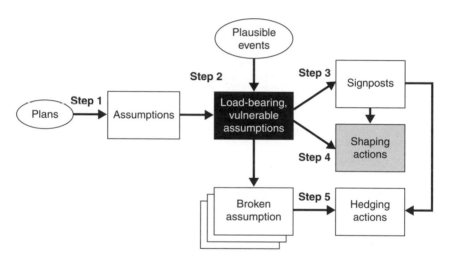

Figure 6.1. Developing Shaping Actions

Shaping actions are a common part of everyday life. Advertising is a shaping action. It helps bolster, or *shape*, an assumption that people will buy the company's products. Branding is an action that shapes people's thinking about a product in a way that makes them want to buy that product instead of another, similar product. Actions that shape the future are generally viewed as success-oriented, a view that is ingrained in American private industry: "The organization knows what it wants and will move mountains [definitely a shaping action] to get it."

It should also be mentioned that shaping actions are an option: They need not be taken. Management may decide that shaping actions, although available, are not required in some situations. Or, planners may fail to come up with any reasonable shaping actions.

After the load-bearing, vulnerable assumptions of a plan have been identified, shaping actions can be developed at any point in the remaining Assumption-Based Planning process. Identifying shaping actions in Figure 6.1 is labeled Step 4 in the ABP process only because, in practice, we have usually developed shaping actions after identifying signposts.

DEFINITION OF *SHAPING ACTION*

To the extent possible, shaping actions are intended to control the future. More specifically, in Assumption-Based Planning,

A *shaping action* is an organizational action to be taken in the current planning cycle and is intended to control the vulnerability of a load-bearing assumption.

Figure 6.2 shows a logical road map for this chapter as it describes the development of shaping actions.

The control of the vulnerability of a load-bearing assumption that shaping actions are intended for can either be to shore up an assumption that the organization likes or to encourage the failure of an assumption that the organization does not like. If an organization assumes that the future will be more competitive and customers less loyal than today, it is well served to gear its plan toward a more competitive world in which customers are less loyal. However, there is much to gain in contemplating shaping actions that would cause the assumptions about future competitiveness and customer loyalty to fail. Acquiring a competitor might be a shaping action aimed at decreasing future competitiveness. Branding might be a shaping action aimed at maintaining or increasing customer loyalty.

Assumptions with two-sided vulnerabilities are taking some risk and could fail either in favor of the organization or against it. For example, an assumption about how many units of a new model will sell could fail on either side. Shaping actions such as advertising and rebates are intended to keep the assumption from failing on the low side. Shaping actions for assumptions with two-sided vulnerabilities are generally aimed at deterring negative consequences.

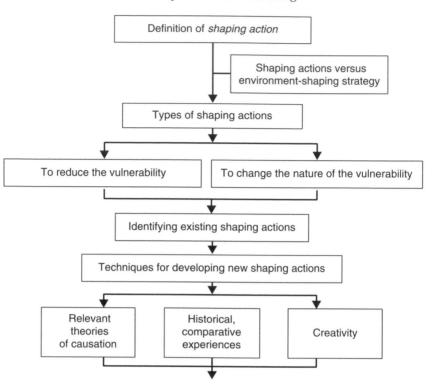

Figure 6.2. Logical Road Map of Chapter 6

That shaping actions are actions meant to be taken in the *current* planning cycle indicates that they are not contingent on signposts. In fact, shaping actions are intended to make signposts unnecessary by reducing or eliminating the uncertainty in a load-bearing, vulnerable assumption. Although, in fairness, shaping actions could be contingent on some future happening, such as the new fiscal year, the results of an election, or a regulatory ruling, they are generally meant to be taken immediately and for the sole purpose of affecting the vulnerability of a load-bearing assumption. The subject of contingency actions is discussed in more detail in Chapter 7.

Whether shaping actions are isolated or coordinated into a strategy, they are all developed in the same ways—a subject we turn to now.

Shaping Actions Versus Environment-Shaping Strategies

In a sense, because they are intended to control the future in favor of the organization, all the actions in a plan are shaping actions. Depending on how coordinated the shaping actions of a plan are, they can be thought of as more than just a set of actions, or more than a *plan for action*. If a set of shaping actions is coordinated into a systematic effort to shape the organization's environment, it is fair to call that set of coordinated actions an *environment-shaping strategy*, forming a continuum from a set of isolated shaping actions to a tightly coordinated, environment-shaping strategy.

At the national security level, for example, the United States has adopted the concept of an environment-shaping strategy. The first such strategy was written about in 1990 (Bracken 1990; Ascher and Overholt 1983), and environment-shaping became part of the military's regional strategy in 1992–1993. By 1997, the United States began treating "shaping the environment" as a top-level component of strategy.

The business literature on coordinated, environment-shaping strategies is generally not labeled as such, so is somewhat harder to track. However, the general trend for business seems to be from the more passive approach of the "adaptive" corporation in the 1980s (Toffler 1985) to the more aggressive shaping approach of *Hypercompetition* (D'Aveni 1994). Among D'Aveni's *Seven S's* are *signals* to be used to manipulate the future moves of rivals, *shifting* the rules of the market to create disruption for competitors, and *simultaneous* or *sequential* thrusts to mislead or confuse a competitor.

TYPES OF SHAPING ACTIONS

Shaping actions can range from the blindingly obvious to the very creative. However, shaping actions can be thought of as having two different aims: (1) to reduce the vulnerability of an assumption or (2) to change the nature of the vulnerability.

To *reduce the vulnerability*

Reducing the vulnerability directly is the most obvious approach to controlling the vulnerability of an assumption. The typical shaping action will take into account the vulnerability of an assumption and the plausible mechanisms that could cause that vulnerability, then would work to thwart those mechanisms.

Advertising is a good example of a shaping action that directly reduces vulnerability in a load-bearing assumption. Most plans involving products assume (and depend on) sales of the products at specific levels. One mechanism that would cause people to stop buying a product would be forgetfulness: out of sight, out of mind. Advertising works to keep the product in the mind—in the public's attention—and acts directly to counter an assumption failure mechanism. Another failure mechanism is that the price gets too high relative to a competitor's price. Here, a shaping action to reduce the uncertainty in sales would be to lower the price, via a sale, rebates, or other money-back mechanism.

Safety precautions belong to a general class of shaping action that works to reduce the vulnerability of assumptions that accidents will not happen. The interesting aspect of safety measures is that they often automatically become part of planning because they are mandated by regulations. As will be covered in Chapter 7, regulations can also mandate hedging actions.

Reducing uncertainty could require a combination of shaping actions, such as those for the Army's assumption that it would go to war in concert with its European allies. There was (and is) serious uncertainty that the Army could conduct such combined operations effectively. To reduce the uncertainty in that assumption, the Army instituted a plethora of shaping actions that included promoting cooperative programs to foster goodwill, providing technologies to ensure compatibility between different countries' weapon systems, and funding exchanges to promote knowledge and familiarity with other nations' doctrine and practices (and vice versa).

To change the nature of the vulnerability

Teisberg (1993) has divided the type of shaping action that changes the nature of the vulnerability into three categories of actions that alter (1) the industry structure, (2) relative position, or (3) knowledge and information of an organization.

Altering industry structure. Changing the nature of the uncertainty by altering the industry structure can be done in a variety of ways, depending on the maturity of the industry, the kinds of changes that are occurring in the industry, and other factors. Teisberg identified a variety of mechanisms for altering industry structure, including creating industry-wide associations, negotiating uncertainty-absorbing contracts, restructuring vertical relationships with suppliers or customers, constructing entry or mobility barriers, or instituting new market mechanisms such as bidding systems.

Teisberg cites a number of examples of altering the industry structure. I include an illustration of the concept here, based on Teisberg's mention of industries' experiencing regulatory change and influencing industry structure by influencing public policy. Although it is not one Teisberg mentioned, a good example of influencing public policy was the Federal Communications Commission's (FCC's) changes to regulatory policy over "enhanced services"—the regulatory structure surrounding computers and cable television (Kellogg, Thorne, and Huber (1992: Chapter 11) summarize the history). All of the major stakeholders, including computer manufacturers and cable television owners, worked diligently not only to influence the FCC's decisions but to help educate the FCC on the emerging technologies that would or should be affected. The stakeholders worked to change FCC policies on regulating enhanced services over the phone lines. Those changes in policy enabled the Internet and World Wide Web, changing the nature of communications.

Altering relative position. Changing the nature of the vulnerability by altering relative position in an industry comes from challenging the conventional wisdom on how to compete. In Teisberg's example, BiC changed the rules of competition in the ballpoint-pen business by introducing an inexpensive, disposable, virtually indestructible pen. It was not the first inexpensive pen, but it became the first to be branded and aggressively promoted, changing the nature of competition in the industry.

Altering knowledge and information. Research and development is one way to change the nature of the vulnerability through altering knowledge and information. An interesting example comes, again, from Royal Dutch/Shell. One of the assumptions Shell sought to buttress, or shape, was that oil prices would remain at high levels. Shell planners looked at specific ways in which oil prices could collapse (and developed hedging actions). The planners recognized that a price collapse would affect all oil companies fairly equally and that Shell would be forced to sell its gasoline for less, unless it could find a unique way to enhance the gas. Shell identified a shaping action to keep gas prices high: It began research on an environmentally clean, high-performance gasoline that could be sold at a higher price than standard gasoline.

Whether shaping actions alter industry structure, relative position, or knowledge and information, they are designed to control the vulnerability of load-bearing assumptions. Since controlling the vulnerability of load-bearing assumptions is a fundamental part of planning, there are undoubtedly some shaping actions already defined in any plan. The overall intent of ABP is to make sure that all load-bearing, vulnerable assumptions are, to the extent possible, bolstered by shaping and hedging actions. Before developing shaping actions to be added to a plan, it is important to understand what shaping actions are already in the plan.

IDENTIFYING EXISTING SHAPING ACTIONS

Knowing what shaping actions are already in a plan will help ensure that additional shaping actions are not redundant. A better reason for understanding existing shaping actions is to forge a deeper understanding of the plan and its uncertainties. Shaping actions are generally tied to a specific assumption or set of assumptions. Changes in the vulnerability of the assumptions can lead to changes in the shaping actions.

In a trivial example, shaping actions designed to ensure the timeliness of the rollout of a new product can be stopped once the product is rolled out. In general, whenever changes take place in the vulnerability of an assumption, the shaping actions associated with that assumption can and should be reviewed to see if they are still appropriate or necessary. Forging that deeper understanding of the existing plan is useful apart from the value of avoiding duplicate shaping actions.

Where should you look for existing shaping actions in a plan? The assumptions most likely to have shaping actions already associated with them are assumptions about solutions, or actions. The instincts of a good planner are to take whatever steps possible to enhance the success of a plan. Motivational actions such as advertising and branding are likely to be shaping actions. Internal motivational actions such as sales campaigns for new-product introductions are also likely to be shaping actions.

More generally, any explicit, load-bearing assumption is a good candidate for already having *some* shaping actions associated with it. The question, "What actions are planned to make sure that this assumption comes true or stays true?" will help identify existing shaping actions.

The assumptions least likely to have shaping actions already associated with them are, of course, the assumptions that were implicit before ABP was applied. Even here, there can be surprises. Implicit assumptions can often be identified by noting that no explicit assumptions have been associated with a given planned action. In one corporation's plan, several actions were related to diversifying the corporation through strategic alliances, but there were no specific assumptions about the coming need to diversify. In conversation, the planners could discuss at length their concerns over the instability of regional economies that made diversification through strategic alliances a good idea. The planners may not have made the justification of the strategic alliance actions explicit, but alliances were intended to do *something*—to shape an assumption that had not yet been called out in the planning documentation. The strategic-alliance actions were shaping actions for an implicit assumption. Making the assumption behind the actions explicit in this case ratified shaping actions already taken.

TECHNIQUES FOR DEVELOPING NEW SHAPING ACTIONS

Within the two major types of shaping actions, reducing the vulnerability and changing the nature of the vulnerability, there are some heuristic rules[1]—or rules of thumb—for generating shaping actions, including

- relevant theories of causation

- historical and comparative experiences

- creativity.

Relevant theories of causation

Shaping actions are supposed to cause (good) things to happen. In any enterprise, there are theories about "how the enterprise works" and there are grander theories about how the world works. These theories form the basis for thinking about shaping actions.

Advertising is a good example of a relevant *theory of causation* in shaping the sales of a product to make good things happen. The theory is that if one puts the word out widely on a product and generates desire for that product, that will cause the product to become better known, which will, in turn, cause more people to buy the product over that of lesser-known competitors. This logic leads to advertising in order to put the word out widely and take advantage of the theory.

---

1   The form of these heuristics was recommended by Yehezkel Dror in a private communication in June 2001.

Using theories of causation is a natural and common part of making *anything* happen in planning. Given a planning goal—say, increased sales—any planned actions are likely to come from theories of causation about how to increase sales. Using theories of causation to increase the chances for success of planned actions is merely an extension of methods that were likely to have been used to generate the planned actions in the first place. Packaging, marketing, adding features to products, and safety and functionality testing are all shaping actions based on relevant theories of causation and are used both to generate planned actions and to buttress assumptions about the chances for success of those planned actions.

Theories of causation—even the most scientific ones—are not infallible. Nonetheless, they became theories either because they capture general existing patterns or because they could be argued sufficiently cogently to be worth acting upon. The classic geopolitical example of the latter was George Kennan's theory on what to do about the Soviet Union in 1947. Writing as "X," Kennan theorized (Kennan 1947) that if the United States and its allies contained Soviet expansion, the USSR would eventually collapse. For four decades, the United States generated plans and shaping (and hedging) actions to contain the Soviet Union based on that theory of causation, and in 1989 that theory finally bore fruit—the Soviet Union collapsed.

Historical and comparative experiences

Historical and comparative experiences are similar to, but not as robust or predictive as, theories of causation. Whereas theories of causation are based on patterns involving from a few to hundreds of examples, *historical experiences* might be useful if there is only one such example. Imagine an organization that had success with company parties as a means of keeping employee morale high during a fondly remembered and successful program requiring several weeks of significant overtime effort to meet a load-bearing, vulnerable assumption about a new-product release date. The organization would certainly think about employing the same means of shaping an assumption about a future crash effort.

Comparative experiences are behaviors that have been successful in similar or comparable situations. They may be based on a single experience or on a theory of causation. The question is, "Are the situations similar enough to be able to say that the experience in one situation will carry over to the other?" An interesting recent example has been advertising on the World Wide Web. There is a theory of causation for advertising in print media, for example, and shaping actions can be developed using that theory. Are those same shaping actions going to have the same effect on the World Wide Web? Similarly, are company parties that were so successful for a crash software effort going to be as successful for a crash manufacturing effort?

Shaping actions based on historical and comparative experiences may not carry the same likelihood of success that shaping actions based on theories of causation do, but historical and comparative experiences are very helpful when there *are* no theories of causation. Advertising on the World Wide Web is a good example. There are no theories of causation for what will work on the Web, so comparative experiences are the best that one can hope for in developing shaping actions.

Creativity

It is always a good idea to try to think about new shaping actions for controlling the vulnerability of a given load-bearing, vulnerable assumption that go beyond the traditional or conventional. Kennan's theory of containment was very creative. Another good example of creativity in generating a shaping action was Shell's researching an environmentally clean, high-performance gasoline as a means of shaping its assumption about gasoline prices' remaining high. Certainly in situations when there are no relevant theories of causation or historical/comparative experiences, creative invention of shaping actions is the only recourse. And, even when there are relevant theories of causation or historical/comparative experiences, searching for creative new shaping actions remains a good idea. It is exactly how both historical/comparative experiences and theories of causation get started in the first place.

* * * *

No matter how clever the shaping actions, there are limits to the control that an organization can exercise over the future. The basic shaping challenge is how to shape uncontrollable vulnerability mechanisms. In the Royal Dutch/Shell example above, there was little Shell could do directly to ensure that oil prices would not collapse. The shaping action it adopted shaped the price of gasoline in a very creative way, but could only control a small aspect of the market.

This brings up another point about the development of shaping actions: Shaping actions do not always work. Worse yet, they can be counterproductive. The organization that threw company parties to help meet one very tight deadline may find that company parties the next time around do not work: Parties are not enough to overcome employee burnout as they did the first time around. On a geopolitical scale, the United States supported the Shah of Iran in the 1970s to shore up its assumption about a relatively peaceful and Western-leaning Middle East. For a while, that shaping action had the desired effect. However, when the Shah fell in 1979, the shaping action turned aggressively counterproductive as evidenced by massive anti–U.S. demonstrations.

Developing a shaping action is not a *guarantee* that a vulnerable assumption has been shored up. Shaping actions are risky but generally worth the effort.

Where control is not possible, organizations must be ready for a world that moves in a way they do not like and over which they have little control. This world demands hedging actions. But before we can look at hedging actions, let us visit the lemonade stand.

Lemonade Stand—4

The plans for Margot's lemonade stand this summer contain six load-bearing, vulnerable assumptions:

- The weather will be nice.
- There won't be any competition from other lemonade stands.
- Margot will be available.
- Margot will be healthy.
- Margot will be allowed to run the stand.
- The stand will draw at least 24 customers at $.25/cup.

While she was identifying signposts, Margot noticed several opportunities for shaping actions and a couple of instances in which shaping or hedging actions seemed like the only hope for handling the uncertainty in the load-bearing, vulnerable assumptions.

She starts out this step of the Assumption-Based Planning process by looking for shaping actions that are already in the plan. Some shaping actions were so straightforward that they were included in the original plans. Others were added as soon as a vulnerable assumption was identified. For example, one shaping action to

(continued)

Lemonade Stand—4 (continued)

control the assumption that she would be available on the big weekend was to mark the weekend on her calendar so that she herself would not inadvertently schedule anything else on that weekend. For ease in the presentation here, let us assume that that is the only shaping action of consequence that is already in the plan.

Identifying shaping actions

- *The weather will be nice.* There is not much that Margot can do about the weather. She can't think of any action she could take that would affect the weather. Not every load-bearing, vulnerable assumption can be shaped. About all Margot can do here in terms of shaping/hedging is to hedge against bad weather (in Step 5).

- *There won't be any competition from other lemonade stands.* Margot is already keeping her ears open at school and in the neighborhood for any talk of a lemonade stand that would compete with hers. She is torn over whether or not to announce that she is going to have a lemonade stand on the last weekend in June. Announcing her plans would be a successful shaping action if it served to discourage competition. Unfortunately, announcing her plans may also encourage competition—a shaping action, but not one that would have the desired effect of buttressing her assumption that there won't be any competition from other lemonade stands.

  This is a serious judgment call on Margot's part. History is not much help here, because Margot has had good *and* bad experiences with similar shaping actions in the past. In this case, she may want to reveal her plan to have a lemonade stand on the last weekend in June (to discourage others), but keep the fact that she will be touting "organic" lemonade a surprise (to try to preserve her uniqueness in case others decide to compete).

- *Margot will be available.* Margot has already set a signpost to check the softball calendar when it comes out. She's pretty sure she *cannot* affect the softball calendar, so she had given up on shaping actions along those lines. She *can* affect whether or not the family vacation takes place during that weekend. In fact, she has already let the vacation planners know (by marking the last weekend of June on the calendar) that it would be nice if the family vacation did not interfere with that weekend. Her other concern is that there will be a "must-go" party invitation that weekend. She thinks about possible shaping actions, but decides against developing any. She'll accept the risks involved at this point.

- *Margot will be healthy.* In the case of illness, Margot's shaping actions are limited to taking care of her health. She has been known to get summer colds. Besides taking care of herself, there's little she can do to specifically avoid getting a cold on the last weekend in June. As to shaping whether or not she has an accident, she resolves not to do any rollerblading during the week leading up to the planned lemonade stand. That should adequately shape her most likely source of self-induced accidents.

- *Margot will be allowed to run the stand.* This is something that Margot has some control over. For example, she can make a note to herself on her calendar (a signpost) to try particularly hard not to get grounded during the week before the big

(continued)

Lemonade Stand—4 (continued)

event. This would be a shaping action. Beyond that, her getting grounded is out of her control and the best she can do is hedge against that possibility.

• *The stand will draw at least 24 customers at $.25/cup.* Here, Margot has historical cases to draw upon. She knows where to advertise, and she knows what customers have said about what attracted them to her previous lemonade stands. Her shaping actions for this assumption are the advertising campaign she and Chloe are going to develop as soon as school is out. They have also kicked around some more creative ideas—such as advertising in the church bulletin—to try to attract customers from farther away.

Margot has reviewed those aspects of the lemonade stand that she can control. Next, she will turn to hedging actions.

7

Step 5: developing hedging actions

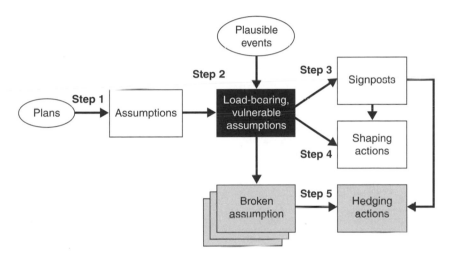

Figure 7.1. Developing Hedging Actions

The first four steps of Assumption-Based Planning have identified the load-bearing, vulnerable assumptions underlying a plan, and have developed signposts for monitoring the vulnerability of those assumptions and shaping actions to control, to the extent possible, the assumptions and their vulnerabilities. The last step in ABP is designed to identify actions that can be taken in the plan to best prepare the organization if a load-bearing, vulnerable assumption fails. As depicted in Figure 7.1, developing hedging actions first requires thinking seriously about what might happen if a load-bearing, vulnerable assumption fails. Means for thinking about the possible consequences of failed assumptions and for identifying appropriate hedging actions are the subject of this chapter.

As depicted in Figure 7.2, hedging actions can be developed either with the aid of scenarios or without. Because we have made significant use of scenarios in developing hedging actions, this chapter contains an extended description of scenarios and their role in developing hedging actions. However, before describing how to develop hedging actions, I need to define and motivate them.

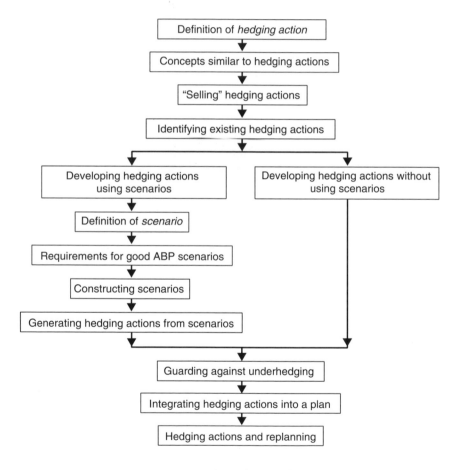

Figure 7.2. Logical Road Map of Chapter 7

DEFINITION OF *HEDGING ACTION*

Although not labeled as such, hedging actions are common in everyday life. We are hedging against the possibility of a crippling accident when we fasten our seat belts in the car. Any insurance we buy is a hedge against some plausible disaster. And hedging is not done just against major disasters. We go to the trouble of carrying an umbrella on a cloudy day to hedge against the possibility of getting wet.

As with shaping actions, hedging actions are an option: They need not be taken. Management may decide that the hedging actions that are available are not required in some situations, or planners may fail to come up with any reasonable hedging actions.

The Tenth Edition of *Webster's Collegiate Dictionary* (1993: 538) includes as one of the definitions of *hedge* "to minimize the risk of a bet"—not a bad definition for hedging actions in Assumption-Based Planning. A load-bearing, vulnerable assumption really is a "bet" with risks. As with shaping actions, hedging actions in Assumption-Based Planning are intended to be specific to the plan under consideration:

> A *hedging action* is an organizational action to be taken in the current planning cycle and is intended to better prepare the organization for the potential failure of one of its load-bearing assumptions.

Perhaps the biggest restriction in the definition is that hedging actions are "to be taken in the current planning cycle." This distinguishes between hedging actions and contingency actions, although not in a simple way.

CONCEPTS SIMILAR TO HEDGING ACTIONS

In addition to contingency actions, hedging *strategies* are related to hedging actions. It is useful to understand the similarities and differences among these concepts before we proceed.

Contingency actions

Throughout the text, I have referred to both hedging actions and contingency actions. They are related, but not interchangeable. Hedging actions are taken as part of the current plan; contingency actions are not to be taken until some likely but not certain event occurs or situation arises. This simple distinction is complicated both by common usage of the term "contingency plans" and by the question of warning time.

Contingency plans are usually lumped together with disaster-recovery and business-continuity plans, which gives contingency actions a connotation of post-disaster actions. Having plans in case of disasters is certainly in keeping with the notion that contingency actions are to be taken after a contingent—likely—event. However, disaster recovery unnecessarily narrows the idea of a contingency action. In this section, *contingency actions* will be used in the broader sense of being dependent on disastrous *or* nondisastrous likely-but-not-certain—contingent—events or situations.

The complication introduced by the question of warning time is trickier to deal with. The main problem is that both hedging actions and contingency actions are likely to cost money. If hedging one's bet is not free, one would like to know what the costs are of acting now (a hedging action) or waiting until some later event or situation (a contingency action), which brings notions such as warning time and signposts into the mix.

A family planning for an impending hurricane is a good example for discussing how warning time interacts with hedging and contingency actions. At this point in the planning, no one knows for sure if or where the hurricane will make landfall. The family's load-bearing, vulnerable assumption is that the hurricane will make landfall near enough to their beach house to cause serious damage. An important signpost will be the hurricane warning siren. That signpost should be sufficient warning to allow the family to move themselves to higher ground and safety inland. From Figure 7.3, which repeats the logic of signposts and warning times, the family can stay at the beach house and listen for the warning siren.

But what about the beach house? If the hurricane makes landfall near the beach house, moving the beach house is not an option. Therefore, preventive actions should be taken. But no preventive actions will guarantee that the house will remain intact after the hurricane hits. The beach house may be lost in the hurricane. If it is, the family is looking at a specific kind of contingency action: the disaster-recovery plan.

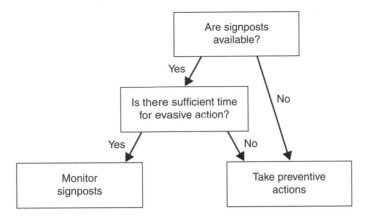

Figure 7.3. The Relationship Between Signposts and Warning Time

This plan will include arrangements for temporary lodging, disaster-relief loans, rebuilding plans (or moving plans), and so forth.

The more interesting case is when there *are* preventive actions that can be taken. These preventive actions are for a hurricane that does not destroy the house, but could do damage if actions—both contingent and hedging—are not taken. To save the windows from being blown in (or sucked out) by the hurricane's winds, a contingent action would be to board the windows up when the hurricane warning is received. The hedging action would be to buy the boards for the windows, today. The family *could* wait until some later signpost before buying the boards. However, the prudent family (and the one with sufficient monetary reserves) will recognize the likelihood of a run on the lumberyards after the hurricane is first spotted heading their way, and will buy the boards ahead of time. Similarly, to keep the house from getting flooded by the waves, contingent actions would be to sandbag the front of the house and dig a trench to encourage the water to bypass the house. Hedging actions would include making sure there are sufficient shovels and sandbags (and raincoats?) to equip the sandbag-filling team.

Why distinguish between hedging and contingency actions? Although both are important, the details of contingency plans can be distracting. Except for natural disasters, detailed contingency plans are often more of a hindrance than a help. As Wells emphasizes in his book on strategic thinking (1998: 189),

Let's be realistic. You do not want detailed contingency plans. When the time comes to change or modify your strategic direction you are not going to search through the office file cabinets to implement what you decided in the past. You will need to respond to the conditions as you face them. Contingency planning has a different value. You may gain some insight about conditions into the future that you want to include in the initial strategy.

Those "insights" that you would want to include in the initial strategy are what hedging actions are intended to capture. Contingent actions will naturally be part of the thinking about the world of a broken assumption, just as having the boards will call to mind putting them over the windows when the hurricane warning comes.

To use ABP is not to preclude developing contingency plans. There are situations, such as disaster recovery, for which it is very important to have contingency plans prepared. In that case, you could consider an appropriate hedging action to be preparing a contingency plan. The arrow in Figure 7.1 from signposts directly to hedging actions is intended to acknowledge a connection between hedging actions and signposts and contingency plans. But the emphasis in ABP is on those things that can/should be done "today"—in the current planning cycle—to help prepare for future contingencies. The definition of a hedging action specifically reinforces that emphasis.

Hedging strategies

The planning literature often talks of hedging "strategies." A proper hedging strategy is more than just a collection of hedging actions, as Microsoft's Comdex booth in 1998 demonstrated. Described as being much more like a Middle Eastern bazaar than a trade show booth (Beinhocker 1999), the space displayed not only Microsoft's second version of Windows, but DOS version 4.0, OS/2 (which it was developing with IBM); new versions of Word, Excel, and other applications for the Macintosh; and a Unix system developed by another company. Beinhocker suggests that, in combining such diversity, Microsoft was revealing a very robust strategy that would pay off no matter what happened in the Windows-DOS and OS/2-Mac-Unix battles. To further hedge its bets, Microsoft invested heavily in building skills in graphical user interface design and object-oriented programming that would be important no matter what operating system won. Does this represent more than just a set of hedging actions?

To my mind, the best explication of hedging strategies is by Hodges (1990), although he does not talk about hedging strategies per se. Hodges's primary intent was to bring management more actively into an ongoing *design* for handling uncertainty rather than passively defining a series of judgments or decisions intended to handle the uncertainties. In this, he anticipated some of the more popular current solutions in today's planning literature, such as "learning organizations" (for example, Senge 1990; Garvin 1993; Mason 1994) and "adaptive enterprises" (for example, Toffler 1985; Haeckel and Slywotzky 1999).

What Hodges describes is a collection of "generic strategies for uncertain situations" that accepts and deals with uncertainty that cannot be controlled or reduced. Although these generic strategies qualify as solutions to the planning problem, Hodges's (1990: 17) primary intent is to expand the class of solutions

> from a search for a better decision rule to a search for a better system, [f]rom sophistication in *judgment* to ingenuity in *design*" [italics in the original].

This search leads him to divide the collection of solutions into passive and active strategies. It is here that his argument takes wing (Hodges 1990: 20):

> Passive strategies rely on size, scale or diversity: Passive systems are *ample*; they *absorb*. Active strategies work on the premise that the future will consist of outcomes following from specific key *events*; the system must recognize those key events and *adapt* in a timely fashion with some activity relevant to the impending outcomes . . . passive strategies emphasize *goods*, and active strategies emphasize *management* of goods [italics in the original].

Hodges describes the strategies generically and gives a nice variety of examples. There are three passive strategies (buy it out, operate on a larger scale, and diversify) and four active ones (get more information [also referred to as procrastinate and react], use general or flexible resources, push the risk onto someone else, and combine strategies). In the past, hedging was often thought of in terms of passive strategies in Hodges's sense.

In any case, hedging strategies are not just collections of hedging actions, but coherent collections of hedging actions that take a more active role in managing uncertainty. In ABP, signposts and hedging actions are intended to support this more active approach to managing uncertainty by helping management recognize key events and having them think about adaptation ahead of time.

That said, hedging strategies are most appropriate not for every planning situation but for very uncertain times. In very uncertain times, the plan itself ought to reflect a hedging strategy, and Step 5 of ABP should make sure the hedging strategy is robust by augmenting it with further hedging actions if necessary. In less uncertain times, a hedging strategy is not necessarily required; a few hedging actions may suffice to buttress the plan against the few important uncertainties.

"SELLING" HEDGING ACTIONS

Hedging actions are rarely cost-free, and they do not usually contribute *directly* to the successful implementation of a plan. Why would anyone want to pay for hedging actions?

It should be clear that shaping actions are easier to sell than hedging actions. Plans most often expand to (over)fill any budget restrictions they are given. Tight budgets work in favor of actions that are likely to make the plan succeed rather than actions that are more contingent on bad things happening.

Particularly in the business world, cultural norms that emphasize taking action and thinking positively view hedging actions as suggesting hesitancy. The heroes in spy movies never hedge their bets. Norman Vincent Peale's original self-help book, *The Power of Positive Thinking* (1952), is still selling well almost 50 years after its first publication. "Just do it" and "No fear" are popular bumper stickers. Sales meetings do not abound with hedging actions.

But hedging actions *can* be marketed, as Thomas Chesnutt (1992) suggests in his light but insightful presentation on the need to market uncertainty. The following are the features of hedging actions that can be promoted:

- Regret avoidance. Hedging actions help avoid later regret.

- Anxiety reduction. An unknown threat produces anxiety. Converting that unknown threat to a known threat produces discomfort. Hedging against that discomfort produces relief.

- Vivid disasters. It is particularly important to make high-consequence, very-low-probability events vivid in order to encourage hedging actions today. The true power of a vivid story is that it helps bring the consequences of low-probability events into sharp focus, enhancing arguments for taking a "stitch in time" to avoid nine later. In some cases, such as the low probability of a nuclear war, the consequences are vivid enough that people can be persuaded to take action. In other cases, it is up to a vivid story to convey the importance.

- Option provision. Rather than just acknowledging the risk of a vulnerable, load-bearing assumption, producing hedging actions provides decisionmakers with options.

Hedging actions are insurance against the uncertainties of the future, and they may need to be sold in the same way that insurance needs to be sold. More generally, actions that look like insurance are likely to be hedging actions. The question, "What actions are planned to prepare the organization for the possibility that this assumption breaks?" will help identify existing hedging actions.

IDENTIFYING EXISTING HEDGING ACTIONS

As with shaping actions, knowing what hedging actions are already in a plan will help ensure that additional hedging actions are not duplicated, and it will help forge a deeper understanding of the plan and the plan's uncertainties.

Hedging actions are generally tied to a specific assumption or set of assumptions. Changes in the vulnerability of the assumptions can lead to changes in the hedging actions. Developing alternative approaches to a new technology is a hedge against the new technology's not working out. If the new technology works out, the alternative approaches can be discontinued. As with shaping actions, whenever changes take place in the vulnerability of an assumption, the hedging actions associated with that assumption can and should be reviewed to see if they are still appropriate or necessary.

Parallel programs—completely separate programs with the same goal, but using different approaches—are likely to be hedging actions for each other. The classic example of parallel programs was the three different approaches to the development of the atomic bomb during World War II. Hedging actions often involve research and development. Organizations often assume *implicitly* that technological breakthroughs will not upset a given technological or market advantage, and they often *explicitly* pursue research and development both to guard against technological breakthroughs and to increase their chances of being the ones to develop the breakthrough if there is one.

Where should you look for existing hedging actions in a plan? The assumptions most likely to have hedging actions already associated with them are assumptions about solutions or actions, as with shaping actions. Those actions that are riskiest are most likely to have some fallback positions or some hedging actions identified.

It will not always be possible to identify appropriate hedging actions. For example, consider a football team assuming that a late-game fourth-down pass play will be completed for a touchdown—an assumption that usually comes in a desperate, losing situation, and, hence, one bound to be load-bearing and vulnerable in planning the play. The consequences of the failure of the assumption are clear: a lost game. No appropriate hedging actions are possible in this situation. The same is true of bet-the-farm kinds of gambles. However, most pass play calls and most business gambles are not quite so consequential or desperate.

When it *is* possible to develop appropriate hedging actions, the difficulty in doing so ranges from trivial to very high. As above, ABP generally encourages the use of scenarios in developing hedging actions. However, scenarios are *useful,* but not *required,* for developing hedging actions. Scenarios are particularly useful for developing hedging actions either when an assumption is particularly risky or when the situation surrounding an assumption is complicated. Scenarios are particularly useful when an assumption is risky, because they aid exploration of subtleties in the risk that should not be overlooked. Scenarios aid particularly complicated situations by providing a grounding for extended discussions on the complexities.

I begin the discussion of defining hedging actions with the case in which scenarios are used and then address the development of hedging actions without using scenarios.

DEVELOPING HEDGING ACTIONS USING SCENARIOS

Many of the techniques found in the literature for developing the scenarios of scenario planning are applicable to developing scenarios for identifying hedging actions. There are differences, however, and typically those differences make the generation of scenarios for hedging actions somewhat easier. The following subsections describe what the planning literature has to say about generating scenarios and some of the specific idiosyncrasies of scenarios for identifying hedging actions in ABP.

Definition of scenario

Before talking about developing hedging actions using scenarios, it would be useful to describe more explicitly what we mean by a scenario. van der Heijden's (1996: 5) definition of an "external" scenario captures what we mean by a *scenario:* "External scenarios . . . are created as internally consistent and challenging descriptions of possible futures. . . . What happens in them is essentially outside our own control." This definition encompasses two commonly held notions of scenarios:

- A scenario is an alternative future.

- A scenario is an alternative future *plus* a description of the path that goes from today to that future.

Both notions of scenarios are useful in developing hedging actions. More often, the scenarios of ABP will include both the future state and the path from today to that future state.

Scenarios, as used in a planning sense, followed an unusual migration pattern from the radio and movie industries before World War II to the military after the war, to government in 1960, and to the business world in the mid-to-late-1960s. Scenarios for explicit planning purposes arose out of wargaming at RAND in Project SIERRA in 1954. Project SIERRA's objectives were "to examine possible limited war situations . . . and . . . to develop a methodology for the study of such situations by small balanced staffs" (Weiner 1960: 4). Scenarios began as simple lead-ins for wargaming exercises that were used to help develop nuclear policy. As wargaming became a two-sided game with the development of Soviet nuclear weapons, the scenarios became more sophisticated, their use expanded, and they began to be studied in their own right.

In 1960, Robert McNamara took scenarios to the Defense Department. By 1964, he was using them not only as a prelude to introducing his defense programs to Congress, but also as a means of testing force postures (DeWeerd 1967: 4). In 1965, Pierre Wack, Edward Newland, and the planners at Royal Dutch/Shell began developing scenarios as a means of handling business uncertainties. By 1971, they began using scenarios in Shell's planning process. The way in which they used scenarios eventually became the basis of "scenario planning" (described in the shaded box) as it appears in the business literature today.

Scenarios to Identify Hedging Actions Versus Scenario Planning

For those familiar with scenario planning, ABP is similar to scenario planning in its use of scenarios. The differences are important to understand, because they lead to differences in how the scenarios are developed in the two approaches. Perhaps the differences are most easily seen by considering the roles that van der Heijden suggests for scenarios in scenario planning (1996: 5):

- Providing a test bed for plans and/or policies
- Stretching mental models as a means of leading to discoveries
- Enhancing corporate perceptions about the future
- Energizing management
- Aiding top management in providing leadership to the organization.

The first two purposes approximate the use of scenarios to help identify hedging actions. Their primary purpose in ABP is for testing plans and/or policies. Using the scenarios of ABP as a test bed for plans/policies is taken up in further detail in Chapter 9. The scenarios generated in the ABP process can, themselves, also be used *in support* of the last three purposes.

Whereas scenario planning is concerned about the process for developing (and "selling") a plan, ABP's use of scenarios is for the more-restricted purpose of improving the robustness of a plan that has already been developed.

The use of scenarios to help identify hedging actions is more similar to the uses of scenarios that Fahey and Randall (1997) describe for scenario *learning*:

- Augment understanding.
- Produce new decisions.
- Reframe existing decisions.
- Identify contingent decisions.

In describing how scenarios are useful in reframing existing decisions, Fahey and Randall say, "Scenarios can provide a new context for existing decisions.... At a minimum, this new context might suggest the need to hedge the original strategy to make it effective across a variety of futures" (1997: 13). These are exactly the types of hedges the scenarios in ABP are intended to suggest.

Another way of describing the difference between the scenarios used for developing hedging actions and those used for scenario planning comes from looking at the primary audiences of the two: upper management and/or the entire organization for scenario planning; planners for using scenarios to develop hedging actions. Constructing scenarios intended for higher management is done differently than constructing scenarios for planning purposes.

In the meantime, RAND researchers continued to develop and study scenarios as a planning tool for the military, which is where the scenarios in Assumption-Based Planning have their roots. Only later did we connect scenario usage in ABP with scenario usage in the business planning literature. The two different development paths show surprising convergence on many elements of scenarios and their uses.

Requirements for good ABP scenarios

The two primary requirements of a good ABP scenario are relevance and credibility. These are requirements for good planning scenarios in general, and they have not changed since scenarios were first introduced into military gaming. Relevance is first among equals. In analyzing scenarios that did not work well, van der Heijden (1996: 43) sees lack of relevance as the predominant cause:

> I discovered that most failures had been produced by scenario planners who had come to the job with a clear preconceived idea of the particular story they wanted to tell. . . . On the other hand, scenario planners who were more interested in working in a client-oriented, consultant frame of mind . . . tried to find out what really mattered to management, including their priorities and frustrations. . . . The latter were more successful than the former.

Independent of their credibility, then, the scenarios tended to succeed or fail according to their relevance to the issues at hand. Beyond relevance and credibility, good scenarios require two additional qualities: detail and the proper number.

Relevance. A scenario is *relevant* if it pertains to the plan under consideration. Scenarios in Assumption-Based Planning are automatically relevant to the plan under consideration because they are generated *from* the failures of the load-bearing assumptions in the plan. If a plan rests on an assumption that could fail, a scenario surrounding the failure of that assumption is highly relevant to the plan.

The built-in relevance of ABP scenarios is a point worth emphasizing. Much of the preliminary work in scenario planning is deciding what scenarios would be relevant. Many of the scenarios in support of planning have been generated by futurists who have a better understanding of the potential futures than do the day-to-day managers of an organization. Having futurists develop the scenarios makes sense from the credibility standpoint of the scenarios. What is often sacrificed or is much tougher to establish is the relevance of the scenarios to the problems of the organization. As van der Heijden suggests, if the relevance is not clear to those who are supposed to use the scenarios, the scenarios are likely to fail despite high credibility.

Relevance of scenarios, then, is built into ABP from the basic concept through the identification of and agreement on the vulnerable, load-bearing assumptions of a plan. By the time the scenarios are built from those vulnerable, load-bearing assumptions, they are highly relevant to the goal of making the plan robust to uncertainty.

Credibility. A scenario must be *credible*—believable—to the people who are going to use it so that they can develop hedging actions or defend the hedging actions that have been developed. These people include the planners involved in developing hedging actions and the decisionmakers higher in the organization.

Credibility of a scenario is more difficult to ensure than relevance (which is why organizations so often turn to "experts" on the future to design scenarios). According to DeWeerd (1973: 12), "people demand a great deal more of it [credibility] from future-oriented scenarios than they do from history. They willingly accept from the hand of history what they would strenuously protest against if offered by a scenario writer."

Not even perfect foresight can *guarantee* the credibility of a scenario. This fact is brought home most vividly by DeWeerd's retelling (1967) of General Matthew Ridgway's story about the skepticism that greeted a scenario Ridgway wrote in 1940 for the opening of a war game. In that scenario, the Japanese went to war with the United States by staging a surprise air attack to immobilize the Pacific Fleet at Pearl Harbor. Ridgway (1956: 46–47) said that his fellow officers told him that his scenario was a "possibility so improbable that it did not constitute a proper basis for a maneuver." DeWeerd goes on to say, "One year later the game players were all involved in playing out in real life the scenario that Ridgway's fellow officers ruled out as 'incredible.'"

To emphasize, relevance is more important than credibility. As DeWeerd (1967) says, "Complete credibility is seldom if ever obtainable in a future-oriented scenario and I think it is a waste of time to strive for it." Instead, DeWeerd recommends (as do we) concentrating on relevance when there is a question about the credibility of individual elements and to remind those who would use the scenario that its purpose is not prediction but insight.

Scenario detail. Once the general outline of a scenario has been developed, it is often easy and fun to add embellishing detail. A good scenario should be just detailed enough—contain the specifics of who, what, when, where, why, and how—to elicit appropriate hedging actions. Including too many details gets in the way of generating as many scenarios as possible with the talent and time available.

The amount of detail required as "enough" can range quite widely. In some cases, merely stating a broken assumption is enough to suggest some hedging actions: "If interest rates go higher than 7 percent, the entire new product line becomes unviable. Because interest rates *could* go that high in the next two years, we should hedge by leasing the fabrication area for the new line rather than purchasing."

For more complex situations, a rather detailed scenario may be required to capture that complexity credibly. In the military, for example, the credibility of a threat posed in a given scenario can depend heavily on specific technical details of an opponent's forces, as well as on the doctrine that governs the employment of those forces.

Two heuristics apply in deciding how much detail to put into a given set of scenarios:

1. The scenario will probably require more detail the less likely it is to happen. If the scenario is unlikely to happen, its associated assumption is on the list of vulnerable, load-bearing assumptions because the consequences of the assumption's failing are dire. The less likely a scenario is, the greater the difficulty in establishing its credibility. Greater detail is likely to add to its credibility.

2. It is generally best to strive for roughly equal detail across the various scenarios. This heuristic, unfortunately, works somewhat in opposition to the first. If the amount of detail across a set of scenarios is very uneven, the scenarios with the greatest detail—although not necessarily representing the most important risks—are most likely to dominate one's thinking about relative risks among the uncertainties.

In general, developing hedging actions from scenarios requires less detail in the scenario than would be typical for a scenario that was to be used in scenario planning. This will be dealt with further in the Constructing scenarios section.

Number of scenarios. In the previous steps of ABP, we have encouraged erring on the side of inclusion in identifying load-bearing assumptions and their vulnerabilities. It is in generating scenarios that the line on inclusiveness must be drawn. Any systematic attempt to generate scenarios from all possible combinations of broken assumptions and/or all possible ways the assumptions could fail will lead to combinatorial explosion—geometric growth in the number of possible scenarios that could be generated.[1] Every planner and planning system that uses scenarios has to deal with this explosion.

Assumption-Based Planning handles combinatorial explosion by addressing two questions: "How many scenarios do you need?" and "How do you reduce the combinatorial explosion of possible scenarios to that number?" It should come as no surprise that the answer to the first question is, "It depends": It depends first and foremost on how well the combinatorial explosion has been reduced, so let me start there.

In Assumption-Based Planning, the combinatorial-explosion problems come from two sources: (1) the number of load-bearing, vulnerable assumptions (and therefore the number of possible combinations of broken assumptions that could form the basis of distinct scenarios), and (2) the fact that each load-bearing, vulnerable assumption could fail in more than one way.

In the first case, if you allow scenarios to be generated from all possible combinations of broken assumptions, $2^M - 1$ possible scenarios could be generated from M load-bearing, vulnerable assumptions. In ABP, we insist that each scenario contain only one broken assumption—dropping the number of possible scenarios from $2^M - 1$ to M. However, understanding the potential synergistic effects of scenarios containing two or more broken assumptions is sacrificed by this necessary reduction. Of course, if there are obviously important combinations of important assumptions, those few could be added without compromising the reduction.

---

1   From M vulnerable assumptions, $2^M - 1$ logical combinations can be made, which means that $2^M - 1$ possible scenarios could be made from M vulnerable assumptions. In mathematics, this is called geometrical growth, or a *combinatorial explosion*. If each vulnerable assumption could fail in more than one way, the mathematical expression gets more complicated and grows even more quickly. The problem of combinatorial explosion is widely recognized in planning, but is not often dealt with explicitly. Perhaps the most explicit method for dealing with the problem (in pairwise comparisons) is the cross-impact matrix. See, for example, Ayres (1969) and Martino (1972).

The second case, addressing the number of ways each assumption could break, is a tougher problem. Experience suggests that, usually, there is a dominant means by which the assumption might fail and that exploring failure through that means is sufficient. We have made exceptions, sometimes exploring two or more means of failure. In a military example, we were exploring the credible failures of the assumption that the United States Army would be forward-deployed in Europe. The two failure mechanisms we explored for this assumption were (1) pulling back from Europe because of domestic political pressures, and (2) being "invited" to withdraw from Europe by the Europeans. Both were important, and both were explored in some detail.

The list of potential scenarios produced by these two means for reducing the combinatorial explosion of possible scenarios is the same order of magnitude as the list of load-bearing, vulnerable assumptions. In scenario planning, the recommended number of scenarios is generally three to five. Since there are often more than three to five load-bearing, vulnerable assumptions, the number of scenarios to be generated would seem to violate the rule of thumb for generating scenarios in scenario planning. Fortunately, the scenarios for developing hedging actions do not need to be as detailed as those for scenario planning; therefore, a greater number can be generated than is common.

Inevitably, judgment must be called on. In practice, we have begun by roughly ordering the list of load-bearing, vulnerable assumptions by *risk* (the notional product of how load-bearing the assumption is and how likely it is to fail within the time horizon of the plan). At this stage, risks associated with formerly implicit assumptions often rise to the top of the pile because they have typically been "underworried." Then, beginning with the highest-risk assumption, we have gone down the list with the intent of generating scenarios as time and resources permitted. There is usually a point in this process at which there is general agreement that the potential benefit from considering the next broken assumption is not worth the time and energy to create a detailed scenario. At that point, hedging actions for the remaining assumptions are developed without resort to scenarios (to be addressed further below, in a separate section).

With these four requirements in mind, it is time to turn to the actual construction and use of scenarios for developing hedging actions.

Constructing scenarios

There are as many ways to construct scenarios as there are scenarios. In our experience, five aspects of creating scenarios for Assumption-Based Planning deserve particular attention:

- Direction
- Focus
- Credibility
- Details
- Relation to other scenarios.

Direction. Scenarios are constructed in two basic directions—backward and forward: either starting with where you want the scenario to wind up and working backward to today or starting with today and working forward to the desired scenario. DeWeerd (1973) calls these two methods "reverse decision-tree analysis" and "trend analysis"; Fahey and Randall (1997) call them the "future backward" and the "future forward" approaches; and van der Heijden (1996) calls them the "deductive structuring" and "inductive structuring" approaches (and adds an incremental method that is useful for challenging an existing scenario).

Because Assumption-Based Planning begins with end states—the broken assumptions—the most common means for constructing ABP scenarios is the backward method. The challenge is then to describe why the world unfolded the way it did and what were the factors that made it unfold that way.

Focus. In scenario planning, Fahey and Randall (1997) describe the four key elements of a scenario as (1) driving forces, (2) logics, (3) plot, and (4) end state. For *driving forces*, Schwartz (1991) describes five basic categories: society, technology, economics, politics, and the environment. The *logics* provide the explanation of why the forces behave the way they do. By *plot*, Fahey and Randall mean the story that connects the present with the *end state*—or outcome.

For ABP scenarios used to develop hedging actions, the primary focus should be on the plot—the story that connects the present with how the load-bearing assumption failed and what that failure led to. The story will require some driving forces and some logics. For the manufacturing company that was assuming in early 2000 that the economy would remain strong, it took little more than a story about the "dot-com" bubble's finally bursting and dragging the stock market down to get the company seriously thinking about what hedging actions might be needed to buttress that assumption.

Credibility. The primary challenge in constructing ABP scenarios is making them credible, since scenarios in ABP are automatically relevant to the planning situation because they stem from broken load-bearing, vulnerable assumptions. Decision theory has some interesting things to say about factors that will influence the perceived credibility of a scenario.

Often, the most credible scenario of the future will be the one that is most like the present. In ABP, since each scenario is built around a failed assumption, each scenario differs from the present in an important way; so, none of the ABP scenarios looks very much like the present. This disparity should decrease the chances that any one ABP scenario will be viewed as particularly more likely than the others.

Decision theory also suggests that people are drawn to either extremely favorable or extremely unfavorable outcomes, although, in a planning context, there is also evidence that people consider negative scenarios—even those they themselves have written—as much less likely to occur than optimistic ones. Since most of the scenarios generated from broken assumptions are likely to be viewed as being negative, they should tend to be treated more equally from this perspective.[2]

As a cautionary note, a very negative scenario is likely to be viewed as less credible than a merely negative one. Even though crisis scenarios can be made very vivid, research on defensive avoidance—the psychological process of rationalizing and avoiding consideration of a topic (Janis and Mann 1977)—suggests that people may view them as implausible or reject them out of hand as impossible. For example, prior to the outbreak of hostilities in the former Yugoslavia in 1992, the State Department presented several scenarios of escalating violence in the region to President George Bush and his staff. These scenarios had no apparent effect on subsequent policy, and it has been suggested that the

---

2 What is considered negative and what is positive may be based on political and other considerations. For example, we have seen the military services exhibit vested interest in using planning scenarios that detail crises with which they are best suited to cope, even if such crises are extremely undesirable. See, for example, Builder (1989).

uniformly dire nature of all the scenarios led to a wholesale rejection of the scenario set.

Cognitive research suggests that presentation style—the framing of the scenarios—can significantly affect credibility. *Framing* refers to the formatting of a particular risk as either a gain or a loss. For example, a surgical operation can be presented as having a 95-percent survival rate or a 5-percent mortality rate—a difference in semantics. But stating mortality rather than survival has been shown to affect actual decisions in a variety of situations (McNeil 1982). Often, decisionmakers will make riskier decisions when operating within a loss frame than within a gain frame. To some extent, ABP scenarios can be framed as either positive or negative. That is, different possible end states could be framed as presenting the organization with threats, opportunities, or both. There is a clear limit to this technique, of course: Many crisis contingencies that the organization must plan for cannot reasonably be reframed as positive.

Another aspect of framing that can be used to make scenarios more credible is the past tense (Mitchell, Russo, and Pennington 1989). For example, "advances in bioengineering *have led* to increased life expectancy" may have a slight credibility advantage over "advances in bioengineering *will lead* to increased life expectancy." Incorporating *some* details from past events into scenarios of the future may also help to make them more credible.

Details. Another factor that influences the perceived credibility of a scenario is the amount of detail included. Although the conjunction fallacy[3] is a relatively well-replicated effect, it may have its limits. With regard to presented explanations of individual past events, it has been hypothesized that the judged probability of an explanation may increase with the number of reasons up to a point; after that point, additional reasons will cause the judged probability to decline (Einhorn and Hogarth 1985). It is certainly true that a particularly weak link in an otherwise strong causal chain can cause an entire scenario to be dismissed as incredible, as in a famous cartoon in mathematical circles: Two professorial types are standing in front of a blackboard full of equations, looking at a step that says, ". . . and then a miracle occurs." Humorous

3 Recall from Chapter 5 that the conjunction fallacy arises because an outcome paired with one likely cause is often judged to be more probable (or, in this case, credible) than the occurrence of the outcome alone.

or sobering, weak links can ruin any otherwise credible sequence of events.

There may be an optimal level of causality. Constructing an explicit causal chain leading from the present to a particular future may make that future more believable, but it also provides more opportunities for rejection. Similarly, there may be an optimal level of detail, such that more vivid scenarios will be more compelling to a point, after which they will seem outlandish.

Relation to other scenarios. Although each scenario would ideally be evaluated on its own particular merits, when all scenarios are presented as a set, they will probably be considered relative to one another. Scenarios should be clearly distinguishable from one another—their main purpose being to stretch imagination and promote awareness of uncertainty. In another sense, they should also be uniform: One scenario should not stick out as being much more or much less credible than the others, or as being of a qualitatively different nature.

The best hope for the credibility of a collection of scenarios is that they be logically consistent. To check logical consistency, van der Heijden recommends two different kinds of consistency checks: quantification and actor-testing.

Not all scenarios will involve a lot of numbers. Those that do involve *quantification* permit a comparison of their numbers with "standard" or baseline numbers. This comparison often produces discrepancies that must then either be explained by the scenario or result in changes in the scenario (van der Heijden 1996).[4]

For scenarios that involve a variety of active and passive participants, consistency checking can be done by actor-testing. *Actor-testing* a scenario involves putting yourself in the mind-set of an actor (either an individual involved in the scenario or an affected bystander) and asking if that actor's behavior makes sense. van der Heijden cites actor-testing as having been responsible for the creation of Royal Dutch/Shell's most famous scenario, which suggested the possibility of an oil crisis.

---

4   Builder (1983) proposes another approach to evaluating scenarios. He develops a two-dimensional structure for evaluating scenarios as an illustration of how formal procedures might be employed to diagram a scenario, much as a sentence or electrical circuit is diagrammed. Such a calculus would enable the defender and critic of a scenario to reason together about its omissions, inconsistencies, and uncertainties.

Beyond paying particular attention to the above five aspects, the creation of scenarios is more art than science. And the ability to create credible scenarios improves with practice.

Generating hedging actions from scenarios

Given a relevant, credible scenario, how do you use it to generate hedging actions? Developing hedging actions requires the same insight and creativity as does planning itself. From our experience, it is important to have the *proper attitude and focus* about generating hedging actions. Beyond that, there are basically two different approaches to generating hedging actions—*BOGSAT* and *gaming*. But before I discuss these topics, an example from Royal Dutch/Shell's experiences in generating hedging actions (Schwartz 1991) provides an excellent overview of the process.

Shell was contemplating building a large, multi-billion-dollar platform to take natural gas from the Troll gas field in the North Atlantic. Among the assumptions underlying the rationale for the platform was that the price of natural gas would stay at levels it had enjoyed for nearly 10 years. However, Shell was worried that, if political relations between the then-Soviet Union and NATO nations changed for the better, the Europeans could drop their informal agreement that no more than 35 percent of their gas and oil markets would be available to the Soviet Union. Doing so would open the doors for cheap gas and oil from the Soviet Union and prices could drop precipitously.

Shell reckoned that any loosening of political control would require a justification akin to the "New Economic Policy" Lenin used in 1920 to combat massive unrest over food rationing. So Shell set up a scenario called the "Greening of Russia," in which the Soviet Union underwent massive economic and political restructuring, including a significant opening up to the West and a cessation of the 35-percent limit.

If the Greening of Russia scenario came about, the Soviet Union would be trying to compete in the European natural-gas market and to get the Europeans to drop the 35-percent ceiling they had placed on purchases of natural gas that could be made from the Soviet Union. This would drive the price of gas down and reduce the economic viability of the Troll platform. Shell also recognized that if the Organization of Petroleum Exporting Countries' (OPEC's) unity collapsed, demand for oil in an age of increasing conservation and energy-efficiency could dwindle.

Because of the plausibility of these two scenarios, Shell developed several hedging actions. One was an extra effort to bring down the cost of the Troll platform project. Two others—not overinvesting in new oil fields and not purchasing other oil companies at premium prices—went against the grain in the oil industry in the late 1970s, a time when oil prices had been high for nearly 10 years and other firms were "drilling on Wall Street," or buying oil companies at high prices to gain their oil fields. When oil prices did fall, Shell was in a much better position than other oil companies and was able to buy oil reserves at half the price that had been available six months before.

These hedging actions are all conservative. However, Shell's experiences also contain a more radical example. As oil prices started to fluctuate more wildly than at any time prior to World War II, Shell challenged the assumption that they would settle down again, devising a scenario in which oil and gasoline became commodities on the world market. This possibility would mean that there might be a good business in trading oil, and a design for a trading system to capitalize on such a change generally takes years. However, the scenario allowed Shell to see that such a system might be useful, and they began to design one. By the time the price of oil collapsed, Shell had a working trading system.

Now let me turn back to the more specific question of developing hedging actions from scenarios. First, it is important that the people who are engaged in developing hedging actions have the proper attitude toward scenarios for this purpose and are focused on the right basic question.

The proper attitude and focus. The proper attitude is to accept the scenario not as a prediction of the future or the most likely future, but as a credible—or plausible—future that may or may not come about. A useful preface to any scenario is one that de Geus (1999: 72–73) says Royal Dutch/Shell used in introducing its scenario with oil prices that were well below where people were thinking they would/could go:

> We don't know the future [the preface said]. But neither do you. And though none of us knows whether the price is going to fall, we can agree that it would be pretty serious if it did. So we have written a case showing one of many possible ways by which the price of oil could fall.

Participants were then asked to give their views on questions relating to the scenario. In general, any preface that gets people past the stage where they fight the scenario is useful.

Once people accept the scenario, the basic question for those trying to develop hedging actions is, "If this scenario were to come about, what, in retrospect, might we have wanted to do (have) that we are not planning on doing (do not have) now?" Focusing on this question gets people thinking along the lines of actions that can be taken in the near future that will better prepare the organization for the possibility of such a scenario.

With the proper attitude and focus on the basic question, there are two approaches that could arguably be called methods for developing hedging actions, the first of which is by far the more common.

BOGSAT. For those unfamiliar with it, this is an acronym for "Bunch Of Guys Sitting Around a Table." It is usually used in a jocular (and sometimes pejorative) way to describe how little analysis went into a given decision. I'm using it here to reinforce the notion of how little analysis generally goes into developing hedging actions. As Mintzberg (1994b) says of strategy formation, developing hedging actions is synthesis, and synthesis cannot be done through analysis. Analysis can (and should) feed the synthesis, but there its contribution ends.

The *B* in BOGSAT is also important. As with any of the judgmental and creative tasks of ABP (or any other planning process), the more people with varied backgrounds and organizational knowledge working the problem, the greater the chance for innovative answers. As long as everyone has the proper attitude toward the scenario and is focused on answering the basic question, little more is needed to set the stage.

As should be clear from the Royal Dutch/Shell examples, what comes out of the process can range from prosaic (not purchasing other oil companies at inflated prices) to inspired (designing a trading system in case oil might be treated like a commodity).

In some cases, it may be possible to bring a more systematic focus to the development of hedging actions, through gaming.

Gaming. In any discussion of scenarios, there are bound to be move-countermove considerations. "What would we do if they did X?" "What if they did Y?" "If we did A, what would they do?" Gaming is basically a more formal way of having those discussions.

As originally applied to planning, scenarios explored potential strategies in military games that were played between two or more teams.

These games generally consisted of alternate or simultaneous moves by the competing teams. A control team was in charge of deciding the results of the moves. Over the years, developers have worked to increase the detail in these military games, primarily through computer modeling. One constant of all gaming has been its experiential benefit: bringing a richer understanding of the competing interests by forcing the teams into the position of various stakeholders and making them react as they think the stakeholders would react to the game conditions.

From the earliest days of formal gaming, it was clear that games were good for providing insights—in particular, for "anticipating contingencies that may arise . . . and would require strategic decisions not easily extemporized on the spot" (Helmer 1958). It is this anticipation, either for hedging or contingency actions, for which gaming provides a more structured, formal approach than BOGSAT discussions.

Although not all situations lend themselves to gaming the way military conflict does, any situation that unfolds iteratively among a few major players or constituents, with generally a small number of moves and countermoves, holds the potential for a gaming approach. One example in the nonmilitary world that might have been formally gamed but was not, centered on the evolving regulations dealing with computers and communications.[5] As the "game" played out, between 1966 and 1991 the Federal Communications Commission made incremental changes in the regulations governing interactions between computers and telecommunications. After the FCC made its "move," industries interested in putting computers into telecommunications equipment and in connecting computers to phone lines made their "moves"—including legal challenges—and waited to see what the new regulations would be.

The FCC purposely (and, in retrospect, wisely) took an incremental approach to these regulations, which accounted for its game-like nature. Similar situations are likely—for example, for businesses dealing with governments in emerging foreign markets. Governments will often take incremental approaches to changes, which lend themselves to gaming about likely moves and appropriate hedging actions.

Another approach to gaming in defining hedging actions is "The Day After . . ." methodology developed at RAND (see, for example, Molander, Riddle, and Wilson 1996: 5–11). During Step One of the exercise

5   The three major changes in that period were called Computer I, Computer II, and The Open Network. For more, see Kellogg et al. (1992).

("The Day of . . ."), participants are presented with a change, or fore-shadowed change, in the current situation. Step Two contains "The Day After . . .", during which the participants are faced with a major strategic event or disaster (or broken assumptions). Participants spend a significant amount of time dealing with the consequences of the event. Step Three returns to "The Day Before . . ." and gives participants a chance to consider measures (hedging actions) that could be taken in the near future to avert such a crisis.

Games are a means of developing insight into appropriate hedging action. As Schelling (1987) has observed about games:

> Games . . . can produce ideas and insights, but the ideas and insights are not validated by having arisen in a realistic game. They are to be vali-dated the way one would validate an insight derived, say, from reading fiction. . . . But new ideas are so hard to come by that one should be ready to take them anywhere one can find them. Whether they are good ideas then depends on whether they stand up to the tests normally applied to new ideas.

* * * *

There's one final point worth making about scenarios before moving on. In addition to being useful for identifying hedging actions, scenar-ios can also be useful for identifying further assumptions, signposts, and, especially, shaping actions. During the development and testing of a scenario built around a failed assumption, it is often much clearer what steps might be taken to prevent the assumption from failing—so much so, in fact, that it is often possible to convince yourself that the scenario *cannot* happen, that the assumption *cannot* fail. This, of course, is counterproductive to the generation of hedging actions. It should be resisted. The best means for resisting the rejection of the sce-nario is to remember that its purpose is to explore the *plausibility* of its occurring and to suspend disbelief in order to consider what you would do if you knew that, despite all indications to the contrary, it *did* occur.

DEVELOPING HEDGING ACTIONS WITHOUT USING SCENARIOS

We have said that identifying hedging actions for a given load-bearing, vulnerable assumption requires contemplating the failure of that assumption. In complex situations or under great uncertainty, we have found that using a scenario to frame the situation is a good means of aiding the contemplation of an assumption's failure and ensuring that subtle but important interactions in an assumption's failure are not overlooked. However, the development of hedging actions does not absolutely require scenarios in *any* case.

There are two common situations in which vulnerable assumptions are so well known that hedging actions are equally well known and do not require elaborate scenarios to develop:

- Insurable risks
- Regulatory requirements.

Insurable risks

Insurance is a general class of hedging action. One generally assumes that accidents will not happen, but that is a vulnerable assumption. To the extent that that vulnerable assumption is also load-bearing—as in the case of a family breadwinner—insurance can be an important hedge against the failure of that assumption. If an accident may involve the family breadwinner, buying accident insurance can better prepare the family for a post-accident situation.

Several types of insurance—property insurance, liability insurance, life insurance, interruption-of business insurance, etc.—are so common as to be an automatic part of most plans. In addition, certain insurance companies, such as Lloyd's of London, are willing to think about insuring nonstandard items, such as an actress's legs or the throwing arm of a professional athlete.

In some cases, such as collision and uninsured-motorist insurance, insurance may be required by law—which brings us to the second common situation in which hedging actions are well known.

Regulatory requirements

Many physical safety-related hedging actions are required by law and usually take the form of equipment or procedures for handling the aftermath of an accident. In some cases, the equipment can be as simple as special clothing to protect workers if an accident occurs. In other situations, such as a scuba-diving incident involving a diver with nitrogen narcosis, equipment such as a hyperbaric chamber can be complicated and expensive both to maintain and to operate. Hedging actions can also include procedures for operating after an accident has occurred. These include, for example, fire-escape markings and instructions in case a fire breaks out.

Regulatory requirements are not restricted to physical safety. Banks, for example, are required to have deposit insurance. Cities are required to have evacuation procedures if they are located in areas subject to hurricanes. In these cases, the hedging actions themselves are usually spelled out in detail. The challenge is to make sure that an organization follows all pertinent regulations. Although it does not require scenarios, it may require someone with broad knowledge of the regulations surrounding a given operation.

But beyond insurable risks and regulatory requirements, hedging actions *can* be fairly easy to discern. In many cases, the identification of a vulnerable assumption itself suggests potential hedging actions without the need for elaborate scenarios. If there is a serious likelihood that it is going to rain today, carrying an umbrella hedges against the assumption that it will not—the statement of the vulnerable assumption itself triggering a hedging action.

As mentioned in the discussion on developing hedging actions using scenarios, at some point in going through the risk-ordered list of load-bearing, vulnerable assumptions, it becomes clear either that there is no time or money to develop further scenarios or that the risk posed by the next assumption on the list is low enough that it does not warrant a scenario.

GUARDING AGAINST UNDERHEDGING

There is a natural tendency in planning to develop too few hedging actions—to "underhedge" plans. This tendency derives both from the desire to be optimistic about the plan's success and avoid negative thinking and from the fact that hedging actions are often seen as unnecessary expenses. It is important to separate the development of a hedging action from the decision about whether to include it in a plan. The development of hedging actions is an exercise in prudence; the decision about whether to include them in the plan involves other matters.

Where might underhedging take place? Explicit, clearly identified, risky, load-bearing, vulnerable assumptions are least likely to be underhedged. If this seems obvious, practice suggests that it is also true and that there are good reasons for it. Explicit assumptions in a plan are most likely to be agreed upon by all planning parties and are most likely to be addressed with respect to both shaping and hedging actions. Because there is agreement on the importance and vulnerability of such assumptions, there is generally agreement on the need to take hedging actions. Further, the consensus is often sufficient to encourage a discussion of the mechanisms by which the assumption could fail, and there is general agreement on the kinds of hedging actions that are appropriate. All of this attention usually leads to sufficient hedging actions. Less risky, explicit assumptions are more likely to lack appropriate hedging actions.

Once-implicit assumptions are most likely to be underhedged, but subtly so. Implicit assumptions are more likely to *have been* implicit because they were contentious or because they were so culturally ingrained that no one thought or dared to expose them. Either reason reinforces the likelihood both that they will remain implicit (and thus underhedged) and that they will be underhedged even after they are made explicit.

INTEGRATING HEDGING ACTIONS INTO A PLAN

Above, I argued that it was important to separate the development of hedging actions from the decision about whether to include them in a plan. In simple terms, it is a planning function to identify potential hedging actions and a planning failure if appropriate hedging actions have not been identified. It is a management function to decide which hedging actions to implement and a management failure if done inappropriately.

The management challenge at this point is relatively clear. A number of hedging actions should have been identified by now—without or without the aid of scenarios. Hedging actions are insurance against the uncertainties of the future. Inevitably, the cost of implementing all the hedging actions will be prohibitive. The management challenge, then, is to find the answer to the question, "How much insurance is enough?" Since there are likely to be some hedging actions already built into a given plan, the question can be more narrowly focused as, "How much *added* insurance is enough?

Experience suggests that the answer is straightforward: (1) Add those hedging actions that fit within the budget and that hedge against the greatest risks, and (2) use good judgment in determining which hedging actions those are.

That said, our experience with ABP suggests two caveats that actually add useful guidance in integrating hedging actions into a plan.

One caveat is that the more compelling a scenario is, the more you are likely to want to hedge against it. That is, if the scenarios are uneven in their detail or exposition, the more detailed or artistic scenarios may sway thinking about appropriate hedging actions. This is another reason for the detail and the tone in the scenarios to be roughly even. And if they are not even, care should be taken to avoid overreacting to the hedging actions developed from a particularly compelling scenario.

The second caveat is that hedging actions can be contradictory, yet appropriate. If, for example, a plan is sensitive to interest rates' going both much higher and much lower, appropriate hedging actions might look contradictory, yet make good sense. Do not be worried, then, about adding hedging actions that contradict other hedging actions, as long as each makes sense in protecting against the failure of a load-bearing, vulnerable assumption.

HEDGING ACTIONS AND REPLANNING

Part of the intent of Assumption-Based Planning is to make clear the uncertainties underlying a plan. At this point in the process, with signposts and shaping actions in place, the plan has been controlled to the extent possible. What remains to be dealt with are the *uncontrollable* uncertainties or vulnerabilities of the plan. Part of the process of developing hedging actions is to reconsider how vulnerable the overall plan is to uncertainty in the face of all the actions taken to control those uncertainties, then to take action to better prepare the plan to operate in the face of those remaining uncertainties.

This raises the question, "How far should a hedging action be expected to go to improve the plan's ability to handle its uncertainties?" Theoretically, a given broken assumption could be so challenging to the plan and likely enough to occur, that planners could decide the only way to make the plan sufficiently robust would be to scrap it and start over (using the added insights of the broken assumption, of course).

The planners, at this stage of the ABP process, should have sufficiently improved insight into the plan and its vulnerabilities to allow them to decide that the best hedging action would be a complete replanning. In practice, this has not happened, although there is no reason for it not to happen. And there is every reason for planners to be on the lookout for such "plan-busting" or showstopper plausibilities. Planners should not fear a showstopper broken assumption that results in a massive replanning effort.

There is no wrong time to scrap a dangerously weak or vulnerable plan—especially when the costs of hedging are considered.

* * * *

It is time to turn, now, to the last of the five ABP steps in the planning of Margot's lemonade stand.

Lemonade Stand—5

At this point in her planning, Margot has done all she can to control the fate of her plans for the lemonade stand. What remains is to hedge against her load-bearing assumptions' breaking despite her best preventive efforts. Recall that her load-bearing, vulnerable assumptions are

- The weather will be nice.
- There won't be any competition from other lemonade stands.
- Margot will be available.
- Margot will be healthy.
- Margot will be allowed to run the stand.
- The stand will draw at least 24 customers at $.25/cup.

Identifying hedging actions

- *The weather will be nice.* Depending on how common rain is at the end of June, this is the riskiest assumption. It is certainly the hardest to shape or control. Are any hedging actions possible? The uncertainty about the prospects for good weather will remain large until the day before the scheduled weekend. By then, the uncertainty will be reduced (although the outcome won't be known until then). But knowing that the uncertainty will be reduced the Friday before the weekend allows for a hedging action to be put into the plan: Obtaining the sugar and cups necessary to make the plan work should not be scheduled until the day before the weekend. At that point, the chances for the success of the stand will be much clearer and a more reasoned decision about whether to buy the sugar and cups can be made.

  Note that, in identifying this hedging action, we have introduced an additional assumption into the plan: Sugar and cups will be available the day before the weekend. Having the lemonade stand on a weekend that close to the Fourth of July may be a problem (particularly for the cups). The hedging action to wait on scheduling the sugar and cups purchase thus introduces a further assumption into the plan that didn't exist before the hedging actions were identified. That assumption should be run through the ABP steps as well. Margot didn't need a full-blown scenario—imagining a rainy day—to identify hedging actions.

(continued)

Lemonade Stand—5 (continued)

- *There won't be any competition from other lemonade stands.* Margot doesn't seriously expect to have competition. But she has some signposts identified to help her determine whether other competition is likely. Should she take any hedging actions? For this assumption, Margot imagines a scenario in which she has competition. She recognizes that the most likely competition will come from the kids down the block, who also have a lemon tree in their backyard. She knows that if they have a lemonade stand, they'll be advertising fresh lemonade. But she knows also that they ordinarily just put up one "fresh lemonade" sign with a price on it and sit behind their stand waiting for customers. Margot realizes that they can't match her "organic lemonade," because their dad uses insecticides in their backyard. This means that Margot's "organic" campaign and advertising on telephone poles already have her somewhat hedged against her likely competition, but not that she'll be able to trump any possible competition. At this point, it's enough to make her comfortable about her plan.

  There's another problem worth raising at this point: What if the kids down the block advertise "organic lemonade" even though their lemonade is not made from organic lemons? In the world of lemonade stands, this kind of unethical behavior is probably not a large problem. In the real world of competitive business, Margot might have had to contemplate taking legal actions if her competitors' behavior was unethical. A reasonable hedging action might have been to have a lawyer on retainer against such a plausibility.

- *Margot will be available.* The one case Margot couldn't control/shape (that wasn't catastrophic) was an invitation she just could not refuse. She created a scenario in which she got an invitation to Alisa's party. She would definitely want to go, but would she have to abandon her lemonade-stand plans? It occurred to her that Chloe wouldn't be invited (because she doesn't know Alisa), and Alisa's parties were never more than two hours. If she promised to take the lemonade stand all by herself for two hours, maybe she could talk Chloe into taking it for two hours while she went to the party. If Chloe would agree to that plan, Margot would have hedged against (at least one) "must-go" invitation. Her hedging actions would be to ensure that the running of the lemonade stand could be done by one person and that Chloe would be willing to do that (and perhaps Brianna, too, to cover for the case where Chloe would be unavailable).

- *Margot will be healthy.* Margot realized there was little she could do if she got sick. She thought about getting Chloe to take the stand over for her, but rejected that idea. She decided that if she was too sick to run the lemonade stand, that she would scrap the plans or postpone them to another weekend. The case of an injury, however, got her to thinking. She imagined a scenario in which she was in a cast from an accident of some kind. There were actually variations. In the case with both arms in casts, she decided she'd just cancel or postpone. In the case with her wrist in a cast, she thought she could probably carry on (with Chloe's help) with the original plans. In the case with a leg in a cast, she imagined herself both in a wheelchair and on crutches. In both cases, she imagined herself going across the grass to get to the stand that she was planning to put under the shade tree. Particularly for the wheelchair case, she thought carrying out her original plan would be awkward. It then occurred to her that if she could get the large umbrella from the table in back, she could set up the stand on the driveway and have the umbrella provide the shade. This was an acceptable contingency plan and required only the

(continued)

Lemonade Stand—5 (continued)

hedging action of making sure she could (and would be allowed to) bring the umbrella from the back. There were some other things that would have to happen (she'd have to rely more on Chloe to move things and set things up), but nothing that required action in the near future. The hedging actions derived from these scenarios adequately protected her against the possibility of a "recoverable" injury.

• *Margot will be allowed to run a stand.* Margot could easily picture being grounded and not being allowed to carry out her plans. Without having to do much more than picture such an event (that is, without developing a full-blown scenario), Margot came up with a clever hedging action. Realizing that not being grounded was a vulnerable assumption, she came up with a means of reducing the vulnerability. She got her parents to agree that if she did do something that was "groundable" for that weekend, they would defer the grounding until the following week. This was a hedging action taken to address the possibility that she would not be allowed to run the lemonade stand and, by it, she managed to reduce this load-bearing, vulnerable assumption to a load-bearing, but not vulnerable, assumption. This action definitely improved the robustness of her plans for a lemonade stand.

• *The stand will draw at least 24 customers at $.25/cup.* It's hard to draw a scenario for this case, but Margot has thought long and hard about her budgetary assumption. That is, it was clear in making her plan that the plan wasn't going to work unless she could make the assumption hold about how many customers there would be. She has already thought of increasing the advertising campaign if the early customer rate is low, of going door-to-door with a pitcher and cups, and of making the stand more portable and taking it over to the softball games on Saturday and Sunday afternoons. In other words, she's spent much more time on shaping and hedging the plan's *performance* than she has on shaping and hedging the assumptions she made about other aspects of the future that the plan could encounter.

8

The art of conducting ABP

Over the years, we have come to appreciate how much art there is to any kind of planning. Mintzberg (1994b) argues convincingly that creativity is at the heart of planning and, further, that any attempt to force planning into a rigid framework is likely to squelch that creativity. *Creativity* is that burst of insight—that "aha!"—that jumps from a thorny problem to its solution. Creativity can be nurtured but not taught. While agreeing with Mintzberg's arguments, I would add that there is an art to planning that is separate from the creativity that he talks about. There is an art to the *conducting* of planning.

Anyone who has done planning has had good and bad experiences. Largely unrelated to the details of the plan, those experiences had more to do with the people involved, or the circumstances in which the planning was done, or the time of the day, week, or year, etc. As you do more planning, the better you begin to understand what is likely to make for good or bad experiences—and how to turn a bad experience into a good one. Art is something that improves with experience, and it can be taught.

This chapter presents some of the major lessons we have learned about the art of conducting ABP. The major lessons break down into four categories:

- Creating the general setup
- Identifying load-bearing, vulnerable assumptions
- Agreeing on signposts
- Introducing scenarios.

Not all of the five ABP steps are represented. The lessons we have learned apply particularly to creating the general setup for doing ABP and identifying load-bearing, vulnerable assumptions (Step 2 of ABP)— the parts of ABP that are least like other kinds of planning and, therefore, where what we have learned will be most valuable to experienced planners.

CREATING THE GENERAL SETUP

Assumption-Based Planning doesn't just happen. There are certain conditions under which ABP should be conducted. These conditions fall under three general headings:

- When to not do ABP
- Who should be involved
- The importance of getting the ABP effort sanctioned.

When to not do ABP

There are good times and bad times to think about doing ABP. It is never a bad time to explicitly understand the load bearing, vulnerable assumptions that underlie a plan. However, any application of ABP requires time (and therefore, money). Further, it is common for an ABP application to result in actions that it would be nice to add to the plan. Adding actions usually adds costs to the plan implementation, monitoring requirements, management oversight, etc. And, ABP works best when it has some kind of plan to go on. All of this makes it easier to talk about when *not* to conduct ABP. It can be too early, too late, or just inappropriate to apply ABP.

Too early. ABP works best when it has a plan to work with, so it can be applied too early in a planning process. In Chapter 9, there is a brief discussion of using ABP as a prelude to a planning effort in order to identify the important issues that planning should address. After the planning is under way, but still at the glossy-brochure-and-stirring-generalities level, it is probably too early to find anything but assumptions with one-sided vulnerabilities. It is best to wait until the planning is far enough along to have produced actions on some tough decisions so that applying ABP is likely to yield value.

Too late. It is generally too late to apply ABP when it is clear that the results will not affect the plan, but it is not easy to tell when that point has been reached. Certainly by the time the plan has been implemented it is probably too late for an ABP effort to affect the plan. If the plan budgeting effort is long and arduous, the plan is not likely to be changed once that effort is complete. In the military, by the time the plan of one subordinate organization has been integrated with the plans of a higher organization, it is usually too late to think about applying ABP. The same is true in large organizations. It is also probably too late to apply ABP once the planning budget has been expended. These are not hard limits, but they decrease the likelihood either of being able to afford an ABP effort or of being able to affect the plan with the results of an ABP application.

Just inappropriate. When is it just inappropriate to apply ABP? This is a judgment call. I can give two examples of when we made judgments not to apply ABP.

In the first example, we recommended against a formal application of ABP to the planners when it was clear that the head of the organization was pleased with the plan and appeared quite defensive about any possible flaws. We recommended that the planners might want to do an informal, abbreviated application of ABP to the plan just to satisfy their own concerns about its robustness.

In the other example, the planners had just finished an exhausting four-month planning effort that included several contentious sessions. We suggested waiting until the people involved had had a chance to recover before thinking about possible changes to the plan.

There are reasons, then, that do not concern the plan itself, for when it is not appropriate to embark on an ABP effort.

Who should be involved

We have made the point several times that it is important to involve a wide variety of perspectives in most of the steps of ABP. The wider the variety of perspectives is, the greater the chances are of uncovering the implicit assumptions, identifying the load-bearing, vulnerable assumptions, and developing adequate signposts and shaping/hedging actions. Further, that variety should be along several dimensions, including (to the extent possible) experience, age, time with the organization, education/training, ethnicity, religion, and disposition.

That said, there are three important qualifications that most or all of the participants in an ABP application should have.

The first is that most or all should believe in the utility of planning. We have found that it is okay to have one or two people who think that planning is "stupid" or "a waste of time." Any more than one or two people like that tends to poison the atmosphere and to seriously hinder or halt any meaningful progress.

The second important qualification is that most or all participants be collegial. The Assumption-Based Planning process is a shared inquiry. Everyone deserves to be heard. We have all had the experience of an overbearing personality effectively stifling contrary opinions in a group meeting. But it is especially important that this not happen in ABP. Identifying assumptions, particularly implicit assumptions, can be a very delicate matter requiring a great deal of trust and openness among the participants. Identifying vulnerabilities is another step at which differences of opinion need to be openly and collegially expressed. Even the development of shaping and hedging actions requires that the participants put their dogmas on a leash. The more the conduct of the ABP process becomes adversarial, the less likely the process is to get at the deeply held, implicit assumptions that are most likely to produce surprises in plan implementation.

It is not always possible to avoid selecting participants who are more confrontational than collegial. When they are selected, it is best to explain the importance of openness and tolerance to the effectiveness of the Assumption-Based Planning process.

The third important qualification is that most of the participants be at about the proper "level": able to converse knowledgeably about the plan. A clerical worker at a small subsidiary is unlikely to be able to talk knowledgeably about a large corporation's strategic plan, just as the CEO is unlikely to be able to talk knowledgeably about the detailed plan of the small subsidiary. However, this qualification should not be enforced too strictly. It is also important to have some diversity in the level of the participants. A few participants from significantly different (typically lower) levels can, if they are encouraged to speak up, provide an important perspective to discussions.

A corollary to being at the proper level is being at the right level for thinking about the organization's problems. We have had the embarrassing experience of conducting a fascinating ABP exercise with a group of enthusiastic participants, only to find out afterwards that the organization's leadership had a totally different concept of what the right problems were. This leads directly into the issue of having the proper sanctions for an ABP effort.

The importance of getting the ABP effort sanctioned

An important general requirement for an effective ABP effort is that it have the support of the organization's leadership. This is not just the approval that is generally required before an ABP effort can be undertaken or funded. The support for ABP should be stronger than that. The participants need to know that the leadership is likely to be receptive to the results of the ABP effort. Without that support, the participants are less likely to put their best efforts into probing the aspects of the plan that come closest to the organization's cultural heritage or soft spots.

It is important that the organization's leadership understand what ABP is and what it is likely to produce. The easiest way to achieve that understanding is to have the leadership participate in the ABP exercise. Failing that, the leadership should be familiar with the ABP process. Sometimes, a brief presentation on ABP suffices. Other times, a written summary with examples is enough. If the leadership cannot participate, it is important to have a message from the leadership, either in person or recorded in some way, emphasizing the leadership's approval of the ABP effort.

Who the leadership is that needs to sanction an ABP effort is usually clear or obvious in a small organization, but may not be in a large organization. The most important person to sanction an ABP effort is the person who is responsible for implementing the final plan. If that is not possible, it is important that at least the leadership of the planning organization sanction the effort. In one military example, we made sure that the commander of the planning section had been briefed on ABP and on the possibility that an ABP effort could return with recommendations that might run counter to the prevailing military opinion. The ABP effort did, in fact, produce a couple of unpopular recommendations, but the planning leadership was prepared for that outcome and carried the recommendations forward in the organization.

Leadership sanction is important if you want to have a positive effect on a plan. In the absence of leadership sanction, an ABP exercise can still be useful, but its positive effect may be restricted to the *planners—*

making them more comfortable with the assumptions they had made in the planning effort.

IDENTIFYING LOAD-BEARING, VULNERABLE ASSUMPTIONS

Much of the art of conducting Assumption-Based Planning surrounds the effort to identify load-bearing, vulnerable assumptions. As detailed in Chapters 3 and 4, there are several means for identifying assumptions, many of them involving the interactions, whether written or face-to-face, of a group of participants. The group setting, then, is a good perspective from which to describe some of the general lessons we have learned about identifying explicit and implicit load-bearing, vulnerable assumptions.

I will take the example, then, of a group of 15 to 20 people who have gathered for what promises to be an all-day session to identify the load-bearing, vulnerable assumptions underlying the recently completed strategic plan for a large organization. There will be a leader of the group, and I will presume to be that leader. In this case, I am quite familiar with ABP, but the lessons we have learned are applicable to any leader. In fact, much of what I discuss can be applied to many of the other forms of identifying assumptions and many other settings. I leave the specific connections up to the reader.

We have learned 10 important lessons about the art of conducting a session to identify assumptions:

- Start with venting.
- Deal with tautologies and circular reasoning.
- Keep the inquiry from getting too closed.
- Keep the inquiry from getting too open.
- Keep the inquiry from stalling.
- Deal with breakdowns in collegiality.
- Deal with conflicting assumptions.
- Pay attention to style in facilitating an ABP session.
- Use interview protocols.
- Assess risk.

Start with venting

We learned the hard way that it is crucial to start any group effort with a venting session. Almost everybody who agrees to participate in an ABP session will have one or more strong opinions about the plan, the planning system, the planners, the organization, planning in general, the quality or absence of refreshments for the ABP session, etc. Those opinions often reveal battles over assumptions or appropriate actions. This information can then be used in the further discussions about load-bearing, vulnerable assumptions.

For an all-day session, we have learned the hard way that it is important to leave the better part of an hour to let people air these opinions. If you do not leave time for venting, you have not prevented the venting, only delayed it. Invariably, the person with a strong opinion will air that opinion at some time during the day, and usually to the detriment of an ongoing discussion. It is best to get that venting out of the way before the more serious work starts.

Often, the venting can be aimed in a useful direction, such as revealing the above battles, by the way the session is introduced. The opening I prefer is, "I'd like to start out the session by just getting your general impressions of the plan and/or the planning process." This introduction gets the discussion aimed quickly at the strong opinions related to the plan itself or the way it was developed.

Closing the venting session is the next responsibility. We have generally found that, after about 45 minutes, the session starts to run out of steam. At that point, it is fairly easy to move the discussion into whatever means has been chosen for identifying assumptions.

Deal with tautologies and circular reasoning

Tautologies and circular reasoning are very common in discussions about the assumptions underlying a plan, especially in the early discussions. For example, to the question, "Why do you do it that way?" it is common to get an answer that boils down to, "because that's the way we do things" or "because it works." It usually takes time to get people to start thinking more deeply about the assumptions they are making in a given plan.

When plans are working—when assumptions are valid—organizations do not tend to worry about what the assumptions are. It is only when plans are not going well that organizations work to figure out what has gone wrong with their assumptions. The assumptions that are currently valid—working—are the most important to identify. It is valid assumptions that organizations most often lose track of, and it is these valid assumptions that are vulnerable to being invalidated in the future that hold the greatest potential for derailing an otherwise good plan. It is essential, then, to get past the tautologies and circular reasoning that generally hide valid assumptions.

The easiest way to get past tautologies and circular reasoning is to help the participants see that other assumptions are possible. If participants cannot come up with reasons for, for example, where something is being done, the facilitator should ask if they could do it anywhere else; if there are advantages or disadvantages to doing it there; if anybody does it (better or worse) anywhere else; if it could be done better (or worse) elsewhere; or where they would do it if they suddenly were forbidden to do it where they are doing it now (and why). Questions of this type get participants thinking about the advantages and disadvantages of doing it where they are doing it. Participants begin to explore the assumptions about why it is being done there or what they are assuming about where it is being done. Such exploration makes asking the journalist's questions a good idea—an idea that will obviously work for any of the journalist's questions, for example. It forms a general approach to getting beneath tautologies and circular reasoning.

In practice, we have found that it may take two or three examples of getting beneath tautologies and circular reasoning before participants begin to see that much of what they think they understand about an organization's actions are based on generally valid assumptions that have become or are becoming implicit. There is then generally an awakening to assumptions, and the discussion begins to have a life and an energy all its own. That awakening is an important aspect of ABP, and one that adds value to the process.

Keep the inquiry from getting too closed

For this ABP session, I am assuming that the means chosen for identifying the load-bearing, vulnerable assumptions is something like the Telling planned actions the long way, or Asking the journalist's questions, or the Core Belief Identification Squad methods discussed in Chapter 3. This means that I am assuming that the group is generally in a relatively free-form discussion of the underlying assumptions. The most common problem in this setting is that the discussion gets too closed: It centers on the well known—the explicit assumptions already called out in the plan.

The plan itself becomes a powerful damper on a discussion of its underlying assumptions. Everyone is inclined to want the plan to work; therefore, they are easily captured by the world in which it *will* work. If someone proposes an assumption by saying, for example, "Aren't we assuming that A won't happen," it is common to hear a quick response along the lines of, "Yes, but is it really likely that A would happen?" It is important for the facilitator to step in at this point and say, "If the plan assumes that A won't happen and A *could* happen, A is an assumption" and to capture that assumption.

There is no guaranteed recipe for "opening up" a discussion that has become too closed. The best means of keeping a discussion from becoming too closed is to recognize when it is becoming closed and stepping in to prevent the closure. Too many *but*s are a good indicator. If someone suggests an assumption and someone else follows that assumption with a sentence that has a *but* in it, likelihood is being brought into the discussion. Nothing closes down a discussion of assumptions faster than bringing likelihood into the picture. This is where I admonish that this is not the place for discussions of likelihood/vulnerability, and capture the assumption on the assumption list. Capturing the assumption on the assumption list usually works to get a discussion that is becoming too closed opened up again.

> **Capturing Assumptions**
>
> In a group setting, it is effective to capture proposed assumptions on large sheets of paper that can be affixed to the walls with masking tape or thumb tacks/push pins. The running documentation allows everyone in the room to keep track of the assumptions already identified, facilitating the further steps of identifying the load-bearing, vulnerable assumptions.

Keep the inquiry from getting too open

Although the most common problem in a group discussion is that it becomes too closed, it can also become too open. For one participant to start talking about the plan's assuming that there will be no alien invasions is all it takes for a discussion of assumptions to degenerate into silliness. In fact, the Assumption-Based Planning process actually encourages the discussion to get too open by emphasizing that vulnerability assessments will come later.

The easiest means for ensuring that a discussion does not get too open is to just write the "silly" assumption on the growing list of assumptions. Recognize that it is indeed an assumption, reemphasize that questions of load-bearing and vulnerability will be discussed later, and ask if there are any other assumptions. Usually after a few more duly recorded frivolous assumptions, the group is ready to get back to more serious work.

Keep the inquiry from stalling

Sometimes a group discussion just loses steam. If it seems as though there are still assumptions to be found, it is up to the facilitator to get the discussion going again, jump-starting the stalled search for assumptions by coming at the plan from a different direction: asking any question that will get participants thinking about some other aspect of the plan. We have developed a few stock questions that will serve this purpose, if they have not already been addressed:

- What does the plan assume about the competition's reaction to the plan?
- Who are the stakeholders in this plan, and what does the plan assume about their behavior?
- Who are the people that will be most important in implementing this plan, and what does the plan assume about them?
- What does the plan assume about timing of planned actions or budget?

Questions of this type will often not only generate answers to the direct question but will also generate similar questions, getting a discussion of assumptions going again.

Another effective means for reviving a discussion, although more difficult to concoct, is illustrated by a session we held with planners in the elite Navy SEAL command. The SEAL's proposed plan called for developing or acquiring a lot of specialized technology. Yet the people in the room were rightly proud of their rigorous training and adaptability to any situation. The juxtaposition of human skills and technology made it seem as though unstated assumptions about how important technology was had been buried in the plan. But the discussion about technological assumptions was stalled. I finally thought to ask, "Do you see yourselves more as MacGyver or James Bond?" Both fictional characters were trained to operate behind enemy lines, as are the SEALs, but MacGyver was famous for using his wits and whatever he found nearby to fashion what he needed; Bond's fame is equated with having the exact, wondrous technological devices he was going to need. By asking a question about two positive, but contrasting, alternatives, we were able to jump-start a useful discussion on the assumptions about technology in the plans. Such serendipitously effective analogies as MacGyver and Bond may not come so readily to mind in every stalled situation, but the search for such examples is a worthy pursuit.

Deal with breakdowns in collegiality

I mentioned in the Who should be involved? section how important it is for the participants in an ABP application to be collegial. In the give-and-take of a discussion on assumptions or load-bearing or vulnerability, parochial interests or personal animosities can lead to friction and a breakdown in collegiality. One of the objectives of starting with a collegial group is to avoid such breakdowns to the extent possible.

The facilitator should be sensitive to the imminence of such breakdowns and move quickly to repair them. Without collegiality, the discussion can break down very rapidly, and recovering from such a breakdown is not easy. In one ABP session, we had to abandon a discussion of assumptions altogether and move to lunch shortly after 11:00 a.m. This physical break, coupled with a reminder of the importance of the shared inquiry and of an objective discussion of the organization's plan, was enough to get the discussion back on track after lunch.

Reminding participants of the goal—not to judge the plan but to identify its uncertainties, ensuring that all are accounted for and dealt with to the extent possible—is the most important tool to employ here. Judgments about the plan, whether implied or explicit, should be avoided in the discussion, nor should participants infer judgments during the discussion. In some cases, this reminder may need to be made more than once over the course of a day's discussions.

Deal with conflicting assumptions

On occasion, discussions aimed at identifying assumptions produce conflicting or contradictory assumptions. As a practical matter, it is best not to dwell on the contradictoriness during a session aimed at identifying as many assumptions as possible. It is better to capture both conflicting assumptions and move on.

At some later point, the conflicts should be discussed seriously. At least two interesting outcomes are possible. One explanation for conflicting assumptions is that they are associated with an action and one or more hedging actions. One of the conflicting assumptions is associated with a primary assumption and planned action; the other conflicting assumption is associated with some failure in the primary assumption and appropriate hedging actions—entirely consistent with good planning practice.

The other explanation for conflicting assumptions is that the planning is confused—not as uncommon an explanation as it should be. A discussion of the conflicting assumptions can usually sort out the confusion and develop a more appropriate assumption and planned actions.

Pay attention to style in facilitating an ABP session

One of the more subtle lessons we have learned about the conduct of an Assumption-Based Planning exercise is that a facilitator's style is important. The journalist's questions that are posed for identifying load-bearing, vulnerable assumptions are a good venue for discussing the importance of style.

In asking the journalist's questions, the facilitator is put in the role of a naive outsider asking fundamental questions about an organization. In fact, the facilitator is being asked to walk two very thin lines between extremes. One fine line is between naiveté and ignorance: If the facilitator behaves too naively, s/he risks one of two reactions: "Come on, *everybody* knows this stuff" or "If you don't even know that, it would take way too long to explain." In either case, the participants get frustrated and the quest for assumptions is jeopardized.

The other fine line is between naiveté and manipulation. If the facilitator does not act naive enough, s/he risks being perceived as trying to steer the discussion to a particular outcome. We have all seen interrogators or lawyers in film or on TV expertly manipulate a witness by asking seemingly naive questions. In practice, appearing manipulative seems to be a somewhat lesser evil than appearing too naive, but both should concern a facilitator.

The primary cure for appearing too naive or not naive enough is to be sensitive to how the participants are reacting. If they appear to be getting either frustrated or wary, the facilitator should be ready to break out of questioner mode and work to remedy the situation. Simply voicing a concern can be effective: "Am I being too naive here?" or "Am I pushing too hard here?" Direct questions such as these have worked particularly well when one or two facilitators were talking with a very small group (in one case, just one person) of participants. It is also effective to remind participants of the value of trying to rethink what "everybody knows" to check for hidden vulnerable assumptions.

One technique for striking a careful balance between being ignorant and being manipulative is to have both an outsider and an insider as facilitators. This practice worked well in our efforts with the Army Noncommissioned Officer (NCO) Corps. We had literally a naive outsider (who knew something about the Army but very little about the NCO education system) and an NCO as the facilitator team. This technique allowed the outsiders to ask naive questions that, if they appeared to be too naive, the insider could "translate," which largely eliminated the worry about manipulation.

Use interview protocols

Many of the methods of identifying load-bearing, vulnerable assumptions involve asking questions of knowledgeable people. This is a form of interview and brings up the question of *interview protocols*—strict formats for ensuring that each interviewee gets the same questions in the same order. Interview protocols are more appropriate in situations where a large number of interviews are going to be conducted and the results are going to be analyzed statistically. Nevertheless, this question has been underaddressed in the development of ABP. In general, we have either employed no protocols or very weak protocols. (The journalist's questions, for example, represent a very crude protocol.) We have justified this lack of protocols with uncertainty: We are not really sure what we are after in the interviews. I do not want to suggest that we have learned that ABP can get by without interview protocols.

However, in our experiences to date, we do not seem to have been hindered by a lack of protocols.

Certainly, protocols would make sense when it is difficult to get participants together, either physically or electronically. The interviews would have to be done in several installments, so that a consistent list of questions for participants to respond to would be critical.

Assess risk

In Chapter 4, we talked about risk as being roughly the product of how load-bearing an assumption is and how likely it is to fail within the time horizon of the plan. We also talked briefly about how risk could be used to rank-order a list of assumptions. Both of these evaluations can be made after load-bearing, vulnerable assumptions have been identified. When conducting these evaluations, the facilitator needs to realize the special challenges they present.

Typically calm and orderly, discussions of risk can, on occasion, become quite animated. The occasion is having to deal with load-bearing, vulnerable assumptions that might be characterized as carrying an important part of the load of the plan and being slightly vulnerable—the assumptions that have high consequences if they break but have a low probability of breaking. Assumptions of this type are seen most dramatically in the medical or military arena. An assumption that has a 1-in-1,000,000 chance of leading to 1 million deaths and an assumption that has a 1-in-100 chance of leading to 100 deaths have the same mathematical expected value: 1. However, these two assumptions lead to very different visceral impressions of risk, and arguments can ensue over which is the more worrisome risk and should, therefore, take precedence in the plan.

The problem can also be stated more positively. Suppose a company must choose to develop one of two prospective products, one with a 1-in-1,000 chance of earning the company $1 billion and one with a 1-in-10 chance of earning the company $10 million. The mathematical expectation of return of each is $1 million, so the risks are equal. But in the company can only choose one, which one should it be? The "correct" choice is likely to rest more on philosophy than on risk. Even though the risks are equal (and therefore, from a risk perspective, a coin toss would be as good a way as any to decide which product to pursue) there is likely to be a battle over the message that the company would be sending with its choice and whether it is a conservative company or an aggressive one.

In ABP, assessments of risk are generally intended only to rank-order a list of load-bearing, vulnerable assumptions. For two assumptions to be tied in terms of risk is not a big problem. The problem arises with extreme cases of drastic consequences and low probabilities of occurrence, such as an invasion by hostile aliens with superior technology. Every plan implicitly assumes that such an invasion will not happen. We might agree that, if it did, human life on earth could be extinguished—an overwhelmingly negative consequence. Even if we decided that the probability of such an invasion was vanishingly small, what should be done about the possibility of a hostile alien invasion? Most rational planners would do nothing.

Where do you draw the line? Historical civilizations, the Aztecs and Incas, for example, *have* been wiped out by "alien" invasions. Should the ancient Aztecs have carried forward the possibility of alien invasions to shaping and hedging actions? Fortunately, most of the high-consequence, low-probability assumptions that have arisen in practice have been fairly easy to handle. In the rare instances when a consensus could not be achieved, we have usually called off discussions of the assumption, maintaining the assumption in question on the list of load-bearing, vulnerable assumptions and involving the organizational leadership in whether to continue to carry the assumption forward into Steps 3 through 5 of the ABP process.

* * * *

The discussion to this point has concentrated on the lessons we have learned about setting up an ABP application and about the first two steps of the process, which identify the load-bearing, vulnerable assumptions. In the remaining three steps, many of the problems are more common to other types of planning methodologies and tools. For example, developing shaping actions and devising hedging actions from scenarios are very much like developing actions for a plan. In the remaining steps, then, there are two areas in which the lessons we have learned might be useful to experienced planners: getting agreement on signposts and introducing scenarios into the ABP process. The remainder of the chapter deals with these lessons.

AGREEING ON SIGNPOSTS

The basic difficulty with signposts comes not with identifying them but with getting *agreement* on them. I mentioned earlier the vice president of a large organization opining that the problem with signposts in his organization was that there was "too much democracy": He could not get agreement on a consensual set of signposts. An ABP facilitator faces the same problem.

Signposts, events or thresholds that indicate important changes in the validity or vulnerability of assumptions, are detailed in Chapter 5, which also discusses several potential biases in recognizing important changes and means for avoiding those biases. Even after all precautions against bias have been taken, a large set of overlapping and conflicting trends and thresholds can remain, purporting to indicate important changes in the validity or vulnerability of load-bearing, vulnerable assumptions. If the group process results in a reasonable number of signposts, that process is complete and has been very successful. More often, going through the group process produces a large set of signposts that represents only a first step in the signpost-identification process. But it is an important first step. The rousing discussion of signposts among participants with differing views is something the above-mentioned vice president did not have. Even in failure to reach a consensus, the discussion itself not only provides an opportunity for participants to come to a consensus, it also provides greater insight into the issues involved.

In the second step in reaching a consensus on a smaller set of signposts, we have yet to find a good substitute for sitting down with a small (3 to 5 people) subset of more senior participants (most often at a different time from that of the signpost-identification process) and distilling out a reduced set of signposts from the larger list. This process works better than asking the full group to stay engaged to derive a smaller list of signposts. We have found that more senior participants typically do a better job of "looking at the big picture" and bringing a broader perspective to what is a process full of judgments about what truly constitutes *significant* or *important* changes to an assumption.

The concluding step is then generally to take the reduced set of signposts back to participants in the first step and ask if they "can live with" the reduced list. With minor changes, the participants generally agree to the reduced list.

There are certainly concerns that this process will throw the baby out with the bathwater by eliminating an important signpost. The trade-off is between being comprehensive in identifying signposts and being successful in producing a list of signposts that can be effectively and efficiently monitored. It is also useful to have at least one member of the group who will monitor the signposts involved in the process that reduces the large list to the smaller one.

INTRODUCING SCENARIOS

Chapter 7 discusses several factors affecting the creation and credibility of scenarios in support of generating hedging actions. The purpose of those discussions was to ensure that the scenarios were adequate for their intended purpose: to make a future plausible situation credible enough to engage ABP participants in the generation of actions that could better prepare the organization if that situation arose. One practical concern that arises in some applications is that one or more of the scenarios become *too* credible. That is, there is the danger that a given scenario is seen as being so realistic that the participants come to believe that that scenario is what will happen.

When participants come to believe the likelihood of a given scenario, they begin planning for that scenario. The role of the facilitator is to keep emphasizing that there is an important difference between planning as though a scenario *could* come about and planning as though it *will* come about: If a scenario *could* come about, the organization takes action today, as it deems appropriate, to prepare itself to more easily change course if it becomes clear that that world is coming about. If an organization thinks a scenario *will* come about, it takes actions appropriate for that scenario. If the organization believes a product *could* become the latest fad, it takes action to facilitate a move toward increasing production, whereas believing a product *will* become the latest fad will cause the organization to be more likely to begin increasing productive capacity now—a more expensive and risky action.

In practice, getting "captured" by a scenario—seeing it as what will happen rather than what could happen—appears to be as likely in the military world as in the business world. In the military world, the Department of Defense generates a (generally pessimistic) "Defense Planning Guidance" scenario that is often taken as a prediction of the future. The business world is more likely to be captured by an overly optimistic scenario, but no less inappropriately.

In ABP, the worry of participants' being captured by one or more scenarios is somewhat reduced because the scenarios generally tend to be sketchier than in scenario planning. As described in Chapter 7, ABP scenarios need be only as detailed as is necessary to engage thinking about the world of a broken assumption. The less well-developed a scenario is, the less likely it is to be taken as a prediction.

In practice, the issue of being captured by a scenario does arise, but not often. The facilitator should be sensitive to the possibility that hedging actions are becoming more like a plan for a given scenario than like actions that would better prepare the organization for the possibility of that scenario. A reminder from the facilitator of the purpose of the scenarios is usually sufficient to get participants back on track.

* * * *

These are the major lessons we have learned about the art of conducting an Assumption-Based Planning exercise. We could have added myriad minor lessons, and the experienced planner could probably add others. Doubtless, we have yet to learn other major lessons about the art of conducting ABP. Nothing is quite so humbling as preparing for the future and then watching to see how those preparations fare as the future unfolds. The major lessons here, then, cannot hope to be comprehensive. However, they should form a good foundation for someone embarking on an ABP exercise.

9

Beyond ABP as a post-planning tool

This book has described a relatively narrow niche for Assumption-Based Planning: as a post-planning tool for testing and improving plans. In our experiences with ABP in a variety of planning situations, we have come to appreciate, somewhat paradoxically, both the utility in circumscribing the role of ABP and the broader utility that can come from paying attention to one's assumptions in planning. This chapter concentrates on the latter.

The broader utility of paying attention to assumptions in planning has two aspects: (1) ABP as a tool can be useful *during* the planning process as well as after, and (2) assumptions can receive attention *apart* from a formal application of ABP—in Assumption-Based *Thinking*. However, before I delve into these two aspects, I want to address why we have worked so hard, up to now, in circumscribing the role of ABP.

WHY WE CIRCUMSCRIBED THE ROLE OF ABP

The two basic reasons for circumscribing the applicability and utility of ABP are

- to avoid overselling ABP
- to emphasize when ABP is most useful.

To avoid overselling ABP

Assumption-Based Planning is not a planning methodology. That is, it is not useful for planning from scratch. It omits too important an in-

172

gredient—the world that planners might consider "most likely," the world of no broken assumptions—to be a complete planning methodology. This omission is purposeful. The world of no broken assumptions is more likely to be a distraction than an aid in thinking about the *uncertainties* of the future. The mind is too easily drawn to the world at which the plan is aimed. The whole point of an ABP exercise is to get planners to consider the frailties of the assumptions underlying the plan, not their likelihood. But, absent the world of no broken assumptions, ABP is looking at a "donut" in the future, concentrating on every future possibility *except* the one the plan is assuming. Adding the donut hole back in weakens the purpose of ABP.

To emphasize when ABP is most useful

After planning is when the assumptions of a plan show themselves best. At the highest level of planning, the goal should be to develop a grand strategy—the ATTAP (All Things To All People) plan that often gets published in glossy brochures—that will handle the worst the world could throw at an organization. This statement is not intended ironically: The organization does not want to come up with a plan that is obviously deficient. However, it is in working through the details that real-world constraints involving money, time, and people begin to generate difficult choices for the grand strategy. Making those difficult choices generally requires making further assumptions, particularly assumptions with two-sided vulnerabilities, and often overlooks implicit assumptions. It is at this stage where the optimism of the grand strategy can lead to decisions that overlook significant uncertainties. This is where ABP is most helpful.

There are good reasons, then, for being careful in describing the nature of Assumption-Based Planning and its utility. Having erred on the side of caution, it is now useful to discuss where else—outside the confines of post-planning improvement—thinking about assumptions has been useful and can be useful. To begin with, as a tool, ABP can be useful *during* the planning process as well as after.

USING ABP *DURING* PLANNING

ABP can be used in at least five ways to help during the planning process, to

- test plan fragments and proposed plans
- identify planning problems
- identify plan problems
- bring fresh perspectives to the planning process
- develop a strategic control system.

Testing plan fragments and proposed plans

The most obvious use of ABP in planning is for its intended purpose: to test plans. The plans to be tested during the planning process are more likely to be plan fragments or rough plans. But at some stage, there will be enough of a plan to run it through ABP. That stage is probably far enough down the planning road for at least a few difficult decisions to have been incorporated into the plan. Until that stage, ABP could be applied, but is not likely to reveal much.

A manufacturing company used ABP to test just its product portfolio and the assumptions underlying it. Only part of the company's overall plan, the product portfolio was thought to be most likely to contain implicit assumptions. ABP was used to try to tease out those implicit assumptions.

Bringing in ABP to test rough plans is how ABP was used in most of its military applications. In the Army in particular, preliminary plans, or *concepts*, are created and circulated widely throughout the Army for comment. The process of incorporating comments and eventually achieving consensus on an official plan is long and arduous. ABP's testing role was a part of that process. ABP's particular strengths were in identifying aspects of the future that had not yet been dealt with in the plan, identifying implicit assumptions being made by the plan, and suggesting shaping and hedging actions for load-bearing assumptions that were vulnerable.

Identifying planning problems

ABP can help identify the problems that planning should address. If an organization is embarking on planning, it is typically doing so because of actual or impending problems in its current plan. These problems are generally well and widely recognized before the planning process begins. Nevertheless, applying ABP to the *current* plan is a way of revisiting a plan's assumptions and providing some assurance that all the broken or breaking assumptions have been identified.

Particularly if some external event is causing the plan unexpected problems, it is possible (perhaps even likely) that there are additional explicit or implicit assumptions underlying the current plan that are broken or at risk.

An example of an overlooked assumption comes from the early 1970s, when Xerox overlooked the Japanese threat in low-cost copiers. Recognizing that the Japanese were producing low-cost, low-volume machines and selling rather than leasing them, Xerox chose to focus on IBM and Kodak, each of which had just come out with its first office copying machines, seriously threatening Xerox's monopoly in that market. Xerox correctly perceived that the assumption that it would continue to monopolize the office copier market was in jeopardy, but it overlooked the implicit assumption that the office copier market was going to continue to be the most important market. As a Xerox executive put it, "It was a question of whether you concentrate on the potential elephants or the mosquitoes that were running around . . . . We focussed on the elephants" (Jacobson and Hillkirk 1986: 71). Their monopolistic position was an assumption underlying their plan, which they were carefully monitoring, and they recognized that it was breaking. However, it was not the only load-bearing assumption underlying their plan that was breaking. A careful scan of the assumptions underlying their plan might have revealed the wider planning problem.

Identifying plan problems

ABP can also be used to help identify holes or weaknesses in an emerging plan. At any stage during the planning process, some aspects of the future are likely to be better addressed by proposed actions than others. ABP can help identify those parts of the plan that are under-addressed.

Particularly effective in identifying plan problems is the Rationalizing a plan method of searching for assumptions. Recall that rationalizing a plan involves making connections between aspects of the future and elements in the plan for dealing with those aspects. In making those connections, some unconnected assumptions about the future usually remain. Elements of the future without connections to planning actions are either holes in the plan—aspects of the future that should be addressed but have not yet been—or are unimportant to the future of the organization. Even when there are actions that connect to assumptions about the future, a review of those actions may reveal that they do not adequately address the assumption about the future. Both holes and inadequate actions reveal weaknesses in the plan itself.

The rationalizing a plan approach was particularly effective in working with the Army: The Army usually does a good job of describing both what it thinks the world is going to look like and what it plans to do about that world. In one instance of an application of ABP to an Army concept of operations, we rationalized the plan, drawing connections between what the Army thought the world would be like and its planned actions. Because a concept of operations is a preliminary product from the Army planning system, our ABP scan was *during* the Army planning process. In this particular concept of operations, there was a clear assumption that the future would require significantly greater Army participation in military operations on urban terrain. However, the plan contained no specific actions to address operations on urban terrain. The planners acknowledged this "hole" in the plan, talked of efforts under way to address the hole, and made sure that they flagged the hole so that the plan would not go out in final form without the hole's being addressed.

A similar rationalization of the (in this case, completed) plan of a large industrial firm revealed a weakness in addressing an implicit assumption that the world economy would remain robust for the succeeding five years. Although there were actions that would hedge to some extent against a dip in the world economy, the vice president in charge of planning conceded that this area of the plan needed more work.

Bringing fresh perspectives to the planning process

ABP can facilitate bringing other people into an ongoing planning process. Suppose you are developing a strategic plan, but you are not entirely comfortable with the expertise on the team that is developing it. You would like to bring in additional people with particular expertise to add their perspectives. Or suppose you yourself want to understand what has been going on in the planning effort. How do you go about it? What is the best way to "get up to speed" on the current effort?

Typically, a newcomer will ask for a complete report from the planning team. With plenty of questioning and interaction, the newcomer is eventually brought up to speed. *At least* as effective a way to come up to speed on a planning effort as questioning the planners is having the assumptions underlying the plan spelled out. Working through the assumptions is an excellent way to get into the planning team's thought processes. Subsequent discussions with the planners can be much more efficient. Asking why the planners chose particular assumptions will very quickly get you inside their thinking.

If the assumptions are *not* written down, any of the ABP techniques for identifying assumptions can either be applied to current written products (and then discussed with the planners) or be used as questions for interviewing the planning team in order to get at the assumptions the members are making. If the team has made its assumptions explicit, using the techniques will bring a newcomer quickly up to speed. If the team has *not* made its assumptions explicit, using the techniques will not only bring the newcomer up to speed but will improve the general planning process by at least making current assumptions explicit. Further, questioning the assumptions could unearth implicit assumptions the team did not realize it was making.

Developing a strategic control system

The signposts that are a part of ABP are intended to monitor the validity or vulnerability of the load-bearing, vulnerable assumptions of a plan. That monitoring is properly a part of a strategic control system. Not all plans have strategic control systems. When such systems do exist, they have been developed during the planning process and are of two basic types: (1) those that are designed to control the implementation of the plan and (2) those that are designed to monitor and control the plan's approach (or strategy). Both are useful products of planning, and ABP can help in the development of each—although more so with the latter than the former.

In a system designed to monitor and give feedback on the progress of the plan implementation, the primary concerns are the plan's goals and being able to measure and track any deviations from progress toward those goals. ABP techniques for identifying assumptions add to an understanding of the assumptions underlying planning actions that can provide insights into both what the action is expected to do and what its limitations might be. For example, a planning action may look innocently like "Ensure that everybody understands the plan and is committed to working it." This kind of action can easily hide a host of assumptions—recognizable beforehand—about some subcultures of a large organization that will find the plan antithetical to their practiced routines and very difficult to carry out. Understanding this resistance beforehand provides the opportunity not only to plan better for those subcultures, but to monitor their progress more closely and specifically.

The true value of ABP techniques, however, lies in developing a control system for monitoring and giving feedback on a plan's approach more so than on its implementation. On a philosophical level, that is exactly what ABP is designed to do. ABP techniques for identifying load-bearing, vulnerable assumptions are aimed precisely at identifying vulnerabilities in the plan's approach to the future. The development of signposts is aimed at identifying means for detecting increasing weakness in the plan's approach and for recognizing when that approach is becoming compromised.

In the strategic control system defined by Lorange (1986), there is an additional step: redevising the approach or strategy if one or more of its assumptions breaks. This step is beyond the direct interest of ABP, although scenarios developed to identify hedging actions can play an important role in any replanning effort. Most of the steps in ABP, then, can contribute directly to the development of a strategic control system that is designed to control the approach/strategy of the plan itself.

* * * *

In addition to the utility that ABP can bring during the planning process, there is a wider utility in thinking about assumptions in general. To discuss this utility, I adopt the term "Assumption-Based *Thinking*."

ASSUMPTION-BASED THINKING

Assumption-Based Thinking (ABT) is about paying attention to *all* the assumptions—load-bearing and non–load-bearing, vulnerable and invulnerable—before, during, *and* after planning. Assumption-Based Thinking is not a tool per se; it is a frame of mind. All of our assumptions, over time, are subject to change. In reality, we should pay attention to all the assumptions we make during planning and monitor them for significant change.

The processes of ABP are useful aids in Assumption-Based Thinking, but ABP is aimed at the load-bearing, vulnerable assumptions of a given plan in order to mitigate the risks to that plan. Assumption-Based Thinking goes beyond the circumscribed role of ABP to contribute to better planning in two ways:

- Monitoring for assumptions to become load-bearing or vulnerable

- Analyzing assumptions for opportunities.

Monitoring for assumptions to become load-bearing or vulnerable

In Assumption-Based Planning, the planner concentrates on the load-bearing and vulnerable assumptions—those most likely to lead to problems with the plan. The purpose of signposts is to provide indications that the validity or vulnerability of an assumption is breaking or becoming less likely to break.

In the same way, load-bearing assumptions could become less load-bearing. For example, a load-bearing assumption about financing could become less critical because of a surge in profits or in the stock market. Logically, this occurrence should perhaps be a part of ABP, but it has been a sufficiently rare event that it has never been a burden to continue to carry a vulnerable assumption that is no longer load-bearing.

In ABP, planners do not pay attention to the possibility that an assumption will *become* load-bearing or vulnerable, and this is where Assumption-Based Thinking can play a role. A formal process for monitoring all of the assumptions of a plan would get quite cumbersome because of the large number of assumptions in a typical plan. One idea behind Assumption-Based Thinking is to do informally for the non–load-bearing or invulnerable assumptions underlying a plan what ABP does formally for the load-bearing, vulnerable ones: to think about whether events or trends in the news might be changing their status.

Analyzing assumptions for opportunities

The other area where Assumption-Based Thinking can supplement Assumption-Based Planning is in paying attention to assumptions that may represent opportunities. ABP is aimed primarily at threats to a given plan. We talked in Chapter 1 about ABP's limited role in identifying opportunities. Thinking more broadly about assumptions can produce better insights into potential opportunities.

Opportunities often come from long-held assumptions that went unexamined despite change. Entrepreneurs who examined long-held assumptions have come up with opportunities where none used to exist. Fred Smith examined the assumptions underlying spare-parts inventories in the age of computers and realized that there was an opportunity for an airline dedicated to overnight delivery of spare parts. Smith developed that idea into Federal Express. Similarly, in light of the advances in miniaturization of computer parts, Steve Jobs and Steve Wozniak examined the assumption that computers would always be large and centralized, and they developed the first Apple computer for home use.

The second main idea behind Assumption-Based Thinking is that there may be opportunities in vulnerable or invulnerable assumptions. The best way to recognize those possibilities is to be aware of all the assumptions—vulnerable *and* invulnerable—that underlie a plan and to continue to question and reexamine their validity.

Monitoring assumptions for opportunities can take on a variety of forms. The examples above are of business opportunities. Analyzing the assumptions underlying an organization's operations can generally improve planning. Some feel for the general value of Assumption-Based Thinking can be seen in a planning effort we did with the U.S. Army Noncommissioned Officer Corps (NCO).

AN EXAMPLE OF ABT—ARMY NCO LEADER DEVELOPMENT

As part of an effort to strengthen the professional development of Army noncommissioned officers, we agreed to help the Army develop an organizational vision for future leader development (Winkler et al. 1998). The NCOs were looking for two essential elements of an *organizational vision*:

- *unique,* shared sense of identity
- *clear,* shared sense of purpose.

This definition of organizational vision comes from RAND work on visions (Setear et al. 1990) and borrows heavily from Vaill (1982). The search for an organizational vision was an essential first step in the

NCO planning process, and, as we have argued elsewhere, developing an organizational vision is a particularly effective—though difficult—planning technique (Builder and Dewar 1994).

If there was a current NCO vision, it was that NCO leaders should be developed in a fashion that paralleled the way in which commissioned officers were developed. Even the mission statement for NCO leader development was a variation of the commissioned officer development mission statement.

To begin with, we wanted to understand what assumptions were behind the current noncommissioned officer development system itself. Over 60 currently serving noncommissioned officers met for a week to discuss the assumptions. They were split into six groups, and two facilitators—one acting as a naive observer of the system and the other an Army NCO—asked the journalist's questions, What? Where? When? How? Who? and Why? (see Chapter 4 for more details on the journalist's questions). Participants were asked to "think hard, think big, discuss."

Of particular importance was the charge not only to answer the journalist's question but also to explain the answer. So, for example, in addition to saying *when* leaders were currently being developed—at what stages in their careers, what time of year/day, etc.—participants had to say *why* each was done then and not at some other time.

Out of the plenary sessions came a comprehensive and shared understanding among the participants of the current system and its rationale. Briefly, the Noncommissioned Officer Education System (NCOES) is built on three "pillars": (formal) institutional education, experience in the NCO's unit, and self-development. The group sessions identified the assumptions underlying each of these pillars and the reasoning behind them.

In plenary sessions, participants were then asked to identify what could change and how—including which changes would be most important and which would be most upsetting to the current system. To focus them on the plausibility of these changes, we asked them to identify "trigger events" that would signify a change had taken place or was taking place. In addition, we asked the participants to identify which assumptions were most important to the NCO corps (in business, these would be the core values or competencies).

Up to this point, the exercise had been very ABP-like, but with a different purpose in mind from most Assumption-Based Planning application. At this point, the participants were asked to stare at the pieces that were before them: their understanding of the current system, the rationale for that system, the changes to that system and its rationale that could occur in the coming years, and the elements the corps held most dear. They were then asked what common threads they could see in that information and what global solutions they could discern to handle all of the future plausibilities. In other words, they were asked to search for a vision—an identity and purpose for NCOs that would honor their heritage and fit the worlds they could face in the future.

In time, they generated a formal vision (Winkler et al. 1998). By presenting the participants with a clear understanding of the assumptions that underlay their leadership development system and what could happen to those assumptions, Assumption-Based Thinking allowed the participants to develop an organizational vision.

That was the original goal, but the participants talked about additional benefits. One was that they had a much better sense of the importance of continuous learning in the coming years. That is, thinking through their assumptions revealed an important aspect of the future—continuous learning—that would become a part of their detailed plan. Also, the participants talked about having a clear sense of the need to improve the incentives and evaluation mechanisms of self-development and to improve its balance with respect to the other two pillars. ABT had helped them see more clearly a problem—self-development—that they had struggled with, but now had a better understanding of what they needed to do. Finally, the ABT session helped the NCOs incorporate one further thought that was not in the original mission statement or thinking: They must be a noncommissioned officer corps that "adapts to a changing world." This thought became a central part of their clear, shared sense of purpose.

There are other ways of producing a reasonable set of the problems and opportunities facing an organization. A process from the business world such as SWOT that develops an organization's Strengths, Weaknesses, Opportunities, and Threats, for example, would suffice. The advantages of an ABT-like approach are twofold:

1. By concentrating on the assumptions underlying the current vision, ABT provides a more systematic look at the problems and opportunities currently facing an organization—important for helping those involved understand the full breadth of challenges to the current vision.

Through the thorough process of explaining the NCOES and defending it, participants in the NCO workshop came to a better understanding of the assumptions that underpinned the NCOES and a better feel for which of those assumptions were vulnerable to plausible future events. Participants recognized, for example, that long-standing assumptions about their select-train-promote sequence, about their up-or-out promotion system, about the utility of the current self-development programs, and about the adequacy of the informal mentoring system were all subject to change in the post–Cold War world. This knowledge gave the participants more specific ideas on what they might need to be flexible about and on what kind of adaptability they might be called upon to develop.

2. The ability to go easily from vulnerable assumptions to scenarios or plausible futures provides additional visualization of the problems and opportunities that an organization must confront.

At one point in the workshop, there was disagreement over whether the long-held assumption that soldiers would have to be able-bodied was vulnerable to future events. The facilitator described a scenario in which physically challenged people argued before the U.S. Supreme Court that many of the desk jobs in the military, far from the battlefield, could actually be better staffed by physically challenged people. Given that similar rulings had been made about blacks and women in the military, the scenario was convincing enough that it promoted general agreement on the vulnerability of the assumption about future soldiers having to be able-bodied.

FINAL WORD

The first eight chapters have made the case for the utility of Assumption-Based Planning as a tool that can help improve plans. This chapter has argued that there is further utility in paying attention to your assumptions in planning. Whether or not you choose to use the techniques outlined here for Assumption-Based Planning or Assumption-Based Thinking, the basic power behind thinking about assumptions in planning is that all planning rests on assumptions: The better you understand and pay attention to the assumptions you are making, the better your planning will be.

Appendix

Assumption-Based Planning and the planning literature

If you are like me, whenever a new planning method or tool is described, you wonder how it relates to those planning methods or tools with which you are already familiar. Usually, the description of the method or tool does little to answer questions of this type. To find out how it relates to other methods or tools (and whether or not it is any good), you must wait, instead, for a review of the method by a planning maven.

A similar, but more awkward, situation occurs if you have been told to evaluate a new method and/or tool for its usefulness in your planning situation. If you cannot find a review of the method/tool, you must either wait for an expert review or you must make the comparisons yourself.

Partly because of the way in which Assumption-Based Planning (ABP) was developed, we have already done that work. ABP started out as the solution to a specific U.S. Army planning problem. When the Army asked us to reapply and document the "method" two years later, we searched through the literature to see how it related to other methods/tools.

Over the years, we have kept up that comparison effort, primarily as due diligence in understanding the literature and, secondarily, as a means of honing our own definitions. As anyone who has looked can attest, there is little standardization of terms and concepts in the large and varied literature on planning. Each new article seems either to introduce new terms or to use existing terms in new ways. Not even ABP is immune to the practice. This Appendix thus serves two purposes.

185

The first purpose is to address how ABP relates to other planning methods/tools in the planning literature. The differences between ABP and other planning methods were highlighted in Chapter 1, but were unsubstantiated. This Appendix will add weight to those claims.

The second purpose is to compare the terms and concepts of ABP with similar terms and concepts in the planning literature. Chapter 1 introduced the basic terms and concepts of ABP. Succeeding chapters presented more precise definitions of those terms. But how are those and similar terms used in the literature? For example, is there anything in the literature similar to ABP? If not, what techniques are most like ABP? How and why might they differ? Where else are the terms and concepts of ABP used and how? What other terms and concepts in the literature are similar to ABP's?

In the vast literature on planning, there is no dearth of adjectives to be found in front of *planning*: Some address time or scope (*long-range, strategic*); others address the type of planning (*business, community, urban, transportation, military*); still others address the level at which the planning is done (*production, financial, capital, corporate, human resources, force*). Given that we have said that ABP is a tool that should be useful for any kind of planning, should all these areas of the literature be covered evenly?

Here, there is a reasonably clear answer with respect to time and scope: Because the roots of ABP are in strategic planning for the military, the birthplace of strategic planning,[1] the terms and concepts in ABP are more likely to be related to those of strategic planning than to those of any other type of planning. Our search through the planning literature generally concentrated on the strategic planning literature, with forays into the remaining planning literature. In what follows, I refer generally to the "planning literature" and use "strategic planning literature" to distinguish that literature specifically. Beyond that, ABP should be applicable to all types and levels of planning.

As with *planning*, the word *strategy* is used in widely different ways in the planning literature: regional strategy, marketing strategy, human

---

1   The word *strategy* derives from the Greek *strategos*, which originally denoted "general of the army." Paul Bracken has pointed out that the meaning of *strategos* has changed over the centuries, mirroring changes in the denotation of *strategic* to mean "the skills of the general," and then to mean "leadership (rhetoric), management, and bravery," implying that strategy was no longer confined to the general.

resources strategy, etc. The strategic planning literature we concentrated on related primarily to the highest level of planning in an organization, and related primarily to the fundamental purposes and plans of that organization.

The remainder of this Appendix, then, will be taken up first with the specific similarities and then with the differences between ABP and the general planning literature. To begin with, I want to give an overall impression of the overlap between ABP and the general planning literature.

OVERLAP BETWEEN ABP AND GENERAL PLANNING LITERATURE

There are three ways to get an impression of how much overlap there is between ABP and the general planning literature.

A direct measure

One reasonably direct measure of the overlap comes from considering what part of the planning process ABP is directed toward. Directed generally toward uncertainties, an unavoidable part of the planning process, ABP is directed specifically toward the uncertainties remaining in a plan that has already been developed. By far the more difficult part of the planning process comes in developing the plan in the first place. In that sense, ABP is akin to checking an answer after it has been devised.

Indeed, a quick review finds that a substantial segment of the literature is aimed not at problem checking but at new problem-solving techniques or ideas: topics such as Total Quality Management, benchmarking, time-based competition, outsourcing, partnering, reengineering, change management, and downsizing. These strategies, or "solutions," sometimes overlap ABP, but the extent of overlap is not large.

In addition to this more direct measure of the general overlap, there are two indirect means of gauging the overlap between ABP and the general planning literature.

Strategic planning habits

The first approximation uses the statistics gathered on the strategic planning habits of 113 firms in the United Kingdom (Glaister and Falshaw 1999). Several of the findings help suggest the relative demand for a tool like ABP. With respect to the firm's commitment to strategic planning, the data "indicate that firms appear to have a greater commitment to formulation aspects of strategy and relatively less commitment to the implementation and evaluation of strategy." With respect to emphasis on areas of strategic planning, the data show that "firms in the sample pay relatively little regard to assessing reasons for actual outcomes not matching anticipated outcomes, or to developing contingencies around these variances" (Glaister and Falshaw 1999: 112). In the question on use of tools and techniques of strategic analysis, only one tool (scenario construction) closely related to ABP was on the list, and the authors were surprised at how far down the list (11th out of 19) it finished.

The demand for tools to evaluate, improve, or monitor strategic plans appears to be lower than the demand for tools to generate such plans in the first place. To the extent, then, that the terms and concepts of ABP-like tools differ from those of tools used to generate strategies, we would expect a more limited overlap between ABP and the general planning literature.

The second indirect means of estimating the overlap between ABP and the general planning literature comes from Mintzberg's comprehensive review of the strategic planning literature since its inception in the early 1960s (1994b: especially 52). The review suggests a large planning literature devoted to what Ginter et al. (1985) found to be planning's underlying sequence of steps: mission, objectives, external analysis, internal analysis, development of strategic alternatives, strategy selection, implementation, and control of the strategy. There is some room for ABP in this sequence of steps—particularly in the implementation and control stages, a particularity that, again, suggests a more limited overlap.

* * * *

These three means of gauging the overlap between ABP and the general planning literature match our experience in looking through the literature. There is definitely an overlap between the terms and concepts of ABP and those of the general planning literature, but it is limited. However, because every term or concept of ABP can be found somewhere in the planning literature, the overlap that exists is worth discussing. Some of the overlaps, particularly in the area of scenarios, depend for their explication on the path we took in developing ABP. For that reason, it is useful, before proceeding, to review the origins of Assumption-Based Planning in some detail.

THE ORIGINS OF ASSUMPTION-BASED PLANNING

In 1987, two of us at RAND (Morlie Hammer Levin and I) were asked to assist the U.S. Army with its strategic planning, which at that point was split into two pieces: AirLand Battle Future, looking 15 years into the future, and Army 21, looking 30 years out. We were asked to assist with the 30-year look. The concept for Army 21 was to develop a "most-likely" world for 2017 (possibly with some excursions) and, from that, to develop a concept of operations.[2]

Even in the fairly stable geopolitical world of 1987, the idea of coming up with a "most-likely" world in 30 years seemed like a stretch, so we received permission to think about an alternative to the "most-likely" world approach. It was in thinking about that alternative approach that ABP came into being.

We started with the well-established idea of using a variety of scenarios to approach the uncertainty of a world 30 years in the future. But the question we struggled with was, "What's the best way to develop those alternative scenarios?" There were two classical approaches to developing scenarios at the time: (1) have futurologists develop a representative group of scenarios, and (2) scan the environment in several dimensions, pick out extremes in each dimension, and develop three worlds—a "worst-case world," a "best-case world," and a world in the middle.[3]

2   Of the military services, the Army is the one most driven by strategy. Army doctrine is an official, detailed document that describes the Army's strategy. Doctrine is developed by starting with a worldview and a concept of operations. That concept of operations is then subjected to rigorous review throughout the Army before it becomes doctrine. The Army uses that doctrine to inform the equipping and training of its forces, so the Army seriously follows through on its strategy.

3   This is a bit overstated. Starting with a set of dimensions and an understanding of the extremes in each dimension that could be reached by the planning time horizon, the subsequent development of scenarios was often a very subtle and intellectually rich exercise. Unfortunately, the results tended to be exactly three scenarios, which could then be easily put into

Examples of the first approach often led to difficulty relating the futurist-generated worlds to the mission of the organization. Examples of the second approach always seemed to leave uncomfortable questions about how to know which dimensions were most important and how far along each dimension to go in selecting a point for inclusion in a world. These difficulties led us to the idea of starting with the assumptions the Army was making about the world and asking which of those assumptions was most likely to change by 30 years out and what effect that change could have. We were encouraged in this endeavor because the AirLand Battle Future work that was looking 15 years out had been reasonably well documented.

We developed one scenario each for what we thought were the failures of the four most significant load-bearing and vulnerable assumptions the Army was making about the world. One of those scenarios was called "Gorbachev works." It took the Army assumption that the Soviet Union would continue to be the implacable foe of the United States into perpetuity. We "broke" that assumption by positing that Gorbachev's incipient *glasnost* and *perestroika* initiatives would really work to fundamentally change the nature of the Soviet Union. In that scenario, we did not foresee the fall of the Berlin Wall. However, as a consequence of Gorbachev's initiatives' working as planned, we did posit a significant rapprochement between the two Germanys. This was, itself, a definite break with writings at that time and a seriously different world for the Army.

Our draft report on this approach and its tentative results reached the desk of the colonel in charge of the Army 21 effort literally the week he cleaned out that desk because the Army had decided to concentrate its strategic planning efforts on the AirLand Battle Future work. With the fall of the Berlin Wall two years later, the Army again came calling and asked if we could resurrect the planning "methodology" we had developed in 1987 to assist them with planning in a radically different and more uncertain world. We did. Over the next 12 years, ABP evolved as we applied it to a variety of military and nonmilitary planning situations.

In writing up Assumption-Based Planning as a planning methodology we began to notice that its strengths were in plan testing, not in plan development. In this way, ABP diverged from the general planning lit-

"Goldilocks" order, leading to the canonical selection criterion, "always pick the one in the middle."

erature that was and is more taken up with *how* to plan or with the correct *kind* of plan/planning for a given situation. Yet, many of the concepts and means that we were using to test plans were similar to, or the same as, means that were used for plan development—although they might be used in different ways. We found that if we wrote up ABP as a planning tool, we could use some of the concepts from the planning literature in support of the tool and we could more easily compare ABP with those parts of the planning literature that were tool-oriented.

ABP AND THE PLANNING LITERATURE

I divide the discussion about Assumption-Based Planning and the planning literature into three major sections:

- ABP-like processes in the literature
- ABP concepts in the literature
- ABP words in the literature.

ABP-like processes in the literature

Our scans of the planning literature have produced two texts that deal with many of the same words and concepts as ABP.

"Maneuvering Through Shifting Terrain." The first example is strikingly similar to ABP and comes from a short chapter, "Maneuvering Through Shifting Terrain," in a book on strategic thinking by Wells (1998: 189–91). Several direct quotes from that chapter capture most of Assumption-Based Planning:

- "We never know the future with certainty, so we use assumptions to move past this and make decisions."
- "The whole trail of the strategic thinking cycle is littered with assumptions."
- "It is important to be absolutely explicit about assumptions to avoid the trap that happens so frequently in people's thinking—they forget that they made assumptions to arrive at their decisions and begin to believe they are operating by unalterable truths."
- "You want to have an assumption list, no matter now extensive."

- "Classify your assumptions using the degree of uncertainty you have about the assumption and the potential impact on your organization if the assumption is incorrect."

- "Clearly you want to look at the high-risk, high-impact assumptions first."

- "We probably want our strategy to be proactive. . . . [M]any of our actions, however, need to be reactive. . . ."

- "What we want to do is get an early warning system in place so that we react before it escalates into an insurmountable hazard."

- "Our thinking should prepare us to respond quickly to signs—observable facts or information—that alert us about a significant move by another player or an environmental shift that will render an assumption incorrect."

- "In addition, we want to go one step further and have some contingency plans—what we will do if a trigger alerts us to an upcoming change."

With the exception of shaping actions, Wells captures the basic elements of ABP in seven pages. He goes little further with them. However, as a description and defense of ABP, it is compact and unerring.

"Strategy Under Uncertainty." The other ABP-like process is less easily recognizable as such, but worth detailing. An article by Courtney et al. (1997) in the *Harvard Business Review* is a nice piece on strategic planning and uncertainty, beginning with uncertainty. It first sets up four levels of uncertainty about the future:

- Level 1 is a "clear enough future" to be able to develop a single forecast for the future that is accurate enough for strategy development.

- Level 2 permits the future to be described in a few alternate, discrete scenarios, such as when the future depends primarily on a regulatory decision or a primary competitor's strategy.

- At Level 3, a variety of alternative futures—defined by a number of key variables—can be identified, but the uncertainties range across a continuum.

- Level 4, called "true ambiguity," is described as rare, and is virtually impossible to predict.

Next, the authors describe three strategic postures—shaping, adapting, and reserving the right to play—and three portfolios of actions—big bets, options, and no-regrets moves. The authors then describe the different posture and action combinations that are most appropriate for each of the four levels of uncertainty about the future.

At Level 3 uncertainty, at which alternative futures can be defined by a few key variables, resonances with ABP are most easily perceived. Those who choose a shaping strategy here are taking actions to "move the market in a general direction." This strategy generally involves shaping actions—"big bets"—with few hedging actions. Both those who choose an adapting strategy and those who choose to reserve the right to play at Level 3 generally take a strategy of keeping their options open, primarily through hedging actions and identifying and monitoring trigger variables or market signals (or signposts) to tell them when and how the situation is clarifying.

The emphasis in the Courtney et al. work is on *making* strategy (including a portfolio of actions) rather than on testing or improving strategy. Further, their key variables are not quite the same as load-bearing, vulnerable assumptions, and what ABP would call shaping and hedging *actions* are split up among strategic postures and actions. Nonetheless, this discussion is full of elements that relate to load-bearing assumptions, signposts, and shaping and hedging actions in a way that pays particular attention to the uncertainty inherent in the planning situation.

This is a good example of how the same concepts and words can be used in slightly different ways.[4] Differences can arise either from differences in concepts or simply differences in word usage. Both kinds of differences are explored further below.

ABP concepts in the literature

At a second level of comparison of ABP and the planning literature are the basic concepts of ABP, which have been discussed in the preceding chapters. What follows is not a thorough recitation either of ABP's concepts or of similarities with those concepts to be found in the litera-

---

4   Moreover, while the handling of Level 3 uncertainty has parallels with ABP, the handling of Levels 1 and 2 might be improved through application of ABP.

ture. Rather, I chose the specific topics because they represent either a critical ABP concept or an important theme to be found in the wider planning literature (or both). My goal is to highlight both important concepts in ABP and in the wider literature.

"Strategic Control." Spurred by the rise in strategic planning, the field of strategic management has evolved into a distinct subdiscipline in management studies. Models of the strategic management process generally show three basic stages: strategy formulation, strategy implementation, and strategy evaluation or control. In the most general sense, strategic control is the feedback mechanism for the strategic management system. It compares strategic goals with progress and exposes shortcomings.

As well as asking whether satisfactory progress is being made toward strategic objectives, much of the literature also includes the element of asking whether the assumptions underlying the strategy are still valid. Schreyogg and Steinmann (1987: 95) identify three different kinds of strategic control mechanisms: premise control, implementation control, and strategic surveillance. They distinguish *implementation control*, which questions the basic direction of the strategy, from *operational control*, which questions whether the strategy implementation is proceeding as planned. *Premise control* checks whether the premises (or assumptions) that were set during the planning process are still valid. In addition, *strategic surveillance* is a wider scan designed to monitor the "full range of events inside and outside the enterprise which are likely to threaten the course of strategic action." Preble (1992: 402) adds a fourth mechanism, special alert control, to deal specifically with low-probability, high-impact threatening events. *Special alert control* includes monitoring for events such as natural disasters, hostile takeovers, court indictments, product defects, and the like.

Assumption-Based Planning has always been aimed more at premise control in this sense, but mainly through ignorance of these subtleties. Its wider interest is in behaving like the full-blown system that Schreyogg, Steinmann, and Preble outline. At this point, ABP explicitly ignores implementation control, but encompasses the other three aspects of this taxonomy.

Muralidharan (1997) also distinguishes between two types of strategic control, one of them similar to Schreyogg and Steinmann's operational control and the other focused on what Muralidharan calls "the control of the strategy content." The process for this second type of control is to "collect data to monitor the validity of planning assumptions and to identify opportunities/threats, interpret the data and respond to the information contained in the data." In its identification and monitoring of load-bearing, vulnerable assumptions, ABP clearly falls under this second type of strategic control.

Much the same way that ABP defines signposts and describes their utility, Lorange et al. (1986) define a *strategic control system* as "a system to support managers in assessing the relevance of the organization's strategy to its progress in the accomplishment of its goals, and when discrepancies exist, to support areas needing attention." Further, they distinguish between two types of strategic control, each of which has elements in common with ABP. The purpose of the first type, *strategic momentum control*, is "to reconfirm organizationally that the critical environmental assumptions behind the particular strategy are still valid." It is akin to premise control above. The purpose of the second type of strategic control for Lorange et al., *strategic leap control*, is to control the strategy by taking on the additional task of replanning it when one of the fundamental assumptions underlying the strategy has broken. One step of ABP is detecting when an assumption might break, but it stops short of strategic leap control. However, ABP uses some of the same techniques as strategic leap control (especially scenarios) to think about broken assumptions and identify actions that would better prepare the organization if the assumption did break.

Plans vs. "planning." ABP's primary emphasis is on testing and improving concrete manifestations of the "planning process": the plans. Although we have described how ABP might and might not be used in the planning process itself, the focus of ABP is clear: Its primary application is for analyzing plans and improving them.

Making a distinction between *plans* and *planning* may seem like a minor issue, but it speaks to deeper definitional issues, the debate over which is ongoing in the planning literature. The deeper disagreement is about where planning stops and programming starts—about where synthesis stops and analysis starts—an endless debate akin to those over strategy-tactics (where does strategy stop and tactics start?) and means-ends (where do means stop and ends start?).

In the field of strategic planning, Mintzberg has made an heroic attempt to answer the planning-programming question, arguing cogently in *The Rise and Fall of Strategic Planning* (1994b) that "strategic planning" has had it wrong since shortly after its early days. Claiming that much of what has historically been called strategic planning has really been strategic programming, he carefully distinguishes between strategy formation as *synthesis* and formal strategic planning (the part he calls "strategic programming"), which Mintzberg characterizes as *analysis,* which feeds the strategy formation process, abets it, and turns its creative output into concrete, realizable steps to implement the formed strategy.

We, as practitioners of ABP, are sympathetic with and mindful of this distinction between *synthesis* and *analysis.* ABP is primarily a tool for *analyzing* the results of a previous synthesis. ABP works to identify load-bearing, vulnerable assumptions in that synthesis and to strengthen their handling. In so doing, ABP may well *require* further synthesis (primarily in the form of shaping and hedging actions), but only *prepares* the way for that further synthesis (primarily through laying the foundations for and actually generating scenarios) and *encourages* that synthesis. It is in that specific way, then, that ABP deals with the planning-programming or synthesis-analysis debate evident in the planning literature.

Long-range vs. strategic vs. other planning. In a sense, ABP sidesteps the planning-programming conundrum by concentrating on analysis and encouragement of synthesis. There is another conundrum—most visible specifically in strategic planning—that ABP tries to shun entirely: planning time horizons. ABP claims to apply to all kinds of planning by accepting and dealing within whatever time horizon has been set by the plans it is analyzing. For financial plans, the implied or explicit time horizon is short and specific, usually measured in quarters of a year. On the other end of the time scale, strategic plans can range decades into the future: I have personally worked on a serious U.S. Air Force planning effort that looked 40 years into the future of space utilization.

The conundrum is not specifically about time horizons but about the reasons for looking out to a particular time horizon (or horizons, just to confuse the matter further). In the 1970s, planners began to explore the important difference between planning to a time horizon and addressing important issues that the organization may face out to that horizon. In simplified form, the conundrum can be seen in the overlap in Figure A.1.

There are good reasons both to think out to some point in the future and to think about those things that are most important to an organiza-

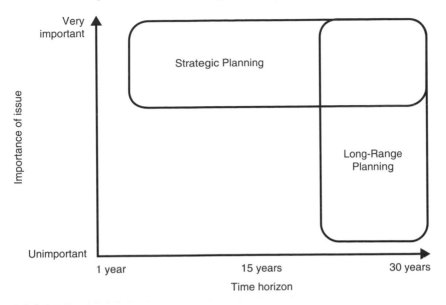

Figure A.1. Simplified Dimensions of Long-Range and Strategic Planning, for Comparison

tion, which can be well out in the future but affecting planning today. For some companies, "well out in the future" may be much less than 30 years. Whatever is specified as "well out in the future," it is important to make sure that such issues that impinge on planning today are considered. For public utilities, the costs and planning for major capital investments in infrastructure have effects 20 to 30 years or more in the future and are an important aspect of planning today. For a "dot com," a concern "well out in the future" may be the likelihood of a subsequent round of funding that is less than a year away. Nonetheless, it should be included in the planning.

In the late 1970s, a shift occurred in the planning literature from long-range planning, which focused on specific time horizons, to strategic planning, which focused more on the "big issues." People stopped worrying about detailed individual plans well into the future and started worrying more about the important issues facing the organization, regardless of their specific time horizons.

This shift in planning seems reasonable for a 30-year time horizon. However, as the time horizon is moved closer to today, the murkier the distinction becomes. At some point, an organization is going to have to work with both the important (broad) issues *and* detailed (specific) plans out to some time horizon. Where is that point? Five years? One year? And what happens to strategic planning at that point?

A specific answer depends, of course, on the exact nature of an enterprise. Part of Mintzberg's complaint is that formal strategic planning generally was becoming more like a mechanism for planning for individual details than it was about planning for the important issues. There seems to be an ongoing tension, in strategic planning, between planning for important issues and detailed planning. Mintzberg does not particularly condemn this tension. He asserts that part of strategy formation emerges from day-to-day operations; part of planning for issues emerges from the process of working with individual details. The trick is not to confuse one for the other.

In general, the question of planning for key issues as opposed to planning for details is one that ABP attempts to avoid entirely. ABP takes the position that *all* plans generally need to make some assumptions about the future, and all are thus vulnerable to surprise—particularly if they are not aware of, or have not taken steps to address, the vulnerability of the assumptions that have been made. By avoiding a conundrum that (unavoidably) affects a part of planning to which ABP does not speak, ABP tries *not* to fit into the planning literature.

Emphasizing uncertainties in planning. ABP concentrates on the uncertainties of a plan. Its goal is to make explicit, plan for, and track all the important uncertainties—behaviors that are generally avoided, according to Chesnutt (1992: 3 ff.):

- "Stakeholders wanting to advance the cause of action have strong incentives to understate uncertainty."

- "Many . . . professions share the common approach of coping with uncertainty by seeking it out, attempting to destroy it, and ignoring what remains."

- "Even the casual empiricist would have to admit that feigned certainty is a wildly popular coping strategy to deal with an uncertain world."

Chesnutt, who advocates the need to market uncertainty, then suggests a variety of means for "repackaging" uncertainty so that people will pay more attention to it. One of those means is as anxiety reduction: "Explain the value of converting unknown threats into known ones: known threats can be hedged against, unknown threats can only give ulcers."

While Chesnutt overstates the avoidance of uncertainty for dramatic effect, there is certainly evidence of uncertainty-avoidance in a good deal of planning and in the planning literature. However, specific areas of the literature concentrate expressly on uncertainty. The entire field of decision analysis, for example, pays particular attention to uncertainty and how to handle it in making decisions. Classic texts include Raiffa (1968; reissued 1997) and March (1994).

The uncertainty in decision analysis is slightly different from the uncertainty that occupies ABP. ABP specifically aims to identify, and may have its greatest utility in identifying, implicit assumptions that frequently have major implications for an organization and its decisions. Beyond that, ABP is more interested in seeing how the uncertainties in the decision have been handled and in monitoring those uncertainties—and perhaps in adding elements to the decision to better shape and hedge the uncertainties.

Decision analysis is more concerned with taking the uncertainties into account in making the decision (plan) in the first place. If the decision needs to be remade (replanned), new information on the uncertainties is taken into account in making the new decision. With respect to replanning, ABP is more interested in checking to see when a new decision might need to be made and in trying to postpone the need to make new decisions by making the current decisions more robust.

Another entire area that arguably emphasizes uncertainty is scenario planning. In the most complete explication of it, van der Heijden (1996) says, "Scenario planning distinguishes itself from other more traditional approaches to strategic planning through its explicit approach toward ambiguity and uncertainty in the strategic question." He echoes Chesnutt when he says,

> The traditional approach tries to eliminate uncertainty from the strategic equation, by the assumption of the existence of "experts" who have privileged knowledge about "the most likely future," and who can assess the probabilities of specific outcomes. Scenario planning assumes that there is irreducible uncertainty and ambiguity in any situation faced by the strategist, and that successful strategy can only be developed in full view of this.

In much the same way that decision analysis does, the scenarios in scenario planning are used to help *create* robust plans (or, more specifically in van der Heijden, to create a robust Business Idea—a concept more akin to a vision for the organization). Another aspect of scenario planning is that it is part of a learning loop that continuously compares the Business Idea with real-world results, so there is an element of learning to scenario planning that is generally missing from decision analysis discussions. In the learning loop, the (potentially new) scenarios are again used to create and/or update the Business Idea.

In addition to decision analysis and scenario planning, other instances in the planning literature emphasize uncertainty (the Courtney et al. (1997) article cited earlier in this Appendix being a good example). Indeed, uncertainty rarely goes *unacknowledged*. Although rarely emphasized as much as in ABP, uncertainty and the role it plays in all forms of planning appear, in fact, to be growing in prominence, dominating the "dot-com" world of the Internet. The world's militaries have clearly faced different and greater uncertainties since 1989 and the disintegration of the Soviet Union than they had during the Cold War. Further, the planning literature is beginning to respond. Harvard Business School Press has, for example, repackaged a series of its historical articles (including the Courtney et al. article) under the title *Harvard Business Review on Managing Uncertainty* (1999).

How government planning handles uncertainty is also receiving growing attention. One means of governmental planning that has several aspects in common with ABP is a method its authors call "Uncertainty Sensitive Planning" (for further details on this method, see Bracken 1990; Davis 1994b, 1989; Davis, Gompert, and Kugler 1996; and Davis and Khalilzad 1990). Its components are as follows:

- Describe the emerging core environment and major uncertainties, particularly in the form of scheduled uncertainties that can be thought of as future branch points, and unscheduled uncertainties in the form of potential shocks.

- Develop a set of alternative grand strategies.

- For each grand strategy, develop a core strategy, an environment-shaping strategy, and a hedging strategy.

- Compare the grand strategies in a summary framework based on differentiating attributes of strategy.

- Consider ways to integrate some of the strategies by exploiting the willingness of proponents of all strategies to acknowledge the need to adapt strategy over time.

Uncertainty Sensitive Planning introduced "environment-shaping strategy" into the government and had an important influence on the Quadrennial Defense Review of 1997 (Cohen 1997).

Also of renewed interest is the notion that the business world is changing so rapidly that the speed of change itself affects uncertainties. D'Aveni (1994) argues that we are entering a new era of "hypercompetition" in which even "certainties" are changing so rapidly that new approaches are required for handling uncertainty. He argues that four kinds of changes—customer changes, including fragmenting tastes; rapid technological change; falling geographic and industry boundaries as markets globalize; and deep pockets among competitors as a result of the rise of giant global conglomerates in a variety of industries—make it impossible to sustain any advantage once gained. His solution[5] is not as important as his inferring that any assumptions made about the future can be overtaken with breathtaking speed. This inference reinforces ABP notions of paying attention to uncertainty and to monitoring uncertainties that are important to the success of a plan.

Planning methodology vs. planning tool. We have described ABP as a tool for testing and improving plans, as though the designation "tool" was important. It is generally more important to us than it is to the rest of the planning literature, primarily because we specifically restricted ABP's utility as a means of developing plans or doing planning in order to enhance its ability to be used to test and improve plans, as discussed in Chapter 9.

The concept of a planning tool can be found in the literature but is commonly lumped together with planning techniques and methodologies. Glaister and Falshaw (1999), for example, asked businesses in the United Kingdom about the strategic planning tools and techniques they used without distinguishing between them, usually referring to both interchangeably. As another example, Courtney et al. (1997: 78), at the tail end of their article, discuss the need for a "more comprehensive strategy tool kit" and recommend adding scenario planning, game the-

---

5   The solution is codified in *Seven S*'s: stakeholder satisfaction, strategic soothsaying, speed, surprise, signals, shifting the rules, and simultaneous or sequential strategic thrusts.

ory, system dynamics, agent-based models, and real options to that "tool" kit.

The issue of "tools" per se has also been at least partially addressed in the literature. Mintzberg (1994b: 50) quotes Peter Drucker as saying that strategic planning "is not a box of tricks, a bundle of techniques." The "tricks and techniques" Drucker addresses are tools for *doing* planning, not, as with ABP, for testing or improving plans. However, as Paul Bracken (private communication) has said,

> While Professor Drucker has a point, it is our experience that tricks and tools often have their greatest value-added as a checklist, much like the checklist a pilot ticks off before a takeoff. All too often there is something "missed" on the checklist. Such "gaffes" are obvious in retrospect. But this doesn't mean they are always caught in time. In this sense, tools (whether checklists or ABP) can be extremely useful.

In general, the "tools" to be found in the literature refer to self-contained and separable parts of planning methods or processes. For example, scenario planning, which is used to develop a greater sensitivity to uncertainty in the process of developing a strategy, might be classified as a "tool" (if it were classified at all). SWOT analysis, which identifies an organization's strengths, weaknesses, threats, and opportunities, is sometimes actually referred to as a planning tool.

In any case, the distinction that ABP makes between a planning methodology and a planning tool is not so clearly made in the rest of the planning literature. For clarity, we might wish that it were.

Identifying key assumptions. The heart of ABP is identifying the load-bearing, vulnerable assumptions that underlie an organization's plans. All else in ABP follows from those key assumptions. Identifying key assumptions and issues is a common concept in the planning literature, but generally takes a different form according to whether it is done in the middle of planning or at the end of the planning cycle. Both forms are worth relating to ABP's concepts, starting with identifying key assumptions at the end of the planning cycle.

Of the two most explicit treatments in the literature of identifying key load-bearing, vulnerable assumptions at the end of the planning cycle, one preceded our development of ABP and the other derived directly from ABP. The latter surveyed how the business community identified and dealt with load-bearing, vulnerable assumptions.

The first treatment comes from the Strategic Assumption Surfacing and Testing (SAST) planning process (Mason and Mitroff 1981: 18), whose developers share our view on the centrality of assumptions in planning: "complex problems depend in countless ways on a host of critical assumptions" and "[M]ost policymakers are unaware of the fact that much of their action rests on assumptions and, moreover, they are unaware of the particular set of assumptions they hold." Further, Mason and Mitroff have a rigorous scheme for surfacing the assumptions underlying a given strategy. The SAST scheme is described in some detail in Chapter 3.

Interestingly, SAST starts out exactly the way ABP does, by identifying the important and uncertain assumptions underlying an extant strategy candidate. Unlike ABP, its purpose is specifically about planning. SAST actually starts with three strategy candidates for the same organization and assigns a team to each. Each team identifies the important, uncertain assumptions underlying its own candidate. SAST then brings the teams together in a structured way to hammer out a consensus set of the most important, uncertain assumptions. They then develop a compromise strategy to address those assumptions. However, the process all starts from the identification of the most important, uncertain assumptions underlying an extant strategy.

The second direct treatment of important, vulnerable assumptions comes from the Corporate Strategy Board's *Proceeding in Daylight: Frontier Practices for Challenging Strategic Assumptions* (1999). From research conducted among more than 150 companies, that work had the specific intent of identifying best practices in successfully challenging strategic assumptions. The assumption-challenging practices are divided into four intellectual tasks, the fourth of which illuminates the overall goal: to assist an executive team in creating "new sets of assumptions to guide future company strategy." Granted, this task directly supports planning, but the first intellectual task is to "force a highly explicit restatement of foundational assumptions underlying current company strategy." These are the important, vulnerable assumptions in an extant strategy, and the study discusses four distinct best practices for identifying them. All four practices are discussed in Chapter 3. One of the four practices is SAST, which, as described above, identifies the most important, uncertain assumptions. The other three do not directly identify important, vulnerable assumptions, but they do identify the *issues* that are most important to an organization. The manner in which one of the methods does so forms a nice segue into a discussion of the slight change observable in the literature when the focus shifts from an extant plan or strategy to planning itself.

In the Annual Key Bets Contract method described in the report, the goal is to identify the key issues facing the organization. The means for doing so were described in Chapter 3. What is important here is that the goal of the Key Bets method is to identify key issues rather than key assumptions. What is the difference?

In a sense, issues are "pre-assumptions." *Issues* are uncertainties about the future that are important to the organization. That is, they are important, uncertain elements of the future. Key issues are the starting point of most planning methodologies. Their connection with load-bearing, vulnerable assumptions can be seen quite clearly in the Key Bets method. Given the important, vulnerable issues facing the organization, this method leads the organization to make "bets" about how those issues will turn out. A key issue might be whether "Russia resumes export of a competing product" and a key bet would be that it would not. This key bet is then automatically a load-bearing, vulnerable assumption of the resulting strategy. Implicitly, then, the Key Bets method produces load-bearing, vulnerable assumptions.

This relationship between key issues and load-bearing, vulnerable assumptions is an important one and will be discussed further below, in the "Assumptions" subsection.

Developing a monitoring system. ABP's position on monitoring systems is clear: The load-bearing, vulnerable assumptions underlying a plan hold the greatest potential for surprise. The best means of preparing for that kind of surprise is to set up and monitor a system of signposts that warn when events may be invalidating a load-bearing, vulnerable assumption.

To understand how the concept of warning systems appears in the planning literature, I distinguish between two parts of a plan: the planning actions and those aspects of the future that gave rise to the actions. That is, a plan contains actions that make up a general solution to the problem, "What should we do about the world as it is and might become to achieve our goals?" There are assumptions in the plan, then, both about what the world is and might be like, and about what it will take to successfully deal with that world. In developing monitoring systems, the planning literature is generally more concerned with warning systems aimed at whether the planning actions are having the desired effect than it is about systems aimed at whether the world is behaving as assumed.

A good example of this preference can be found in Discovery-Driven Planning (McGrath and MacMillan 1999). This planning method (discussed in Chapter 3) is aimed at new business ventures for which there are many unknowns. Through the use of a "reverse income statement," Discovery-Driven Planning derives all the activities required to run the new venture and a set of minimum performance measures (which then become the assumptions of the plan) required to achieve an acceptable level of profitability. It then sets up a monitoring system to carefully track all the performance assumptions. A shortfall in any performance assumption is cause for serious concern.

Note that there is no apparent concern for what is happening in the world, except through the performance assumptions. In this sense, Discovery-Driven Planning does not seem to care what is going on in the world. In the extreme, the world could change completely and, if the performance assumptions were being met, the plan would not notice. Similarly, the world could play out just as the planners might hope, but if a performance assumption fails to hold or obtain, serious changes may need to be made.

This is an extreme example of most financial plans. The focus of financial plans is ultimately the performance of the plan elements, not the performance of the assumptions about the world that led to the plan elements. In Discovery-Driven Planning, the performance assumptions are set up as minimum-allowable performance standards: Anything short of those standards brings the entire viability of the planned enterprise into question and signals an important decision point (in this sense, they are very much like ABP signposts associated with load-bearing, vulnerable assumptions).

Generally, it makes sense for an organization to pay more attention to the performance of its plan elements than to changes in the world that might affect that performance. The performance of its planning actions *should* be a primary concern, but not the *only* concern. It is clear from the Corporate Strategy Board's work on stall points that failing to monitor assumptions about the world can deny the organization a chance to catch a planning surprise in the making. ABP, of course, advocates monitoring all the load-bearing, vulnerable assumptions whether they are about the world or about the organization's planned actions for handling that world.

The monitoring systems mentioned in the Wells quotes earlier in this Appendix make it clear that some writers in the literature, especially the strategic control literature, are aware of the need to monitor the wider set of assumptions made in the formation of a plan or strategy. The importance of monitoring is also clear in the work of the Corporate Strategy Board, which documents no fewer than five "best practice" monitoring systems—Critical Issue Monitoring, Risk Outlook Committee, Real-Time Market Briefings, Web-Enabled Signposting, and Trajectory Mapping—all aimed specifically at external parameters and/or events. Without going into details, I note that the names themselves suggest a variety of approaches about both what and how to monitor.

Further evidence of this kind of strategic control can be found elsewhere in the planning literature. In his article about the dynamics of strategy, Markides (1999: 61) says that the first step in preparing for the "inevitable strategic innovation that will disrupt a company's market" is to "[B]uild an early monitoring system to identify turning points before a crisis occurs," emphasizing that the company should "regularly monitor indicators of *strategic* rather than *financial* health" [emphasis in the original]. In their book on scenario learning, Fahey and Randall (1997: 4) suggest one of the indications that scenario learning is taking place in an organization is when the organization "scans changes in the environment to determine whether further strategy change or adaptation is required."

Recent works on adaptive organizations—those designed to adapt more quickly and incrementally to changes in the external environment than traditional organizations—suggest that signposts as a monitoring technique are "old think" and that companies need something different in today's constantly changing business environment. Even so, the system recommended by Haeckel and Slywotzky (1999), for example, monitors the external environment, although in a somewhat less structured way than signposting. More so than ever, these works suggest the need to sense and interpret[6] data, which are at the heart of any mon-

---

6 Sense-and-interpret is part of a SIDA (sense, interpret, decide, act) system and is akin to the military OODA (observe, orient, decide, act) system and similar systems such as the SIER (sense, interpret, evaluate, respond) model. Another similar construct is the learning loop of scenario planning (see van der Heijden 1996), which can be broken down roughly into observation, reflection, formation and testing of concepts, and implementation/concrete experience.

itoring system. Signposts are simply a predetermined set of interpretations used to help with the sense-and-interpret function of any monitoring system.

Another thread in the literature from the 1980s that relates to monitoring systems centered around Strategic Issue Analysis (SIA) and Strategic Issues Management (SIM). Strategic Issue Analysis (King 1982) seeks to break down strategic issues (those that are "important," about which there is "controversy," and that have "strategic impact") into successively more specific categories so that data might be collected and assessed. Strategic Issues Management (Ansoff 1980: 134) "is a systematic procedure for *early* identification and *fast* response to important trends and events both inside and outside an enterprise" [emphasis in the original]. SIM is the wider system for periodically reviewing and updating a key strategic issues list. Its proposed intent was to "prevent strategic surprises and respond to threats/opportunities" (Ansoff 1980: 132).

Finally, monitoring of the environment may be on the rise in businesses. The president of a futures organization is quoted in the Corporate Study Board report (1999: 207), "We have long advocated the systematic monitoring of one's environment for trigger events and trends that indicate a need for a modification in a company's strategic direction. It's encouraging to see that management—at least in some cases—is coming around to this critical addition to the planning cycle" (Corporate Strategy Board 1999: 207).

Making plans robust. The stated goal of ABP—to reduce the potential for, and consequences of, surprises to an organization's plan—is to make the plan more robust and adaptive, a goal quite common in the planning literature. But the approach ABP takes is not common. Perhaps the best way to distinguish ABP's approach from the general approach is to say that ABP's approach is to make plans robust, whereas the more common approach is to make robust plans. If that makes the difference seem subtle, the practical implications are less so.

Every good planner works to make robust plans in the face of uncertainties. This is most evident in decision analysis. Recall that decision analysis pays particular attention to uncertainty and how to handle it during the making of decisions. If the decisions need to be revisited, the implication in decision analysis is that they should be revisited using decision analysis again. Left out of the decision analysis approach is consideration of how to know it is time to redecide. Decision analysis is just about the decisionmaking process itself, and is one approach to making plans robust.

If decision analysis is about taking a step back from the planning process to think about uncertainty, another step back is to the more general topic of risk management. At its most fundamental level, making a plan robust is about managing the risks inherent in the plan. In his bestselling and award-winning book on risk, Bernstein (1996)[7] says that while the concept of risk goes back indefinitely, the notion that risk can be understood and measured, and its consequences weighed, was revolutionary and distinguishes modern times from the past.

A more contemporary approach to making strategies robust is suggested by Microsoft's booth at Comdex 1998, as described in Chapter 6. To recall, it displayed Microsoft's second version of Windows, but it also had displays of DOS version 4.0; OS/2 (which it was developing with IBM); new versions of Word, Excel, and other applications for the Macintosh; and a Unix system developed by SCO. Beinhocker (1999) suggests that Microsoft was revealing a very robust strategy that would pay off no matter what happened in the Windows-DOS and OS/2-Mac-Unix battles. Beinhocker goes on to suggest the formation of a population of strategies in much the same way that Microsoft did as a means of providing a robust, adaptive approach to the future. One of the questions he explicitly asks about a candidate population of strategies is, "Does the population includes shaping, hedging, and no-regrets moves?"

Beinhocker also values scenarios in the creation of robust, adaptive strategies. This use of scenarios is echoed in scenario planning. For example, van der Heijden (1996) talks about using scenarios as a test bed for policies and plans—much, as he says, like using a wind tunnel to test aerodynamic designs, with the goal of producing more robust designs.

As suggested by Wells (1998), another means for building strategies robust is to develop contingency plans. This is a popular means for tactical planning in the military and can be found in some of the business literature as well. *Contingency plans* are actions to be taken in the event that something goes wrong. Their relation to hedging actions is explored further below. Here, they provide a plan with actions to take

---

7 Bernstein's book was on *Business Week*, *New York Times Business*, and *USA Today* bestseller lists and won the Edwin G. Booz Prize in 1997 for the most insightful, innovative management book.

in contingent situations, which in itself makes a plan more robust to uncertainty.

To bring this discussion full circle, ABP's goal of making plans robust should result in robust plans. Thus, ABP becomes one of several means identifiable in the literature for making plans robust. If there is a notable difference between ABP and other approaches, it is that ABP is designed to act at the end of the planning process; the others generally act during the process.

Planning in uncertain times. Businesses are accustomed to planning in uncertain conditions, but the magnitude of those uncertainties varies with time and enterprise. One of the best things about the Courtney et al. article, "Strategy Under Uncertainty" (1997), discussed above, is that it breaks down uncertainty into different levels, with appropriate planning means for each level. When times change, uncertainties change; when uncertainties change, they may change enough to require different planning means. This was certainly true in our work with the U.S. Army both just before and after the collapse of the Soviet Union. Before 1989, the Army was faced with greater uncertainty in looking 30 years out than it was willing to admit, a misunderstanding of uncertainty that led to the development of Assumption-Based Planning. However, what encouraged the Army to pay attention to ABP's handling of uncertainty was the collapse of the Soviet Union in 1989 and the concomitant jump in uncertainty (not to be confused with the significant drop in danger) that it then faced. ABP became a planning tool not just for the uncertainty of the long range future but for the uncertainty of the much-closer-range future as well. Part of the challenge of developing ABP for the Army was helping the Army realize just how much more uncertain the times had become. Part of the utility of ABP was in making concrete and compelling the uncertainties the Army now faced.

In much the same way, the Courtney et al. article helps businesses think differently about the particularly profound uncertainty that they face in thinking about doing business on the World Wide Web. In a similar vein, in 1966 James R. Schlesinger (before he was Secretary of Defense) tried to help the Defense Department change its thinking about how much certainty there was in its planning.

Schlesinger, then at RAND, wrote a paper on defense planning (1966) that distinguished between Cook's tour planning and Lewis and Clark's tour planning. In *Cook's tour planning*, the future was sufficiently certain that one could chart a straight course years in advance, the way Captain Cook did in circumnavigating the globe. By contrast, *Lewis and Clark's tour planning* "acknowledges that many alternative courses of action and forks in the road will appear, but their precise character and timing cannot be anticipated." The choice between straightforward planning and planning that factors in alternatives should be determined by the magnitude of uncertainties about the future. Even as far back as as 1966, Schlesinger thought the DoD should be doing Lewis and Clark's tour planning. He went on to advocate "(1) facing uncertainties (i.e., not pushing them aside) and (2) hedging against uncertainties." Also, "[A]ttention should be given to the flagging of decision points and the building in of options." Finally, the measure of success of doing Lewis and Clark's tour planning was "to stumble fewer times and in less important ways than one's national rivals."

We were pointed toward Schlesinger's article well into our work on ABP, but it was striking to find the echoes of ABP in his planning suggestions for uncertain times. He urges facing uncertainties rather than shrinking from them; explicitly mentions hedging actions; talks about flagging decision points (ABP's signposts); and recognizes that the ultimate goal is to reduce surprises rather than hoping or expecting to eliminate them.

ABP words in the literature

The third level at which to compare ABP with the literature is at the level of words. ABP uses specific words—carefully defined—that can be found in the planning literature. Those words may be used in very much the same way or in slightly different ways in the wider literature, and different words may be used in the literature that mean the same or similar things. This section explores the major ABP words and their use in ABP; their use in the wider literature; similar or different words used in the literature that mean generally the same thing as the ABP words; and words commonly used in the literature that are related to ABP words.

Assumptions. As defined formally in Chapter 2, an *assumption* is a judgment about the future that a planner makes during the process of deciding what actions to take to affect that future. From the Wells quote earlier, "[W]e never know the future with certainty, so we use assumptions to move past this and make decisions." Assumptions, then, are ubiquitous in planning.

They are almost as ubiquitous in the planning literature. From earlier, we have seen them discussed at some length by Wells, Drucker, McGrath and MacMillan, Mason and Mitroff, and in the Corporate Strategy Board report. It is more common to see assumptions explicitly acknowledged, but only in passing, with phrases such as, ". . . challenging the existing operating assumptions . . ." or ". . . and the implicit assumptions they make about their industry, technologies, and the economy . . ." or ". . . to make explicit the assumptions that key employees have about . . ." and then never see assumptions explicitly mentioned again.

However, it is rare to see any word in the planning literature used in place of *assumption*. The exception that proves the rule is Simpson's (1998a,b) insightful two-part article reflecting on the practical aspects of strategic planning. In it, he mentions words such as *beliefs, truths,* and *facts,* which could substitute for *assumptions*. In decision analysis, assumptions are akin to rational choices and a nice alternative to *assumptions* about the world might be *strategic choices* (Child 1972, as quoted in Wilson et al. 1996). In strategic control, they are referred to as *premises*.

The idea that an assumption is related to a strategic choice brings in a concept common in the planning literature that is similar to, but used slightly differently than, an assumption: an issue or an uncertainty about which an assumption could be made.

As above, an *issue* or *uncertainty* can be thought of as part of the strategic problem to be solved. Making an assumption about that issue and planning for that assumption is one way to deal with that issue. Another is to adopt temporizing measures and to wait and see how the issue or uncertainty evolves. An issue, then, may or may not lead to an assumption. Further, not all assumptions will come from the issues that have been identified for a given planning effort. Some assumptions will come from old issues that have not been resolved; other assumptions will be implicit and thus derived from "forgotten" issues.

That said, it is typical to make assumptions about issues and to plan on that basis. This tendency draws a strong connection between load-bearing, vulnerable assumptions and what the literature refers to generally as *key* issues.

Load-bearing and vulnerable assumptions. Load-bearing, vulnerable assumptions are assumptions that are both important to the success of the plan and uncertain enough to threaten the success of the plan. Most of the literature that discusses assumptions at any length eventually gets around to some concept of load-bearing and vulnerability, although by differing names. In SAST, they are called the *important, uncertain assumptions*; Wells calls them *high-impact, high-risk assumptions*; in the Corporate Strategy Board report (1999) they are referred to as being of *high importance* and *high uncertainty of understanding.*

The more common notion in planning is not load-bearing, vulnerable assumptions, but key issues or uncertainties. The issues are *key* both because of their uncertainty and because of the sense that they are the most important determinants of the organization's future. In a sense, then, they are the load-bearing, vulnerable *issues* facing planners.

Many planning methodologies start with some variation of key issues. The opportunities (O) and threats (T) of SWOT analysis, for example, are key issues, as are the driving forces of Driving Force Analysis (Christensen 1997). Other methods refer to "critical" issues. In the Annual Key Bets Contract mentioned earlier, the first part of the process is a thorough search for the key uncertainties facing the company. The second part of the process is about negotiating key bets to be made against these key uncertainties, and, as above, this is the connection with load-bearing, vulnerable assumptions.

As soon as a plan or strategy makes a bet or a strategic choice on a key issue, that bet or choice becomes a load-bearing, vulnerable assumption. There is not a one-to-one correspondence between key issues and load-bearing, vulnerable assumptions, but the overlap is generally large—so large, in fact, that one way to translate issues into assumptions (as described in Chapter 3) is to look in the plan for how an issue has been handled. In many cases, an assumption will have been made and planned for.[8] Key issues, then, are a common element in the planning literature. Although they are not the same as load-bearing, vulnerable assumptions, they are to planning what load-bearing, vulnerable assumptions are to plans.

Signposts. Signposts in ABP are the parts of a strategic monitoring system that indicate a significant change in the validity or vulnerability

---

8   If the organization has *not* placed a bet on a given key issue, it certainly is not off the hook. It should have at least taken temporizing action on that issue or its plan is incomplete—a point also discussed in Chapter 3.

of load-bearing, vulnerable assumptions. They can be either specific events or trends that have reached a critical level.

Even in the limited literature on strategic control, the word *signpost* rarely appears. What does appear is usually something more focused than a signpost. The Corporate Strategy Board (1999: 42) captures this difference in its definitions of signposts and tripwires:

> *Signposts*—Measurable phenomena or events that serve to validate or invalidate certain assumptions or to act as harbingers [of] specific scenarios. Companies define signposts to facilitate the monitoring of critical external factors; changes in the signposts indicate important changes in global assumptions or scenarios.

> *Tripwires*—Threshold levels determined for each signpost indicate certain assumptions are being invalidated or certain scenarios are unfolding. Companies use tripwires as objective warning signs to indicate that certain phenomena or events have progressed sufficiently (beyond the threshold level) to warrant immediate review or action.

It is tripwires that are more often found in the literature. Wells (1998) calls them *key events*; Muralidharan (1997) calls them *triggers*; Markides (1999) calls them *turning points*; and Fahey and Randall (1997) refer to identifying "appropriate indicators to track."

The signposts in ABP are meant more as true signposts on the highway, to include indicating both a general change in direction (a la the Corporate Strategy Board's signposts) as well as the arrival at a destination (a la the Corporate Strategy Board's tripwires).

Shaping and hedging. In ABP, *shaping actions* are actions to be taken to control the vulnerability of a load-bearing, vulnerable assumption. *Hedging actions* are actions to be taken to better prepare the organization in case such an assumption fails despite attempts at control.

Often found together in the planning literature, shaping and hedging are more often in the older literature, and in military or geopolitical planning literature. In some of the business literature, *shaping* and *hedging* are associated with planning actions. For example, among the questions Beinhocker (1999) asks about the robustness and adaptability of plans is whether a population of strategies includes "shaping, hedging, and no-regrets moves." Particularly in the more recent literature, there is greater emphasis on shaping and hedging as general strategies than as types of planning actions, but the intentions are the same. So, for example, Bracken (1990) talks about a core strategy, an environment-shaping strategy, and a hedging strategy.

With regard to strategies, other variations in the terms and concepts used can also be found. Courtney et al. (1997: 74), for example, talk about three kinds of strategic postures: shaping, adapting, and reserving the right to play. *Adapting* reacts to current market conditions and opportunities, while *reserving the right to play* is described as a special form of adapting that involves "making incremental investments today that put a company in a privileged position." ABP would consider both of these hedging actions (and would appreciate the distinction).

Hedging is more often found by itself in the literature than is *shaping*. Hedging strategies are particularly prominent in the investment (or portfolio planning) literature and in the geopolitical literature. However, while most of the strategies mentioned in the planning literature, such as Total Quality Management, benchmarking, time-based competition, and outsourcing, could, in fact, be argued to be shaping strategies, they are rarely referred to as such.

One variation of hedging actions, contingency plans, can also be found in the literature, prominent particularly in the military planning literature but also in the business literature, and particularly in strategic management and strategic control. *Contingency plans* are generally thought of as plans to be implemented once a trigger or tripwire event occurs—a slight, but important, difference from hedging actions, which are meant to be taken *today* or in the current operations cycle to better prepare the organization for the potential failure of a load-bearing, vulnerable assumption. The philosophy of a hedging action is to make current planned actions more robust. The same is generally true of contingency plans. As Markides (1999: 62) puts it, "Among equally capable generals, the one with the best contingency plans will usually win the battle." Contingency plans are hedging actions in that sense, but are generally only appropriate if a signpost has been passed or a trigger event fires, as discussed at some length in Chapter 7.

Another slightly different use of contingency plans can be found in Uncertainty Sensitive Planning, mentioned earlier in this Appendix, in which Davis (1989: 3; see also March and Simon 1993) uses two different kinds of uncertainties—scheduled and unscheduled uncertainties. *Scheduled uncertainties* can also be thought of as *branch-point uncertainties*, or uncertainties whose possibilities can be foreseen reasonably well. For example, we do not know what will happen with North

Korea, but we know the choices reasonably well: It could disintegrate, unite with South Korea, or hang on. These three choices can be dealt with by means of contingency actions predicated on a change, or branch, in North Korea's future. *Unscheduled uncertainties* are more akin to ABP uncertainties, requiring hedging actions.

Scenarios. ABP uses scenarios primarily to help develop hedging actions. Scenarios, which are generated from broken load-bearing, vulnerable assumptions, are a means of bringing a plausible plan-threatening situation into vivid focus, to better engage planners in devising actions for inclusion in the current plan to improve organizational preparations for potential assumption failures.

Originally developed as planning aids at RAND in the 1950s, scenarios stayed in the realm of military and geopolitical planning until Pierre Wack and the planners at Royal Dutch/Shell transformed them into a business planning tool with demonstrable benefits. Since then, scenario planning has become a visible part of the planning literature and landscape, and anything that uses scenarios in planning tends to get labeled "scenario planning" (probably to its and scenario planning's mutual detriment).

Part of the problem is that scenarios are used for a variety of purposes. For example, van der Heijden (1996) talks about five distinct uses for scenarios. In addition to their first, earlier-mentioned use as a test bed for strategy candidates, he cites using them for stretching mental models as a means of leading to discoveries, for enhancing corporate perceptions about the future, for energizing management, and for use by top management to provide leadership to the organization. All these uses are basically in the service of improving strategic planning or decisionmaking, but lead to a variety of subtle differences in the way scenarios are discussed in the literature. Another interesting use of scenarios is "The Day After . . ." methodology (Molander, Riddle, and Wilson 1996) described in Chapter 7. During Step One of the exercise ("The Day of . . ."), participants are presented with a change or foreshadowed change in the current situation. Step Two contains "The Day After . . .", during which the participants are faced with a major strategic event or disaster. Participants spend a significant amount of time dealing with the consequences of the event. Step Three returns to "The Day Before . . ." and gives participants a chance to consider measures that could be taken in the near future to avert such a crisis.

Further, a variety of means is mentioned in the literature for how to develop scenarios. Most of that literature is applicable to the scenarios of ABP, given that the starting point in ABP is a broken assumption. In addition, once developed, the ABP scenarios are useful for the other purposes to which scenarios can be put, but, again, their primary function is in support of developing appropriate hedging actions.

The development of scenario planning has done one thing in the literature: It has standardized usage around the word *scenario*. *Worlds* in the earlier literature (particularly in the military literature) and *environments* have faded into disuse.

Bibliography

Ansoff, I. H., "Strategic Issues Management," *Strategic Management Journal* 1 (1980): 131–48.

Ascher, William, and William H. Overholt, *Strategic Planning and Forecasting: Political Risk and Economic Opportunity*, New York: John Wiley & Sons, 1983.

Ayres, R. U., *Technological Forecasting and Long-Range Planning*, New York: McGraw-Hill, 1969.

Baets, Walter, "Corporate Strategic Planning in an Uncertain Environment," *European Journal of Operational Research*, 32 (1986): 169–81.

Barnett, W. P., and R. A. Burgelman, "Evolutionary Perspectives on Strategy," *Strategic Management Journal*, 17 (1996): 5–19.

Bartlett, C. A., and S. Ghosal, "Changing the Role of Top Management: Beyond Strategy to Purpose," *Harvard Business Review* (November/December 1994): 79–88.

Beinhocker, Eric D., "Robust Adaptive Strategies," *Sloan Management Review* (Spring 1999): 95–106.

Bernstein, Peter, *Against the Gods: The Remarkable Story of Risk*, New York: John Wiley & Sons, 1996.

Bonn, I., and C. Christodoulou, "From Strategic Planning to Strategic Management," *Long Range Planning* 29(4) (1996): 543–51.

Boshoff, H., "Testing Plans Against Alternative Futures," *Long Range Planning* 22(5) (1987): 69–75.

Bracken, Paul, *Strategic Planning for National Security: Lessons from Business Experience*, Santa Monica, Calif.: RAND, N-3005-DAG/USDP, February 1990.

Brauers, J., and M. Wever, "A New Method of Scenario Analysis for Strategic Planning," *Journal of Forecasting* 7 (1988): 31–47.

Breheny, M. J., "The Renaissance of Strategic Planning?" *Environment and Planning B: Planning and Design* 18(2) (1991): 233–49.

Bryson, John M., and William D. Roering, "Initiation of Strategic Planning by Governments," *Public Administration Review* 48(6) (1988): 995–1004.

Builder, C. H., *The Masks of War*, Baltimore, Md.: The Johns Hopkins Press, 1989.

Builder, C. H., *Toward a Calculus of Scenarios*, Santa Monica, Calif.: RAND, N-1855-DNA, 1983.

Builder, Carl H., and James A. Dewar, "A Time for Planning? If Not Now, When?" *Parameters* (Summer 1994).

Bungay, S., and M. Goold, "Creating a Strategic Control System," *Long Range Planning* 24(3) (1991): 32–39.

Capon, H., and J. Hulbert, "The Integration of Forecasting and Strategic Planning," *International Journal of Forecasting* 1 (1985): 123–33.

Chesnutt, Thomas W. (A&N Technical Services, Inc.), "Marketing Uncertainties in Policy Analysis: Why It Does Not Sell and How to Repackage It into Something That Does," paper presented at the Association for Policy Analysis and Management Conference in Denver, Colorado, October 30, 1992.

Child, J., "Organizational Structure, Environment and Performance: The Role of Strategic Choice," *Sociology* 6 (1972).

Christensen, Clayton M., "Making Strategy: Learning by Doing," *Harvard Business Review* (November–December 1997): 141–56.

Cohen, William S., Secretary of Defense, *Report of the Quadrennial Defense Review*, Washington, D.C., May 1997, at http://www.defenselink.mil/pubs/qdr.

Collis, D. J., "The Strategic Management of Uncertainty," Cambridge, Mass.: Harvard Business School, Working Paper 89-019, revised March 1991a.

Corporate Strategy Board, *Proceeding in Daylight: Frontier Practices for Challenging Strategic Assumptions*, Washington, D.C.: Corporate Executive Board, 1999.

Corporate Strategy Board, *Stall Points: Barriers to Growth for the Large Corporate Enterprise*, Washington, D.C.: Corporate Executive Board, 1998.

Courtney, Hugh, Jane Kirkland, and Patrick Viguerie, "Strategy Under Uncertainty," *Harvard Business Review* (November–December 1997): 67–79.

Dalkey, Norman C., *The Delphi Method: An Experimental Study of Group Opinion*, Santa Monica, Calif.: RAND, RM-5888-PR, June 1968.

Das, T. K., "Time: The Hidden Dimension in Strategic Planning," *Long-Range Planning* 24(3) (1991): 49–57.

D'Aveni, Richard A., with Robert Gunther, *Hypercompetition*, New York: Free Press, 1994.

Davis, Paul K., *National Security Planning in an Era of Uncertainty*, Santa Monica, Calif.: RAND, P-7605, 1989.

Davis, Paul K., "Protecting the Great Transition," in Davis, Paul K., ed., *New Challenges in Defense Planning: Rethinking How Much Is Enough*, Santa Monica, Calif.: RAND, MR-400-RC, 1994b.

Davis, Paul K., ed., *New Challenges in Defense Planning: Rethinking How Much Is Enough*, Santa Monica, Calif.: RAND, MR-400-RC, 1994a.

Davis, Paul K., David Gompert, and Richard Kugler, *Adaptiveness in National Defense: The Basis of a New Framework*, Santa Monica, Calif.: RAND, IP-155, 1996.

Davis, Paul K., and Zalmay M. Khalilzad, *A Composite Approach to Air Force Planning*, Santa Monica, Calif.: RAND, MR-787-AF, 1996.

Davis, Paul K., and Zalmay Khalilzad, *Strategic Planning for Southwest Asia and the Central Command*, Santa Monica, Calif.: RAND, R-3978-USCC/JCS, 1990.

de Geus, Arie P., "Planning as Learning," *Harvard Business Review on Managing Uncertainty* (1999): 51–67.

Deshpande, R., and A. Parasuraman, "Linking Corporate Culture to Strategic Planning," *Business Horizons* (May/June 1986): 28–37.

Dewar, James A., Carl H. Builder, William M. Hix, and Morlie H. Levin, *Assumption-Based Planning: A Planning Tool for Very Uncertain Times*, Santa Monica, Calif.: RAND, MR-114-A, 1993.

Dewar, J. A., and M. H. Levin, *Assumption-Based Planning for Army 21*, Santa Monica, Calif.: RAND, R-4172-A, 1992.

DeWeerd, H. A., *A Contextual Approach to Scenario Construction*, Santa Monica, Calif.: RAND, P-5084, September 1973.

DeWeerd, H. A., *Political-Military Scenarios*, Santa Monica, Calif.: RAND, P-3535, February 1967.

Dixit, A. K., and B. Nalebuff, *Thinking Strategically*, New York: Norton, 1991.

Dixit, A. K., and R. S. Pindyck, *Investment Under Uncertainty*, Princeton, N.J.: Princeton University Press, 1994.

Dror, Yehezkel, "Beyond Uncertainty: Facing the Inconceivable," *Technological Forecasting and Social Change* 62(1&2) (1999): 151–53.

Dror, Yehezkel, "Statecraft as Fuzzy Gambling with History," *Futures Research Quarterly* 9(3) (1993): 95–107.

Dror, Yehezkel, "Uncertainty: Coping with It and with Political Feasibility," in Miser, Hugh J., and Edward S. Quade, eds., *Handbook of Systems Analysis: Craft Issues and Procedural Choices*, New York: North Holland, 1988, pp. 247–81.

Drucker, Peter F., *Managing in a Time of Great Change*, New York: Truman Talley Books, 1999.

Duncan, N. E., and P. Wack, "Scenarios Designed to Improve Decision Making," *Planning Review* (July/August 1994): 18–25.

Dutton, J. E., and R. B. Duncan, "The Influence of the Strategic Planning Process on Strategic Change," *Strategic Management Journal* 8 (1987): 103–16.

Dutton, J. E., and E. Ottensmeyer, "Strategic Issues Management Systems: Forms, Functions, and Contexts," *Academy of Management Review* 12(2) (1987).

Einhorn, H. J., and R. M. Hogarth, "Ambiguity and Uncertainty in Probabilistic Inference," *Psychological Review* 92 (1985): 18–46.

Fahey, Liam, and Robert M. Randall, *Learning from the Future: Competitive Foresight Scenarios*, New York: John Wiley & Sons, 1997.

Fischhoff, B., P. Slovic, and S. Lichtenstein, "Fault Trees: Sensitivity of Estimated Failure Probabilities to Problem Representation," *Journal of Experimental Psychology: Human Perception and Performance* 4 (1977).

Ford, H., *My Life and Work*, Garden City, N.Y.: Doubleday, Page and Company, 1922; reprinted Salem, N.H.: Ayer Company Publishers, 1987, pp. 67–68.

Freudenburg, W. J., "Heuristics, Biases, and the Not-So-General Publics: Expertise and Error in the Assessment of Risks," in Krimsky, S., and D. Golding, eds., *Social Theories of Risk*, New York: Praeger, 1992.

Garvin, D. A., "Building a Learning Organization," *Harvard Business Review* (July/August 1993): 78–91.

Ghosal, S., and C. A. Bartlett, "Changing the Role of Top Management: Beyond Structure to Processes," *Harvard Business Review* (January/February 1995): 86–96.

Ghosal, S., and C. A. Bartlett, *The Individualized Corporation : A Fundamentally New Approach to Management*, New York: HarperBusiness, 1999.

Ginter, P. M., A. C. Rucks, and W. J. Duncan, "Planners' Perceptions of the Strategic Management Process." *Journal of Management Studies* XXII (1985): 581–96.

Glaister, Keith W., and J. Richard Falshaw, "Strategic Planning: Still Going Strong?" *Long-Range Planning* 21(1) (1999): 107–16.

Godet, M., *Scenarios and Strategic Management*, London: Butterworths Scientific, Ltd., 1987.

Gordon, Theodore J., "Futures Research: Did It Meet Its Promise, Can It Meet Its Promise?" *Technological Forecasting and Social Change* 36 (1989): 21–36.

Gordon, T. J., and O. Helmer, "An Experimental Application of the Delphi Method to the Use of Experts," *Management Science* (April 1963).

Gray, Daniel H., "Uses and Misuses of Strategic Planning," *Harvard Business Review* 64(1) (1986): 89–97.

Haeckel, S. H., and A. J. Slywotzky, *Adaptive Enterprise: Creating and Leading Sense-and-Respond Organizations*, Cambridge, Mass.: Harvard Business School Press, 1999.

Hamel, G., and C. K. Prahalad, *Competing for the Future*, Cambridge, Mass.: Harvard Business School Press, 1994.

Harvard Business Review on Managing Uncertainty, Cambridge, Mass.: Harvard Business School Press, 1999.

Hayes, R. H., "Strategic Planning—Forward in Reverse?" *Harvard Business Review* (November/December 1985): 111–19.

Helmer, Olaf, *The Use of War-Gaming in RAND's Limited-War Studies*, Santa Monica, Calif.: RAND, D-5799, December 4, 1958.

Heracleous, L., "Strategic Thinking or Strategic Planning?" *Long Range Planning* 31(3) (1998): 481–87.

Hiam, A., "Exposing Four Myths of Strategic Planning," *Journal of Business Strategy* 11(5) (1990): 23–28.

Hill, C. W. L., and G. R. Jones, *Strategic Management Theory: An Integrated Approach*, 3rd ed., Boston: Houghton Mifflin, 1995.

Hitch, C., *Uncertainties in Operations Research*, Santa Monica, Calif.: RAND, P-1959, April 1960.

Hodges, James S., *Onward Through the Fog: Uncertainty and Management Adaptation in Systems Analysis and Design*, Santa Monica, Calif.: RAND, R-3760-AF/A/OSD, July 1990.

Hogarth, R. M., and S. Makridakis, "Forecasting and Planning: An Evaluation," *Management Science* 27 (1981): 115–38.

Huss, William R., and Edward J. Horton, "Scenario Planning: What Style Should You Use?" *Long Range Planning* 20(4) (1987): 21–29.

Igor, H., "Conceptual Underpinnings of Systematic Strategic Management," *ANSOFF European Journal of Operational Research* (1985): 2–19.

Ives, Jeanette R., "Articulating Values and Assumptions for Strategic Planning," *Nursing Management* (1991): 38–39.

Jacobson, Gary, and John Hillkirk, *Xerox: American Samurai,* New York: Collier Books, 1986.

Janis, I., and L. Mann, *Decision Making,* New York: The Free Press, 1977.

Kahn, H., and A. J. Wiener, *The Year 2000: A Framework for Speculation on the Next Thirty-Three Years,* New York: The Macmillan Company, 1967.

Kahneman, D., and A. Tversky, "The Simulation Heuristic," in Kahneman, D., P. Slovic, and A. Tversky, eds., *Judgment Under Uncertainty: Heuristics and Biases,* Cambridge, UK: Cambridge University Press, 1982.

Karagozoglu, N., and R. Seglund, "Strategic Planning for a Public Sector Enterprise, *Long Range Planning* 22 (1989): 121–25.

Kay, Alan C., "Predicting the Future," 1989, at http://www.ecotopia.com/webpress/futures.htm.

Kellogg, M. K., J. Thorne, and P. W. Huber, *Federal Telecommunications Law,* Boston, Mass.: Little, Brown and Company, 1992.

Kennan, George (identified as "X"), "The Sources of Soviet Conduct," *Foreign Affairs* 65 (July 1947): 566–82.

King, W. R., "Using Strategic Issue Analysis," *Long Range Planning* 15 (1982): 548–70.

Kotter, J. P., *Leading Change,* Cambridge, Mass.: Harvard Business School Press, 1996.

Krimsky, S., and D. Golding, eds., *Social Theories of Risk*, New York: Praeger, 1992.

Kukalis, Sal, "Strategic Planning in Large US Corporations—A Survey," *Omega—International Journal of Management Science* 16(5) (1988): 393–404.

Langley, A., "The Roles of Formal Strategic Planning," *Long Range Planning* 21(3) (1988): 40–50.

Lanning, Michael Lee, *Senseless Secrets: The Failures of U.S. Military Intelligence from George Washington to the Present*, New York: Birch Lane Press, 1995.

Leemhuis, J. P., "Using Scenarios to Develop Strategies," *Long Range Planning* 18(2) (1985): 30–37.

Levin, Benjamin, "Squaring a Circle—Strategic Planning in Government," *Canadian Public Administration* 28(4) (1985): 600–605.

Liedtka, J. M., "Linking Strategic Thinking with Strategic Planning," *Strategy and Leadership* (September/October 1998): 30–35.

Lorange, P., F. Scott Morton, and S. Ghoshal, *Strategic Control Systems*, St. Paul, Minn.: West Publishing Company, 1986.

March, James G., *A Primer on Decision Making: How Decisions Happen*, New York: The Free Press, 1994.

March, James, and Herbert Simon, *Organizations*, 2nd ed., Oxford: Blackwell Publishers, 1993.

Markides, Constantinos C., "A Dynamic View of Strategy," *Sloan Management Review* (Spring 1999): 55–63.

Martino, J. P., *Technological Forecasting for Decisionmaking*, New York: Elsevier, 1972.

Mason, D. H., "Scenario-Based Planning: Decision Model for the Learning Organization," *Planning Review* (March/April 1994): 6–19.

Mason, Richard O., and Ian I. Mitroff, *Challenging Strategic Planning Assumptions: Theory, Cases and Techniques*, New York: John Wiley & Sons, 1981.

McGrath, Rita Gunther, and Ian C. MacMillan, "Discovery-Driven Planning," *Harvard Business Review on Managing Uncertainty* (1999): 107–30.

McNeil, B. J., "On the Elicitation of Preferences for Alternative Therapies," *New England Journal of Medicine* 306 (1982): 1259–62.

Milburn, M. A., "Sources of Bias in the Prediction of Future Events," *Organizational Behavior and Human Performance* 21 (1978).

Mintzberg, Henry, "The Fall and Rise of Strategic Planning," *Harvard Business Review* (January/February 1994a): 107–14.

Mintzberg, Henry, *The Rise and Fall of Strategic Planning*, New York: The Free Press, 1994b.

Mintzberg, H., and J. Lampel, "Reflections on the Strategy Process," *Sloan Management Review* (Spring 1999): 21–30.

Mitchell, D. J., J. E. Russo, and N. Pennington, "Back to the Future: Temporal Perspective in the Explanation of Events," *Journal of Behavioral Decision Making* 2 (1989): 25–38.

Mitroff, I. I., and R. O. Mason, "Business Policy and Metaphysics: Some Philosophical Considerations," *Academy of Management Review* 7(3) (1982): 361–71.

Molander, Roger C., Andrew S. Riddle, and Peter A. Wilson, *Strategic Information Warfare: A New Face of War*, Santa Monica, Calif.: RAND, MR-661-OSD, 1996.

Muralidharan, Raman, "Strategic Control for Fast-Moving Markets: Updating the Strategy and Monitoring Performance," *Long-Range Planning* 30 (February 1997): 64–73.

Murphy A. H., and R. L. Winkler, "Reliability of Subjective Probability Forecasts of Precipitation and Temperature," *Applied Statistics* 26 (1974): 41–47.

Newman, W. H., E. K. Warren, and J. E. Schnee, *The Process of Management: Strategy, Action, Results*, Englewood Cliffs, N.J.: Prentice-Hall, 1982.

Pascale, R., M. Millemann, and L. Gioja, "Changing the Way We Change," *Harvard Business Review* (November/December 1997): 127–39.

Peale, Norman Vincent, *The Power of Positive Thinking*, Englewood Cliffs, N.J.: Prentice Hall, 1952.

Peters, John E., Eric V. Larson, and James A. Dewar, *Futures Intelligence: Assessing Intelligence Support to Three Army Long-Range Planning Communities*, Santa Monica, Calif.: RAND, MR-995-A, 1998.

Peters, T., *A Passion for Excellence*, New York: Warner Books, 1989.

Pinchot, G., and Elizabeth Pinchot, *The End of Bureaucracy & the Rise of the Intelligent Organization*, San Francisco: Berrett-Koehler, 1994.

Pistorius, Carl W. I., and James M. Utterback, "The Death Knells of Mature Technologies," *Technologies Forecasting and Social Change* 50 (1995): 133–51.

Porter, M. E., *Competitive Strategy: Techniques for Analyzing Industries and Competitors*, New York: Free Press, 1980.

Porter, M., "Towards a Dynamic Theory of Strategy," *Strategic Management Journal* 12 (1991): 95–117.

Preble, J. F., "Toward a Comprehensive System of Strategic Control," *Journal of Management Studies* 29 (1992): 391–409.

Raiffa, Howard, *Decision Analysis: Introductory Lectures on Choices Under Uncertainty*, College Custom Series, New York: McGraw-Hill, 1997; first published in 1968.

Ridgway, Matthew B., *Soldier: The Memoirs of Matthew B. Ridgway*, New York: Harper, 1956.

Roush, C. H., and B. C. Ball, "Controlling the Implementation of Strategy," *Managerial Planning* (November/December 1980): 3–12.

Rowe, A., R. Mason, and K. Dickel, *Strategic Management and Planning: A Methodological Approach*, Reading, Mass.: Addison-Wesley, 1982.

Russell, Colonel W. N., "Strategic Planning for the Armed Forces," *Long Range Planning* 19(4) (1986): 41–46.

Sackman, Harold, *Delphi Critique*, Lexington, Mass.: Lexington Books, 1975.

Schaars, S. P., "How to Develop and Use Scenarios," *Long Range Planning* 20(1) (1987): 105–14.

Schelling, Thomas C., "The Role of War Games and Exercises," in Carter, Ashton B., John D. Steinbruner, and Charles A. Zraket, eds., *Managing Nuclear Operations*, Washington, D.C.: The Brookings Institution, 1987: 426–45.

Schilit, W. K., "What's the Logic of Strategic Planning?" *Management Review* (November 1988): 41–43.

Schlesinger, James R., *Organizational Structures and Planning*, Santa Monica, Calif.: RAND, P-3316, 1966.

Schoemaker, P. J. H., "Multiple Scenario Development: Its Conceptual and Behavioral Foundation," *Strategic Management Review* 14 (1993): 193–213.

Schoemaker, P. J. H., "Scenario Planning: A Tool for Strategic Thinking," *Sloan Management Review* (Winter 1995): 25–40.

Schoemaker, P. J. H., "When and How to Use Scenario Planning: A Heuristic Approach with Illustration," *Journal of Forecasting* 10 (1991): 549–64.

Schreyogg, G., and H. Steinmann, "Strategic Control, a New Perspective," *Academy of Management Review* 12 (1987): 91–103.

Schwartz, P., *The Art of the Long View*, New York: Doubleday, 1991.

Senge, P. M., *The Fifth Discipline: The Art and Practice of the Learning Organization*, New York: Doubleday/Currency, 1990.

Setear, J. K., C. H. Builder, M. D. Baccus, and W. Madewell, *The Army in a Changing World: The Role of Organizational Vision*, Santa Monica, Calif.: R-3882-A, June 1990.

Shaklee, H., and B. Fischhoff, "Strategies of Information Search in Causal Analysis," *Memory and Cognition* 10 (1982): 520–30.

Shipley, R., and R. Newkirk, "Visioning: Did Anybody See Where It Came From?" *Journal of Planning Literature* 12(4) (1998): 407–15.

Simons, R., "How New Top Managers Use Control Systems as Levers of Strategic Renewal," *Strategic Management Journal* 15 (1994): 169–89.

Simpson, Daniel G., "Why Most Strategic Planning Is a Waste of Time and What You Can Do About It," *Long Range Planning* 31(3) (1998a): 476–80.

Simpson, Daniel G., "Why Most Strategic Planning Is a Waste of Time and What You Can Do About It—Part II," *Long Range Planning* 31(4) (1998b): 623–27.

Sloman, S. A., "When Explanations Compete: The Role of Explanatory Coherence on Judgments of Likelihood," *Cognition* 52 (1994): 1–21.

Smith, P. M., J. P. Allen, J. H. Stewart II, and F. D. Whitehouse, *Creating Strategic Vision*, Washington, D.C.: National Defense University Press, 1987.

Stubbart, Charles, "Why We Need a Revolution in Strategic Planning," *Long Range Planning* 18(6) (1985): 68–76.

Sullivan, G. R., and M. V. Harper, *Hope Is Not a Method,* Times Business, New York: Random House, 1996.

Taylor, B., "The Return of Strategic Planning—Once More with Feeling," *Long Range Planning* 30(3) (1997): 334–44.

Teisberg, E. O., "Strategic Response to Uncertainty," Cambridge, Mass.: Harvard Business School, Case 9-391-192, revised April 9, 1993.

Thompson, A. A., and A. J. Strickland, *Strategic Management: Concepts and Cases*, 10th ed., New York: McGraw-Hill, 1997.

Toffler, Alvin, *The Adaptive Corporation*, New York: McGraw-Hill, 1985.

U.S. Army, *A Concept for the Evolution of Full-Dimensional Operations for the Strategic Army of the Early Twenty-First Century*, Fort Monroe, Va.: U.S. Army Training and Doctrine Command, TRADOC Pamphlet 525-5, August 1994.

U.S. Army, *Intelligence Preparation of the Battlefield*, Washington, D.C.: Headquarters, Department of the Army, FM 34-130, July 8, 1994.

Vaill, P. B., "The Purposing of High Performing Systems," *Organizational Dynamics* (Autumn 1982): 23–39.

van der Heijden, Kees, *Scenarios: The Art of Strategic Conversation*, New York: John Wiley & Sons, 1996.

van Schie, E. C. M., and J. van der Pligt, "Influence Diagrams and Fault Trees: The Role of Salience and Anchoring," in Borcherding, K., O. I. Larichev, and D. M. Messick, eds., *Contemporary Issues in Decision Making*, New York: North Holland/Elsevier Science, 1990.

Wack, P., "Scenarios: Shooting the Rapids," *Harvard Business Review* (November/December 1985): 138–50.

Wack, P., "Scenarios: Uncharted Waters Ahead," *Harvard Business Review* (September/October 1985): 73–89.

Webster, James, William E. Reif, and Jeffry S. Bracker, "The Manager's Guide to Strategic Planning Tools and Techniques," *Planning Review* (November/December 1989): 4–13.

Weiner, M. G., *Gaming Limited War*, Santa Monica, Calif.: RAND, P-2123, October 27, 1960.

Wells, Stuart, *Choosing the Future: The Power of Strategic Thinking*, Boston: Butterworth-Heinemann, 1998.

Wernerfelt, B., and A. Karnani, "Competitive Strategy Under Uncertainty," *Strategic Management Journal* 8(2) (1987): 187–94.

Wilson, David C., David J. Hickson, and Susan Miller, "How Organizations Can Overbalance," *American Behavioral Scientist* 39(8) (1996): 995–1010.

Wilson, I., "The State of Strategic Planning—What Went Wrong? What Goes Right?" *Technology Forecasting and Social Change* 37(2) (1990): 103–10.

Wilson, I., "Strategic Planning for the Millennium," *Long Range Planning* 31(4) (1998): 507–13.

Wilson, I., "Strategic Planning Isn't Dead—It Changed," *Long Range Planning* 27(4) (1994): 12–24.

Winkler, J. D., H. J. Shukiar, J. A. Dewar, M. W. Lewis, B. Benjamin, J. M. Sollinger, J. E. Peters, and H. J. Thie, *Future Leader Development of Army Noncommissioned Officers: Workshop Results*, Santa Monica, Calif.: RAND, CF-138-A, 1998.

Wirtz, James J., *The TET Offensive: Intelligence Failure in War*, Ithaca, N.Y.: Cornell University Press, 1994.

Glossary

Actions (planned). Those elements of an organization's plan that detail what the organization will do.

Actor-testing (of a scenario). The act of putting yourself in the mind-set of an actor (either an individual involved in a scenario or an affected bystander) and asking if that actor's behavior makes sense.

Adaptability (of a plan). The ability of a plan to handle unforeseen or unexpected events.

Addressed assumption. An assumption is addressed in a plan if there are actions in the plan directed at its validity.

Aimpoint. A goal, target, and/or objective. Important to the outputs of any plan. If met, it will make the plan a success.

Annual Key Bets Contract. A technique for identifying and monitoring the most vulnerable decisions of an organization (Corporate Strategy Board 1999).

AOI. Area of Interest

ABP. Assumption-Based Planning

ABT. (see) Assumption-Based Thinking

Assumption (planning). A judgment, or evaluation, about some characteristic of the future that underlies the plans of an organization.

Assumption-Based Thinking. The process of paying attention to all the assumptions—load-bearing and non–load-bearing, vulnerable and invulnerable—of a plan before, during, and after planning.

Availability heuristic. A bias whereby an assumption's failure will be determined by the possible causes of failure that a person can imagine.

BOGSAT. Bunch Of Guys Sitting Around a Table. Another name for a group discussion.

229

Combinatorial explosion. Geometric (very rapid) growth—in this case, in the number of possible scenarios that could be generated from a growing number of assumptions.

Confirmation processing. A bias whereby people pay more attention to evidence that confirms their views than to that in conflict with their views.

Conjunction fallacy. The mental process wherein an outcome paired with one likely cause is judged to be more probable than the occurrence of the outcome alone—a logical fallacy.

Contingency action/plan. An action not to be taken until some likely but not certain event occurs or situation arises.

Core Belief Identification Squad. A means of identifying the core beliefs of an organization through brainstorming sessions involving broad organizational representation (Corporate Strategy Board 1999).

Culture (of an organization). The habits and attitudes that define how and why things are done in an organization.

Decision analysis. The field of endeavor that studies taking uncertainties systematically and analytically into account in making the decision.

Defensive avoidance. Ignoring important signals because unfavorable events begin to unfold that run counter to one's expectations. This is a cause for missing important signposts.

Delphi methodology. A means of obtaining group opinion and running a group discussion anonymously and from a distance. Opinions are solicited separately; interaction among participants takes place in several iterations; feedback is carefully controlled between iterations. A method for determining load-bearing and vulnerability of assumptions at the same time.

Dialectic debate. A structured means for examining a situation systematically and logically from two or more points of view.

Directed assumption. An assumption that is dictated/provided by upper management.

Discovery-Driven Planning. A systematic means of uncovering dangerous implicit assumptions underlying the plans for a new venture (McGrath and MacMillan 1999).

Driving Force Analysis. A technique for getting at the root causes of the issues a company needs to address in planning (Christensen 1997).

Driving forces. In Driving Forces Analysis, the economic, demographic, technological, or competitive factors in the company's environment that either constitute threats or create opportunities.

Elected assumption. An assumption that is chosen by planners.

Environmental scanning. The process of searching the organization's milieu for opportunities and threats.

Explicit assumptions. Assumptions that are documented.

External environment. Generally considered to be those elements of the world that are outside an organization's control.

Facilitator. Person familiar with Assumption-Based Planning who assists in an ABP application.

Failure (of an assumption). That point at which the assumption will no longer be able to support the weight of the plan and replanning will be necessary.

FCC. Federal Communications Commission

Framing (a scenario). The formatting of a particular risk as either a gain or a loss. Can affect the perceived credibility of a scenario.

GBN. Global Business Network

Growth stalls. Serious flattenings or downturns in corporate growth.

Hedging action. An organizational action to be taken in the current planning cycle and intended to better prepare the organization for the potential failure of one of its load-bearing assumptions. An action that prepares for the possibility that an assumption will fail, despite efforts to shore it up.

HTML. Hypertext Markup Language

I&W. (see) Indications and Warning

Implicit assumptions. Uncertainties that are hidden in a plan; an assumption that planners are not (yet) consciously aware they are making.

Indications and Warning. Military methodology for determining a potential threat, through analysis of indicators—military, political, or social changes—of a possible increase in imminent danger to U.S.

forces or national security interests, and issuance of appropriate levels of warning.

Interview protocols. Structured means for questioning respondents so that each gets the same questions in the same order—eliminating potential biases.

Invulnerable. An assumption for which no plausible means of failure can be found or for which all potential means of failure strain credibility within the expected lifetime of the plan.

IPB. Intelligence Preparation of the Battlefield

Issue. Uncertainties about the future that are important to the organization. "Pre-assumptions."

LEI. Leading Economic Indicators

Level (of assumptions). Roughly, the amount of abstraction or generality of an assumption. Assumptions at lower levels are more likely to be load-bearing and vulnerable.

Likelihood. The probability of an assumption's being true or coming about.

Load-bearing assumption. The assumption upon which the success of the plan most heavily rests and whose failure would require significant changes in the organization's plans.

Monitoring (of signposts). A formal means for tracking and testing the signposts identified in the ABP process.

Most-likely scenario. A depiction of a possible future that is deemed the most likely future to occur. Often used for single-future planning.

NCO. Noncommissioned Officer

NCOES. Noncommissioned Officer Education System

One-sided vulnerability. A vulnerability that can cause an assumption to fail, usually, to the company's advantage. In that case, it is the same as a worst-case assumption.

Organizational vision. A unique, shared sense of identity and a clear, shared sense of purpose in an organization (Setear et al. 1990).

Plan. The collection of planned actions; the concrete manifestation of the planning process.

Planning. An iterative process of synthesis and analysis aimed at developing organizational actions for the future.

Premise control. The process of checking whether the assumptions underlying the strategy are still valid.

Retrospective futurology. A method of determining load-bearing and vulnerability of an assumption simultaneously by asking the planner to describe a scenario of how a company or division will go broke within a specific time frame.

Rip Van Winkle technique. A method of determining load-bearing and vulnerability simultaneously that forces participants to concentrate on the more distant future.

Risk. The notional product of how load-bearing an assumption is and how likely it is to fail within the time horizon of the plan. A measure of the danger to a plan represented by a load-bearing, vulnerable assumption.

Risk management. A field of endeavor in which the possibility of catastrophic accidents is identified, their occurrence mitigated, and their consequences planned for.

Robust, robustness. The ability to handle unforeseen or unexpected events; "uncertainty-sophisticated."

SAST. (see) Strategic Assumption Surfacing and Testing

Scenario. An internally consistent and challenging description of a possible future.

Scenario learning. The use of scenarios to augment understanding, produce new decisions, reframe existing decisions, and identify contingent decisions.

Scenario planning. The use of scenarios as a test bed for plans and/or policies; for stretching mental models as a means of leading to discoveries; for enhancing corporate perceptions about the future; for energizing management; and for aiding top management in providing leadership to an organization.

SEAL. Sea, Air, and Land. Elite Navy unit.

Shaping actions. An organizational action to be taken in the current planning cycle and intended to control the vulnerability of a load-bearing assumption. Actions intended to help shore up uncertain assumptions by controlling the future as much as possible.

Signpost.　An event or threshold that indicates an important change in the validity or vulnerability of an assumption.　Warning signs that can be used to monitor those assumptions that are most likely to produce surprises.

Special alert control.　A strategic control mechanism that includes monitoring for events such as natural disasters, hostile takeovers, court indictments, and product defects.

Strategic Assumption Surfacing and Testing (SAST).　A planning technique that includes a process for determining load-bearing, vulnerable assumptions.　The group identifies assumptions underlying the group's particular strategy, then numbers and arrays those assumptions on a matrix, by importance and certainty.

Strategic control.　Part of strategic management that compares strategic goals with progress toward those goals.　The feedback mechanism for the strategic management system.

Strategic control system.　A formal system that monitors and manages a plan after its implementation has begun.

Strategic planning.　The highest level of planning in an organization. Sets the fundamental purposes and goals of that organization.

Strategy.　An overall approach to an organization's future. A coherent collection of means to achieve the strategic ends of the organization.

Theory of causation.　An all-encompassing notion, based on historical patterns, about how an organization's enterprise works and how the world works.

Trigger event.　An event that signals an assumption has broken.

Two-sided vulnerability.　A vulnerability that can cause an assumption to fail in either good or bad directions.

Unaddressed assumption.　An explicit assumption about the world at which no known planned actions are directed. Indicates either that further planning is required or that the assumption is not crucial to the organization.

Unconnected actions.　In Rationalizing a plan, organizational actions that do not appear to be responsive to any specific assumptions about the future; strong candidates for implicit assumptions.

Unconnected assumptions.　In Rationalizing a plan, assumptions to which no actions appear responsive; indicate either that planners have some serious additional planning work to do or that that aspect of the future is not very important to the organization.

Validity (of an assumption). The soundness or truth of an assumption.

Vulnerable assumptions. Assumptions that could plausibly be overturned by future events within the expected lifetime of the plan.

Weakly connected assumptions. In Rationalizing a plan, assumptions with which an organization's actions can be associated but to which the actions appear to be only partially responsive; they suggest areas where planners may want to do additional shoring up of the plan.

Well-connected assumptions. In Rationalizing a plan, assumptions about the future for which the planned actions appear to be adequately responsive.

Index

reserving-the-right-to-play posture, 214
retrospective futurology, 83, 233
reverse decision-tree analysis, 138
reverse income statement process, 52, 205
Ridgway, Matthew, 134
Rip Van Winkle technique, 79–82
The Rise and Fall of Strategic Planning
  (Mintzberg), 195–96
risk management, 104, 208, 233
risks
  assessment of, 167–68
  assumptions and, 1, 28
  definition of, 86, 233
  insurable, 147
  of load-bearing, vulnerable assumptions,
    85–87, 167–68
  recognizing, 12–13
  robustness and, 23–24n3
  scenarios for, 130, 135, 137
robustness, 12–13, 26, 69
  contingency plans for, 208–9
  decision analysis and, 207–8
  definition of, 233
  literature on, 207–9
  load-bearing, vulnerable assumptions
    and, 87
  risks and, 12–13, 23–24n3
  scenarios for, 26–27, 132, 199–200
  testing, 11, 33
Royal Dutch/Shell
  conjunction fallacy and, 77
  hedging actions for, 142–43
  scenarios for, 9, 68–69, 131–32, 141,
    142–43, 215
  shaping actions of, 113, 117–18
  time horizons and, 72

safety measures, 112, 147–48
SAST, *see* Strategic Assumptions Surfacing
  and Testing (SAST)
scenario learning, 132, 200, 206, 233
scenario planning, 132, 199–200, 233
scenarios, *see also* worst-case scenarios
  actor-testing method for, 141, 229
  alternative, 189–90
  attitude for, 143–44
  best-case, 189–90
  captured by, 170–71
  causation and, 140–41
  consistency of, 141, 150
  credibility of, 133, 134, 135, 139, 170
  decision theory and, 139
  for decisions, 132
  definition of, 131–32, 233
  details of, 135, 140–41
  developing, 9, 10, 138–42
  direction of, 138

evaluation of, 141, 141n4
from failure, 133
focus of, 138–39, 144
framing, 140
gaming for, 144–46
global, 18
for hedging actions, 130–46
for hedging strategies, 128–29
introducing, 170–71
lesser-included case, 27n7
likelihood of, 170
literature on, 192, 199–200, 208,
  215–16
for load-bearing assumptions, 10, 133
from load-bearing, vulnerable
  assumptions, 136–37
for the military, 131, 133, 135, 170–71
most-likely, 189, 232
negative, 139–40, 139n2
number of, 135–37
quantification of, 141
relevancy of, 10, 133–34
for risks, 130, 135, 137
for robustness, 26–27, 132, 199–200
for Royal Dutch/Shell, 9, 68–69, 131–32,
  141, 142–43, 215
for shaping actions, 131
for signposts, 131
uses of, 215
scheduled uncertainties, 214–15
Schelling, Thomas C., 146
Schlesinger, James R., 209–10
Schreyogg, G., 194
Schwartz, P., 138
Sea, Air, and Land (SEAL) unit, 163–64,
  233
SEAL unit, 163–64, 233
seminars, 82
sense-and-interpret, 206–7
sense, interpret, decide, act system (SIDA),
  206n6
sense, interpret, evaluate, respond system
  (SIER), 206n6
Shah of Iran, 118
shaping actions, 10, 18, 108–20
  causation and, 115–16
  counterproductive, 118
  creativity for, 117
  definition of, 109–10, 233
  developing, 115–18
  vs. environment-shaping strategies, 111
  experience and, 116–17
  flowchart of, 110
  hedging actions and, 4, 130
  identifying, 114–15
  literature on, 193, 213–14
  for load-bearing assumptions, 114